TRACKING MENTAL HEALTH OUTCOMES

TRACKING MENTAL HEALTH OUTCOMES

A Therapist's Guide to Measuring Client Progress, Analyzing Data, and Improving Your Practice

Donald E. Wiger
Kenneth B. Solberg

John Wiley & Sons, Inc.

New York • Chichester • Weinheim • Brisbane • Singapore • Toronto

This book is printed on acid-free paper.♾

Published simultaneously in Canada.

Note about Photocopy Rights

The publisher grants purchasers permission to reproduce handouts from this book for professional use with their clients.

Library of Congress Cataloging-in-Publication Data:

Wiger, Donald E., 1953-
Tracking Mental Health Outcomes / Donald E. Wiger, Kenneth B. Solberg.
p. ; cm.
Includes bibliographical references.
ISBN 0-471-38875-0 (alk. paper)
1. Mental health services. 2. Outcome assessment (Medical care) I. Solberg, Kenneth B. II. Title.
[DNLM: 1. Mental Health Services—standards. 2. Outcome Assessment (Health Care)—methods. WM 30 W654m 2001]
RA 790.5.W545 2001
362.2—dc21

00-063350

Printed in the United States of America.

10 9 8 7 6 5 4 3 2 1

CONTENTS

QUICK REFERENCE GUIDE TO SAMPLE FORMS

PREFACE

Most professions have some recognized measure of effectiveness. An effective server in a restaurant measures customer satisfaction by tips received, while some artists measure talent by sales or perhaps by attendance at art gallery showings. Teachers are commonly rated by student progress on standardized tests and/or faculty ratings by their students. Mental health practitioners do not receive 15 to 20 percent tips, have a tangible product to sell, or report all of their clients' test scores to a specific outside agency. There is currently no universally accepted metric for evaluating client progress.

Consider the fee policies of some attorneys, who advertise that clients "pay only if we win your case." That is, if the results of the attorney's work are not successful, no fee is collected. It is no wonder that most lawyers are careful in choosing their cases when they are being paid on a contingency basis. Mental health professionals do not win or lose cases, though, nor do they typically have the convenience of handpicking clients who appear to have the most potential.

Mental health practitioners are not paid in proportion to their effectiveness; rather, the standard by which they are reimbursed is gradually changing from a fee for service per session to an outcome criterion. Although reimbursement is not yet based on outcomes on a client-to-client basis, clinicians with a record of ineffectiveness are less likely to remain on managed care panels or employed for extended periods.

Demonstrating effectiveness in the mental health field is difficult due to varying definitions of terms, nonstandardized procedures, different measurement techniques, conflicting views as to what constitutes client change, and lack of documentation training. To further complicate the issue, most mental health professionals have little or no training in how to document clinical outcomes (Clement, 1999; Wiger, 1999a). Therefore, even if their services are effective, they may not possess the necessary skills to provide adequate written evidence of therapeutic progress. Few therapists know how to demonstrate their effectiveness to others (Clement, 1996; Shulman, 1994). Hartman-Stein (1999) cites a number of cases in which psychologists have been audited and consequently have been required to pay back substantial sums of money to Medicare due to poor documentation. She further notes that psychologists should be much better informed about how to properly document their work.

Historically, the field of mental health has been characterized as in transition from a philosophy to an art to a science. Today there are many theoretical orientations in the field. Some schools of thought are technique oriented, whereas others are based on the client's thoughts, behaviors, past experiences, and future plans, or the relationship between the client and therapist. Early literature described theoretical issues and new treatment strategies; however, as the field grew, researchers examined specific aspects of well-established and newer theories.

Therapists' views of outcomes have been understandably influenced by their theoretical stance. Early psychometric tests further backed various foundational beliefs. Both the National Institute of Mental Health (NIMH) and the American Psychological Association (APA) have investigated the feasibility of developing a core battery of tests in outcome assessment (Lambert & Lambert, 1999). Regardless of their theoretical approach, practitioners are being asked to document outcomes in their local settings. This requires a scientific attitude in the context of their clinical work. The approach taken in this book is consistent with a view of professional functioning termed the *local clinical scientist* model (Stricker, 2000; Stricker & Trierweiler, 1995; Trierweiler & Stricker, 1998). This model does not view the clinician as a scientist functioning in a traditional research setting. Rather, the clinician is described as a critical observer of local phenomena in the actual clinical setting—precisely the attitude necessary for successful outcome assessment.

Generally accepted procedures for outcome assessment in mental health are not clearly defined. Nonetheless, standards are emerging. The present text presents a thorough description of state-of-the-art procedures for assessing outcome in clinical settings. The focus is on procedures that can be readily implemented in applied contexts. This is not a book on how to do outcome *research*. Rather, it is a book about outcome *assessment* that describes procedures for determining whether individual clients have changed over the course of treatment. The text is written from the viewpoints of two psychologists involved in different aspects of outcome assessment. A well-rounded presentation of outcomes from the perspectives of both intraclient change and normative measures is presented.

Donald Wiger presents training in outcome assessment from the perspective of intraclient change, focusing on outcome indicators that are assessed session by session. Outcome measurement becomes part of typical clinical procedures rather than increasing the time the clinician spends on paperwork. Documenting outcomes is demonstrated in the initial assessment, treatment plan, progress notes, and other clinical procedures. Each procedure incorporates the *Diagnostic and Statistical Manual of Mental Disorders* (*DSM*) as the standard for making outcome decisions.

Kenneth Solberg provides the perspective of normative outcome measures based on procedures for evaluating clinically significant change developed by Jacobson and Truax (1991). The use of four commonly employed and widely applicable outcome instruments (the Symptom Checklist-90 Revised [SCL-90-R], Beck Depression Inventory-II [BDI-II], Outcome Questionnaire-45 [OQ-45], and Behavior and Symptom Identification Scale-32 [BASIS-32]) is illustrated in detail. The procedures described for these tests serve as models for the use of other instruments as well. Sources for obtaining other instruments are listed, with a sampling of such measures described in more detail. Finally, technical issues are thoroughly discussed, enabling practitioners to apply these methods in the context of their unique practice settings.

TEXT ORGANIZATION

This text is divided into four parts. Part I provides definitions, history, and current needs for outcome assessment, followed by a description of two separate but interrelated outcome assessment approaches. Several examples of various means of assessing outcomes are included. Training is provided in how to convert client behaviors into simple yet meaningful data. Part II covers assessing outcomes of intraindividual progress. It provides practical training that integrates outcome material into everyday clinical procedures, rather than treating outcome assessment methods as separate, time-consuming procedures. Ongoing outcome measures through coordinated efforts from intake information, treatment plan, and progress notes are provided. Part III addresses a commercially available normative outcome measures assessment in which various standardized tests are reviewed. Concepts such as clinically significant change versus statistically significant change are compared. Practical data collection procedures are described. Various outcome measures are evaluated, and the analysis and reporting of data using these measures are described in detail. Part IV concludes the text by integrating both methods of outcome assessment (intraindividual and normative). Throughout the text, the ongoing charting of a hypothetical client, "John Adams," serves to illustrate the various procedures as they are introduced. Samples of clinical forms are included, demonstrating documentation of the assessment, treatment plan, progress notes, charting, and evaluation of outcomes. A computer disk containing the forms is included with the text.

The authors have made a concerted effort to ensure that the book is clinician-friendly. We hope that we have succeeded, and that you will find the book useful as a guide to assessing outcomes in your clinical practice.

I

DEFINING MENTAL HEALTH OUTCOMES

1

INTRODUCTION AND HISTORICAL OVERVIEW OF OUTCOME RESEARCH AND ASSESSMENT

How do mental health therapists know the extent to which their therapy is effective and the degree of improvement their clients experience? Answers to these and similar questions have been forming for the past several years. Most outcome research is relatively recent.

How do third-party payers, managed care companies, prospective employers, or clients determine a therapist's effectiveness? The typical indices historically have been the therapist's education and experience. Nevertheless, we have been encouraged for decades to monitor outcome (Hyman & Berger, 1965; Sanford, 1962, Shlien, 1966; Truax, 1966) in that it is the only way the client's welfare and the public good can be adequately served. Treatment effectiveness is intended to benefit the client, but it cannot be assessed without monitoring therapists in outcome studies.

Are the most effective therapists those who receive the most referrals? Attain the most repeat business? Earn the most money? Receive the most letters of appreciation? Prevent the most suicides? Attain the highest number of services authorized by managed care? A clinic owner may view such measures as effective because of increased business. However, they may have little to do with factors viewed as effective by third-party payers, gatekeepers, and regulatory agencies. In fact, some outside sources may view such indicators negatively. For example, the CEO of a clinic desires increased numbers of visits for fiscal reasons, whereas a managed care director desires decreased numbers of visits for the same reasons. The tug-of-war on the almighty dollar affects both perspective and decision-making processes in gauging effectiveness. The concepts of therapeutic effectiveness and financial effectiveness, therefore, may be confusing due to conflicting self-interests.

The formula that compares the concepts of therapeutic effectiveness and cost-effectiveness is termed the *cost-benefit ratio.* The monetary cost of therapy is not difficult to calculate, but the benefits of therapy are not self-evident. Consider two clients, each claiming to have undergone successful mental health treatment as evidenced by a return to adequate full premorbid functioning. If, for example, Client A requires 20 sessions to be restored to adequate mental health functioning and Client B requires only 10 sessions, the cost-benefit ratio for Client A will be twice that for Client B. Factors that increase the costs of therapy include, but are not limited to, inpatient versus outpatient treatment, number of sessions, cost per session, adjunctive therapy, and medications. Indirect costs include factors such as loss of wages, decreased productivity, and any other setbacks due to the client's impaired condition. The means or rationale for measuring outcome is therefore highly dependent on the rater's perspective. Economics are thus an important factor in evaluating treatment efficacy.

There are conflicting demands on the therapist when providing treatment. Even if the client does not have health insurance, payment for services, rent, utilities, or related expenses must come from somewhere. Only so many clients can be seen pro bono. The third-party payer demands effective treatment in fewer sessions. The clinic owner is concerned about making a profit; therefore, more sessions may be encouraged. The authors know of more than one clinic that pays therapists a bonus for seeing clients beyond a certain number of sessions (a quota system). The client just wants to get better, trusting that the therapist genuinely cares about his or her wellbeing and that others do not have a financial incentive in the case. Therapists go into the field to help people, but, like others, they must make mortgage and car payments, feed the children, and have a life. The clinic and third parties are concerned about the therapist outcome, while the client's significant others are interested in the outcome for the client.

Years before the current impetus of outcome and accountability, Carter (1983) warned that resistance within an agency should be expected when the necessary changes of documenting outcome are implemented. He further added that most of the documentation requirements will be perceived by therapists as unnecessary, time-consuming, and of little use in helping clients, only bureaucracies. Carter (1983, p. 122) suggested following these five steps when introducing new procedures into an agency:

1. The commitment of top management
2. The transfer of this commitment throughout the organization
3. The development of a strategy to implement an outcome monitoring system
4. Implementation
5. Integration of new information

The change in the focus of mental health treatment from a service to a business has increased the importance of total quality management (TQM), in which variables such as client satisfaction and therapist involvement are utilized in improving the quality of services (Eisen & Dickey, 1996). The client becomes an active participant in making decisions regarding treatment options and evaluation of outcome. Previously the client's role was that of passive patient.

Recent years have seen increased emphasis on the documentation of outcome in clinical settings. The demand for outcome documentation and research cuts across the field of health care, affecting professions such as medicine, nursing, social work, and clinical psychology. At the same time, providers of health services are often uncertain as to what the assessment of outcome really means in their local clinical settings, and often lack resources to conduct such research. This book provides practical, easy-to-use tools for assessing, tracking, and analyzing clinical outcome in mental health settings.

The terms *outcome assessment* and *outcome research* in the context of mental health treatment have been used to refer to a number of different, but related, concepts and research paradigms in the mental health literature. For the purposes of this text, four different uses of the term *outcome* are considered. First, psychotherapy *process research* compares variables within the clinical situation to determine which factors lead to the best outcome. Second, *efficacy research* studies compare a specific treatment against a control group under highly controlled conditions to determine whether the treatment is efficacious in causing the desired therapeutic outcome. Third, *effectiveness research* studies treatment outcome in real-world clinical settings. Fourth, *outcome assessment* involves tracking individual client outcome in clinical settings. This text focuses on techniques for outcome assessment, the fourth meaning of the term *outcome.* It also considers techniques that provide information about the effectiveness of treatment programs, the third meaning of the term. In the remainder of this chapter, these various uses of the term *outcome* are explored further.

OUTCOME AS A PROCESS

Much research over the past 50 years has attempted to further understanding of the process of psychotherapy. Process research attempts to identify the factors within the therapeutic context that are associated with more positive outcome. These factors might include client characteristics, therapist characteristics, characteristics of the therapeutic relationship, and specific therapeutic techniques and strategies. Often, process research has focused on a search for common factors in therapy that cut across different schools of thought. The literature abounds in identifying variables that affect the outcome of therapy. For example, Orlinski, Grace, and Parks (1994) identified five basic processes that affect therapeutic outcome: (1) quality of the therapeutic relationship, (2) skill of the therapist, (3) level of client cooperation, (4) level of client openness, and (5) length of treatment. Walborn (1996) identified four process variables that tie together the various schools of thought, including (1) the therapeutic relationship, (2) cognitive insight and change, (3) emotions in therapy, and (4) client expectations. Goldfried (1980) noted two process variables common between therapies: (1) the client is provided with new corrective experiences and (2) the client is given direct feedback. Bergin and Garfield (1994) and Hubble, Duncan, and Miller (1999) provide a thorough review of the role that process variables play in psychotherapy.

Client and therapist variables have often been examined in process research. For example, Moras and Strupp (1982) reported that clients who were more affiliative and less hostile prior to counseling were more successful in terms of treatment outcome. Conte, Plutchik, Buck, and Picard (1991) noted a number of personality traits and other variables that adversely impact the outcome of therapy. Such processes are confounding when comparing various types of treatment modalities, because they are likely common between the therapies. For example, if two therapies are being compared, but the skill level of the therapist, the number of sessions, or any other aspects of treatment differ, results will not be valid.

Process research has often attempted to identify the common positive elements of different therapies. Effective therapies emphasize the common processes that are helpful. Although therapeutic procedures and terms may appear to vary, the underlying psychological mechanisms of change are common among them; therefore, the specific treatment employed is not as important as the underlying processes that are common to successful treatment. Patterson (1974) stated that the differences between therapies are accidental and that a therapy may be effective in spite of its uniqueness.

The process approach to examining outcome contrasts with the efficacy approach, which attempts to identify which treatments are beneficial for specific disorders. The aim of process research cuts across treatment modalities and diagnostic categories, investigating the processes within psychotherapy itself.

Outcome as Efficacy

The first efforts at conducting outcome research on psychological interventions attempted to ask the question, "Do patients who receive psychotherapy fare better than those who do not?" The classic Eysenck (1952) evaluation of 24 studies concluded that the effects of psychotherapy are no greater than the effects of time itself. Eysenck (1952) described his findings as follows:

> Patients treated by means of psychoanalysis improve to the extent of 44 percent; patients treated eclectically improve to the extent of 64 percent; patients treated only custodially or by general practitioners improve to the extent of 72 percent. There thus appears to be an inverse correlation between recovery and psychotherapy; the more psychotherapy, the smaller the recovery rate. (p. 322)

Writers such as Bergin (1971), McNeilly and Howard (1991), and Walborn (1996) noted several statistical and methodological problems in the Eysenck study. Nevertheless, the nature of psychological interventions has changed considerably since the time of Eysenck's initial work. His ideas provided argument for several years to those who questioned whether psychotherapy was a worthwhile endeavor. Prior to Eysenck's critiques of the benefits of psychotherapy, Fuerst (1938) stated, "Unfortunately there exists a great deal of confusion and contradiction about what really can be accomplished by psychotherapy" (p. 260). Little (1972) noted that the executive director of the American Psychological Association stated, "Our credibility is in doubt" (p. 2).

After Eysenck, efforts to demonstrate the efficacy of psychotherapy emphasized well-controlled studies where some individuals received treatment while others (a control group) did not. Many of these studies utilized traditional experimental control procedures like randomization in an effort to enhance their validity. Although there was consistent progress in psychotherapy outcome research using these methodologies in the two decades after Eysenck's article, the results of these studies were inconsistent. Some studies showed statistically significant differences between treatment and control groups, while others did not yield statistically significant differences. It appeared that treatment worked sometimes and did not work at other times. This state of affairs existed until the advent of metanalytic approaches in the 1970s.

Beginning with the seminal work of Smith and Glass (Smith & Glass, 1977; Smith, Glass, & Miller, 1980), the results of metanalyses of large numbers of individual outcome studies demonstrated conclusively that most consumers of psychotherapy fared consistently better than those who did not receive treatment. Smith and Glass's (1977) original finding indicated that those who received psychotherapy scored about two-thirds of a standard deviation in a psychologically healthier direction than those who did not receive therapy. Lambert, Shapiro, and Bergin (1986) similarly reported an improvement of close to one standard deviation. Others have offered similar conclusions based on metanalysis (Andrews & Harvey, 1981; Lipsey & Wilson, 1994; Prioleau, Murdock, & Brody, 1983; Smith, Glass, & Miller, 1980). Whiston and Sexton (1993) noted that approximately 65 percent of those receiving psychotherapy improved, but about 6 to 11 percent got worse.

Although the metanalytic studies provide convincing evidence that, in general, individuals who receive psychotherapy are better off than individuals who do not receive therapy, this finding is not necessarily generally known or accepted. Speer (1998) pointed out that the public wonders whether psychotherapy works, stating that in mental health clinics 50 percent of clients obtain four or fewer sessions and 25 percent do not return after the first session. Fifty percent of clients do not discuss with their therapists that they are discontinuing services (Phillips, 1991). Andrews (1991) criticized psychotherapists for not conducting outcome evaluations. Without empirical research that shows psychotherapy is effective, there will continue to be a crisis in the public's confidence in psychotherapy (Krawitz, 1997). Recently, disagreement as to whether or not psychotherapy works has not been a major issue (Lambert, 1991); rather, the multifaceted, interrelated variables affecting the outcome of therapy are under scrutiny. Confounding findings such as notable differences in outcome in laboratory versus clinical settings further hinder conclusions.

Although the metanalytic studies have provided strong evidence that individuals receiving therapy do in fact fare better than those who do not receive therapy, the evidence for the differential efficacy of various therapies for various disorders has been less convincing. This is despite considerable research designed to begin to answer the question stated by Paul (1967), who argued that the appropriate questions are not those such as, "Does psychotherapy work?" or "Does client centered . . . (or) behavioral . . . therapy work?," or even, "For what (problem areas) does it work?" (p. 111). Rather, Paul argued, the appropriate question is, "*What* treatment, by *whom,* is the most effective for *this* individual with *that* specific problem, and under *which* set of circumstances?" Although the evidence from metanalysis showed clearly that psychotherapy was better than no psychotherapy, research did not yield consistent evidence for the differential effectiveness of different types of psychotherapy for different types of disorders. This lack of evidence for differential effectiveness was termed the "Dodo bird verdict" by Luborsky, Singer, and Luborsky (1975). They suggested that, as in the outcome of the circular race led by the Dodo bird in *Alice in Wonderland,* in the race to determine which therapeutic technique is most effective, "All have won and all must have prizes" (Carroll, 1981).

The Dodo bird verdict became increasingly more unsatisfactory as pressure grew in mental health to provide more definitive lists of which therapeutic techniques were effective in the treatment of specific diagnostic categories. When managed care companies asked therapists to identify treatments of proven efficacy for specific *Diagnostic and Statistical Manual of Mental Disorders*—Fourth Edition (*DSM-IV*) disorders, the answer "Everything works equally well" was not deemed satisfactory, especially when the medical profession was quick to identify lists of medications that did have such specific applications. In response to this pressure, a task force of the American Psychological Association's (APA's) Division 12 (Society of Clinical Psychology) has compiled a listing of treatments that are empirically supported—that is, whose efficacy has been established through testing in a randomized clinical trial (Nathan & Gorman, 1998). Although the work of this group remains somewhat controversial, it has succeeded in compiling considerable evidence that certain psychotherapeutic interventions are efficacious in the treatment of specific psychiatric disorders.

OUTCOME AS EFFECTIVENESS

In both metanalytic reviews of psychotherapy outcome and efforts to establish empirically supported therapies, the assumption has usually been that the gold standard for establishing efficacy is the well-controlled randomized clinical trial. The problem is that efficacy research is conducted under idealized conditions incorporating methodological features such as random assignment to treatment or control groups, carefully monitored treatment conducted according to a treatment manual, and homogeneous client populations presenting with single, well-established diagnoses. While these features are essential to demonstrate whether a particular treatment produces a desirable outcome, they also distance the efficacy study from the actual practice of psychotherapy.

The distinction between efficacy and effectiveness research was initially made in the context of medical research (for example, Brooks & Lohr, 1985). *Efficacy* is defined as outcome within a clinically controlled laboratory setting in which optimal conditions are prevalent in demonstrating treatment outcome. *Effectiveness* is defined as the outcome of treatment in a real-world setting, in which results are generally much more variable than in laboratory settings. Because research on treatment outcome has traditionally focused on efficacy rather than effectiveness, its external validity is compromised (VandenBos, 1996). Efficacy studies have traditionally been conducted using experimental or scientific methods in which subjects are assigned to random, discrete treatment groups. Highly controlled laboratory procedures are employed that attend to the specific diagnostic category being studied. Treatment is conducted strictly according to a treatment manual. Homogeneous client populations are randomly assigned to experimental groups. Clients meeting criteria for more than one diagnosis are not included in the studies (Seligman, 1995, 1996).

Calls to implement the effectiveness approach have appeared in journals of preventive medicine (Flay, 1986), neurology (Holloway, 1988), and psychiatry (Wells, 1999). Each article argues that outcome research must be applied to actual delivery of medical services. The fact that a treatment has been demonstrated to be efficacious in a randomized clinical trial does not necessarily guarantee that the same treatment will be effective in an applied clinical setting. Weisz and Weiss (1989) added that it may not be possible to generalize research findings to treatment settings unless clinical practice includes the same controls as experimental research. Perhaps such controls, from the point of view of the therapist, would mechanize and degrade therapy to a point of going through the motions of compliance.

Studies of clinical effectiveness differ substantially from efficacy studies in that effectiveness studies measure client change in typical or real-life clinical situations. Atkisson et al. (1992) referred to the efficacy/effectiveness distinctions as *clinical research* and *clinical services research.* There are few experimental controls for variables such as number of sessions, multiple diagnoses, or other factors as in efficacy studies. Seligman has been a strong advocate of effectiveness research within psychology (Seligman, 1995, 1996; Seligman & Levant, 1998). He argued that efficacy research sacrifices external validity for the sake of internal validity, and that this is the wrong emphasis from the viewpoint of the practitioner. To achieve high internal validity, efficacy studies must utilize randomization, treatment manuals, single diagnoses, specific lengths of treatment, and other controls to isolate the effects of treatment. Seligman concluded that efficacy studies are not the best measures of psychotherapy outcome because they do not represent actual clinical situations. He asked how many clients are typically seen who are randomly assigned to a therapist, receive treatment for a prescribed number of sessions according to a treatment manual, and receive treatment only if they present with one clearly defined diagnosis.

There is an increasing emphasis on the effectiveness approach to research of mental health outcomes (Foxhall, 2000). The National Institute of Mental Health (NIMH) has issued a call for grant proposals that focus on testing the effectiveness of interventions in the actual settings in which they are delivered. Although NIMH will continue to fund the randomized clinical trials it has traditionally favored, the shift to a public health model is a major change in the funding criteria of the agency (Norquist, Lebowitz, & Hyman, 1999). Similarly, accreditation bodies generally require documentation of the effectiveness of the treatment programs to be offered by the agency or institution under review. For example, the Rehabilitation Accreditation Commission (Slaven, 1997) specifically prescribes the effectiveness (as opposed to the efficacy) approach as the appropriate standard for documentation of outcomes.

Although looking at outcome in terms of effectiveness brings the assessment process into the clinical setting, the effectiveness approach still emphasizes outcome evaluation at the level of the agency or overall treatment program. In other words, the effectiveness approach tends to ask whether a particular treatment approach really works in an applied setting, or whether clients in general appear to benefit from a particular treatment program. However, the starting point for assessing outcome for most clinicians is at the level of the individual client. In other words, the clinician must provide evidence about treatment outcomes for "Jane Doe" or "John Doe," who are clients in treatment. It is possible that at some point the clinician will also want to look at aggregate individual outcome data for evidence of program effectiveness. However, the first step is always looking at individual outcome assessment.

The dose-effect model of Howard, Kopta, Krause, and Orlinski (1986) has provided evidence of increased benefits of therapy as the number of sessions increases up to a certain point, at which the rate of improvement decreases. Kopta, Lueger, Saunders, and Howard (1999) concluded that effectiveness studies have demonstrated that there are different improvement rates depending on the degree of client distress: (1) acute distress—fastest; (2) chronic distress—intermediate, and (3) characterological—slowest. They further add that for most clinical syndromes, 50 percent of clients return to normal functioning by the 16th session and 75 percent return to normal functioning between sessions 26 and 58. A phase model of improvement rates (Howard, Krause, & Lyons, 1993; Howard, Orlinsky, & Lueger, 1994) is described as having three incremental stages. The first, *remoralization,* is described by clients feeling demoralized. Their level of personal distress significantly impairs their functioning. Alleviation of subjective levels of stress often begins within a few sessions of supportive therapy. Some clients terminate therapy when they have dealt with current stressors. The second phase of treatment, *remediation,* spotlights symptom reduction. Treatment focuses on reducing symptoms by working on coping skills. The course of therapy lasts about 16 sessions or three to four months. Termination takes place when current symptomology is reduced. Clients who work through this phase, but want to prevent relapse or repetition of previous ongoing patterns that have regularly interfered with their adaptive functioning (e.g., social, occupational, etc.), may continue to the next phase. *Rehabilitation,* the last phase, may last several months or years. Clients work on unlearning maladaptive behaviors that have become lifelong habits and learning new behaviors that are more adaptive. Howard, Lueger, Maling, and Martinovich (1993) described the three phases as "sequentially dependent," requiring different treatment goals and outcome measures. Howard et al. (1994) held that remoralization is accomplished by encouragement and empathic listening, remediation takes place with interpretations and clarifications, and rehabilitation is aided with assertiveness training. Thus, generic or global measures of outcome provide little help to the client.

INDIVIDUAL OUTCOME ASSESSMENT

Mental health professionals are currently involved in the painful process of changing roles from theoretical to scientific practitioners. The number of PsyDs, typically considered a credential of more practice-focused professionals, has increased substantially compared to PhDs as evidence of current transitions from research-focused to clinically focused graduate education. Lambert, Okiishi, Finch, and Johnson (1998) stated, "It appears that psychotherapists will be involved in outcome assessment either by choice or default. Professional psychologists are seemingly well suited to the task of being practitioner-scientists and using outcome assessment to the advantage of their patients" (p. 63). Sederer, Dickey, and Herrman (1996) observed that the goals of mental health research have changed in focus from process variables to benchmarking, profiling, report cards, and instrument panels, suggesting that outcome studies must go beyond the laboratory into the field.

Clement (1996) stated that most graduate professors and clinical advisors fail to integrate research and practice, and that those who teach and maintain part-time practices usually do not blend their research into their practices either. Traditional clinical training tends to separate rather than integrate research and practice (Black, 1991; Clement, 1988; Moldawsky, 1992; Talley, Butler, & Strupp, 1994; Tyler & Clark, 1987). Strupp (1989) stated, "Although I have greatly profited from the investigation of others, nothing is as convincing as one's own experience" (p. 717).

Clinicians do not necessarily need to become outcome researchers, but all should be involved in assessing the outcome of their clients' therapy (Eisen & Dickey, 1996). Clement (1996) argues that private practice settings do not reinforce clinical psychologists' conducting research or systematic evaluation. The lack of reinforcement has led to general disdain for integrating research and practice. Clement adds that therapists may be interested in finding better ways to help people but that correlations between research findings and actual practice are discouraging (Goldfried & Wolf, 1996; Kopta, Lueger, Saunders, & Howard, 1999; Morrow-Bradley & Elliott, 1986).

Recent literature such as that of Speer (1998), Sperry et al. (1996), and Wiger (1999a) attributes the need for outcome assessment to the rise in demands for clinical accountability. Managed care companies, the self-proclaimed efficiency experts of modern mental health treatment, are often described as the culprits, requiring therapists to document their effectiveness without providing clear criteria about how this should be done.

Demand for individualized outcome measures has increased over the last 20 years. Persons (1991) pointed out that standardized outcome measures do not adequately bridge the gap between actual clinical practice and research. Clients have specific problem areas that are addressed by the therapist but may not be measured by tests. Persons suggested that outcome measurement must be individualized rather than solely standardized.

Kopta et al. (1999) have held that rising demands for accountability in clinical practice, along with recent advances in biological psychiatry, have increased the pressure to provide specific therapeutic interventions that have been empirically validated. Without such validation, several problem areas arise when attempting to continue receiving third-party payment (Barlow, 1994; Broskowski, 1995). The scientific model requires replication, evidence, and openness to scrutiny. Dornelas, Correll, Lothstein, & Wilber (1996) state that many of the outcome variables considered important by third-party payers are viewed as reductionistic by mental health therapists.

The effects of mental health treatment are both difficult to measure and complicated by lack of agreement as to what to measure and how to measure it. Misapplication of statistical procedures has led to questionable interpretations. Prior to the requirement to demonstrate outcome, therapeutic effectiveness was important, but it was not measured empirically, as in today's trends. Previous indirect measures included indices such as (1) whether clients returned for more sessions, (2) referrals, (3) client feedback, (4) session content, and other informal indices. None of these measures was formalized, making it difficult if not impossible to track clients' progress with any level of certainty. It was often assumed that client satisfaction ratings signified client progress, but this has not been consistently verified.

There is no universally agreed-upon rating system in mental health care to indicate effectiveness. It is not possible to directly count units of client progress. Even client satisfaction ratings do not necessarily imply effective treatment, due to confounding variables (Attkisson & Zwick, 1982; Campbell, Ho, Evensen, & Bluebird, 1996; Carscddon, George, & Wells, 1990; Edwards, Yarvis, Mueller, & Langsley, 1978; Greenfield & Attkisson, 1989; Lambert, Salzer, & Bickman 1998; Pekarik, 1992; Pekarik & Wolff, 1996; Vuori, 1999; Williams, 1994). Many therapists are simply likable people, and may be rated equally highly by clients who have experienced either little or much significant therapeutic change.

Mental health professionals care about their clients' well-being; therefore it seems intuitive that outcome measures would be welcomed with open arms. This has not been the case, however. Most therapists have actively resisted increased requirements in outcome documentation. It can be threatening for a therapist to have cases scrutinized by others for reasons other than case conceptualization. In the past, client records were considered private. (See Wiger, 1999a, for a discussion about how to clearly document mental health records yet preserve confidentiality.) Hawkins, Mathews, and Hamden (1999) pointed out, ". . . [C]linicians have relied too much on questionable information, such as retrospective reports. Retrospective reports often contain biases and other errors, due to such influences as clients' failure to notice important recent events when they occurred, forgetting, being unduly influenced by one or two salient events, attempting to make things look better or worse than they really are, and trying to please the clinician" (p. 2).

Hawkins et al. (1999) have further argued that a number of current documentation systems are based on intermittent measurement systems that use general indices of adjustment. Two problems exist in this paradigm. First, when client progress and setbacks are measured intermittently, clinical effectiveness may be compromised as more time lapses between measures. "The more frequent, relevant, credible, and specific the feedback, the more it 'teaches' the clinician how well s/he is doing at achieving the objective of the treatment" (p. 5). A second concern in current outcome techniques is the choice of tests. Too often, general or global tests of adjustment are used because they can cover a wide range of client problem areas. The trade-off is vague information by which outcomes are measured. (See Ogles, Lambert, and Masters, 1996, for a more detailed discussion.)

Dornelas et al. (1996) have suggested that in order for client change to be measured over time, multiple measurement points are essential. The procedure for collecting the data is as important as the data themselves. Concerns are noted, however, due to the added time and costs of additional data collection. Dornelas et al. suggest a shift in thinking about outcome assessment from an additional procedure to a part of routine treatment that contributes to the clinical care of the client. Informed consent in all procedures, especially after termination, is crucial due to ethical responsibilities.

Global measures are appropriate when employed periodically as measures of overall well-being, or as comparisons to normative groups, but they are not very helpful as means of measuring problem areas specific to a client. General tests cannot measure progress on specific treatment plan objectives. The clinician must decide whether to use the outcome procedures that are designed to track client-specific concerns as identified in the treatment plan, or to measure predetermined global measures, or both. Each method measures outcome, but the more vague or global the measurement instruments used, the more vague the interpretation of results.

The outcome measurement system in this text is in agreement with Hawkins et al. (1999) and Clement (1999) in that the quality of outcome information must be specific to the client and must be measured on an ongoing basis. The frequency of measurement depends on the cooperation, time availability, and accuracy of information provided by the client, collaterals, and therapist. The more feedback the therapist receives about, and obtains from, the client, the more specific information is available to fine-tune therapeutic interventions. Few would disagree that ongoing specific feedback is of higher quality than occasional general feedback when considering the individual client's best interest. Ongoing assessment monitors interventions and aids in deciding to continue, modify, discontinue, or add new procedures. This text suggests procedures in which both global and specific measures of outcome are incorporated to objectively view client progress from more than one perspective.

Howard, Lueger, et al. (1993) suggested a three-phase model of psychotherapy outcome that proposes progressive improvements of subjective well-being, reduction in symptoms, and enhanced life functioning. Improvements were noted in each area as a function of time. Initial improvements were found especially in subjective well-being. Gradual improvements took place in symptomatic distress and in life functioning. Improvements in well-being preceded reductions in symptomatic distress.

Outcome data may come from a variety of

sources depending on the client's level of functioning, environmental supports, age, and other factors. Some procedures are standardized—that is, clients are compared to normal and clinical populations—while others measure changes within the individual. Both indices are helpful in outcome assessment.

Sources of Data for Outcome Indicators

Lambert and Lambert (1999) have suggested that an ideal study of change would comprise multiple perspectives including sources of information such as the client, therapist, relevant others, trained observers, and social agencies that store information. Speer (1998) pointed out that in any clinical situation clients will improve in some areas and regress in others. When only one outcome measure is used, it might reveal areas of progress or regression, depending on the measurement conducted. Other important areas might be overlooked. Thus, even therapy that is highly effective in several areas may appear ineffective due to a poor choice of outcome indicators. Outcome indicators incorporating multiple measurements, multiple perspectives, and multiple points in time will best aid in assessment.

Clement (1996) described traditional experimental research strategies as resulting from collection of data on large groups of subjects, in which analysis is between and within groups. The individual clinician, though, is interested in assessing changes within the individual. Most clinicians are not trained in such procedures, nor is there adequate time to closely monitor client behaviors. Therefore, information from multiple sources is necessary in outcome assessment. The scientific model requires replication, evidence, and openness to scrutiny.

The various schools of thought do not agree on which outcome measures are most effective. Walborn (1996) pointed out, for example, that the psychodynamic camp favors global measures of client change, while cognitive behaviorists prefer a symptom reduction approach to assessing outcome. Steuer et al. (1984) have suggested that several dependent measures should be taken to provide an objective perspective.

Lambert and McRoberts (1993) reviewed 116 outcome studies reported in the *Journal of Consulting and Clinical Psychology* (JCCP) between 1986 and 1991. They found that outcome measures were classified into five source categories including (1) self-report, (2) trained observer, (3) significant other, (4) therapist, or (5) instrumental (e.g., societal records, physiological recording devices). Client reports were most often used. Twenty-five percent of the studies involved using solely client self-reports, three-fourths of which used more than one self-report index. The next most popular procedure was using two sources simultaneously. Self-report and observer ratings were used in 25 percent of the studies, self-report and therapist ratings in 15 percent, and self-report and instrumental sources in 8 percent. Ninety percent of the studies contained a self-report alone or used in combination with other ratings. Significant other ratings were rarely employed. Thirty percent of the studies used six or more types of ratings.

The use of multiple raters generally leads to similar results, but at times may lead to different conclusions due to the perspective of the rater. Massey and Wu (1994) found a high correspondence between client ratings of functional scales by consumers, family members, and case managers, although slight differences were noted in that case managers rated consumers somewhat lower than others in vocational abilities and community living skills. Massey and Wu concluded that multiple perspectives are helpful in determining appropriate treatment and discharge readiness, and may help reduce tragic errors in determining accessibility to services.

When a multidisciplinary approach to treatment is taken, outcomes are especially difficult to track. For example, a client may be involved in individual and group therapy in addition to taking medications. Changes in one form of treatment may affect other modes. An alteration in medications may prove to be quite helpful, but if a change in talk therapy takes place at the same time, it is difficult to make any causal connections or attribute outcome indicators to a particular therapist or treatment variable.

Whether the primary cause of the mental disorder is biological, social, characterological, or some combination of factors is difficult to determine. However, the mode of treatment can be crucial depending on the etiology of the disorder (Pearsall, 1997). Outcomes, therefore, are highly affected by numerous variables that may be outside the therapist's control. It is extremely difficult to compare the effectiveness of therapists when the nature of the severity of the clients' problems differs. For example, therapists primarily seeing clients with acute problem areas (e.g., outpatient, brief therapy) may appear on paper to be more successful than therapists seeing clients with severe, chronic disorders (e.g., inpatient, long-term) if the number of sessions is a criterion for clinical effectiveness.

INCORPORATING THE *DSM-IV* AND USUAL CLINICAL PROCEDURES INTO OUTCOME ASSESSMENT

This text aims to reduce or eliminate redundant paperwork in all areas of documentation by incorporating outcome assessment into usual clinical procedures. Too many outcome systems rely on additional outcome paperwork, significantly increasing and complicating the therapist's administrative duties. Some outcome systems contain several pages of questions designed to cover a wide range of problem areas. Such systems may be convenient for the test designer, but are often extremely burdensome for the client and therapist. Some other outcome measurement systems provide several separate questionnaires to cover a number of different problem areas. Problems exist in that these predetermined questions do not necessarily match individualized client problem areas. The authors know of a number of clinics and individual therapists who have purchased elaborate outcome measurement systems, but have discontinued their use due to the excessive time and effort required.

This text provides training in unbiased, standardized, and atheoretical outcome assessment that encompasses an empirically based model earlier suggested by Boorse (1976) and Persons (1991). It differs from most previous texts by its insistence on incorporating the *DSM-IV* as the standard. Clearly, the *DSM-IV* is not an outcome measurement tool or system, but it does operationally define the basic criteria for mental health disorders.

The *DSM-IV* is not based on underlying psychological mechanisms, but rather on observable and measurable mental health symptoms and impairments. Outcome measures, no matter how elaborate or accurate, must remain secondary to the *DSM-IV.* There are several excellent measurement indices available, but their proper place is to support the *DSM-IV.* They must never become the primary diagnostic instruments. The variables, measures, and tests may be quite helpful, but the *DSM-IV* remains the standard. Other outcome measures are interchangeable (i.e., several choices of diagnostic, personality, behavioral, and cognitive tests are available) depending on the therapist's needs and the validity and reliability of the instrument for the intended population.

The several therapies, theories, and schools of thought provide different modalities by which psychological problems are alleviated. The *DSM-IV* is the hub by which those with different or conflicting viewpoints of what works in therapy can communicate. Without the *DSM-IV* it is likely that poor communication between professionals would take place due to the influence of specific theoretical assumptions that are not universally shared. The assessment and treatment aspects of mental health services have both commonalities and distinct differences.

The *DSM-IV* is atheoretical; thus it avoids incorporating any one school of thought or causal inferences in diagnosis. The various theories abound in such speculations; therefore, therapists must be especially careful not to allow a theoretical perspective to influence their diagnoses. For example, concluding that a client is depressed solely because of a disruptive childhood (psychodynamic), lack of reinforcers (behavioral), dysfunctional thoughts (cognitive), lack of positive regard (client-centered), lack of meaning or purpose (humanistic/existential), and so forth, may be helpful in treatment, but the causalities in themselves do not provide sufficient information to form a diagnosis. Although not all agree in full with the *DSM-IV* nosology, it is the current standard in mental health diagnosis.

The client's *DSM-IV* diagnostic information is subsequently incorporated in writing treatment plan objectives. The treatment plan objectives (client-generated) are also atheoretical. However, the treatment strategies (various means by which the therapist will intervene to attain the objectives) are highly influenced by the therapist's school of thought. The bulk of outcome studies have focused on which treatment variables are most effective. The system presented in this text is designed to augment and clarify the ongoing clinical documentation in a manner in which the therapy is regularly fine-tuned and thus remains on target due to helpful outcome data. Ongoing measures are based on the client's specific problem areas within a *DSM-IV* standard. The information used in the diagnostic interview and treatment plan is the same information needed for ongoing outcome assessment. In addition, the therapist may choose to periodically administer brief global tests of well-being or pathology in which the client's condition can be compared to normative samples.

The relatively small amount of time required to document clinical effectiveness is easily made up in timesaving measures when the therapist is adequately trained in effective documentation techniques. This text is not designed to specifically teach documentation methods; the reader is referred to *The Psychotherapy Documentation Primer* (Wiger, 1999a) for such training.

SUMMARY

Mental health professionals are under increasing pressure from a variety of sources to document outcome. However, the term *outcome* has been used to describe very different kinds of research endeavors. Two of these approaches, process research and efficacy research, have tended to utilize traditional experimental methodologies. Process research has investigated variables within the context of therapeutic intervention to determine which factors are associated with more positive outcomes. Some success has been obtained in identifying factors that seem to be common to various approaches to psychotherapy (Hubble et al., 1999). Efficacy research has considered various therapeutic techniques or approaches in an effort to determine whether clients who receive treatment do better than similarly distressed individuals who do not receive treatment. Metanalysis of efficacy studies has convincingly demonstrated that individuals who receive therapy experience better outcomes than those who do not receive therapy. Efficacy studies have been less successful in demonstrating that certain therapeutic techniques work better with certain diagnostic categories. However, progress is being made in developing a set of empirically supported therapies (Nathan & Gorman, 1998).

The results of both efficacy research and process research have important implications for the practitioner. Competent clinicians should be knowledgeable about both process and efficacy research findings because such findings are relevant to their clinical work. However, practitioners are unlikely to engage in this kind of research in the context of their everyday practice, and this text is *not* about how to conduct the kinds of studies described earlier as process research or efficacy research. Experimental methodologies utilizing randomly assigned control groups, treatment manuals, and carefully selected subject samples are simply not feasible in most applied settings. Advocates of effectiveness research (Seligman, 1996) have argued that for these kinds of reasons the results of efficacy studies may have limited applicability to the actual clinical setting. Rather, Seligman and others have emphasized the importance of conducting outcome research in the actual setting in which services are delivered.

Most clinicians are now required to document outcomes for individual clients as part of their provider contracts. Individual outcome assessment can be conducted utilizing global measures given before and after intervention. However, the long time periods between testing do not aid in the client's treatment. More current outcome procedures incorporate both normative and individualized measures. Data from multiple sources provide a wide perspective when assessing individual outcome. The *DSM-IV* provides a reference point that gives the various schools of thought and outcome measurement tools common ground. Because the *DSM-IV* is the primary criterion for receiving and continuing mental health services, it should also be the crucial element in outcome assessment. This text presents procedures for clinicians to use in assessing individual client outcome.

It may also be possible to combine the results of individual outcome assessments in evaluating the effectiveness of a treatment program or agency. Some suggestions for this kind of analysis are also presented in this text, and procedures for documenting the outcome of treatment programs are provided. Procedures for conducting effectiveness research are also presented.

2

THE NEED FOR OUTCOME ASSESSMENT

"At one time, therapists had the luxury of needing only devotion and faith to testify regarding the efficacy of counseling and psychotherapy. However, the honeymoon is over; times have changed. The public is psychologically more sophisticated; a wider array of different styles of therapy is now available; policy makers are demanding accountability; and third-party payers want results" (Walborn, 1996, p. 80).

"Clinicians who are not committed to a large network that requires and/or generates data pertaining to cost and therapeutic effectiveness will see a rapidly shrinking number of referrals. . . . It is likely that the next critical wave in mental health quality programs will come from demonstrating value in outcomes. . . . Without outcomes research, justification for the claim of value-added services is lacking" (Ericson, 1995, pp. 8, 9, 11).

Times Are Changing

In today's era of accountability (Ellwood, 1988), both the rules and the paradigm have changed. Vague and generic treatment modalities that never attempted to systematically measure outcomes are no longer acceptable if third-party payment is to be obtained. Fonagy (1996) holds that the age of generic psychotherapy is dead. Pearsall (1997) adds further, "We can no longer afford the blithe assumption that the simple act of talking with people in distress can be equated with treatment of mental illness. We cannot afford any treatment that lacks a sound theoretical base, a replicable methodology, and a measurable outcome" (pp. 599–600).

The increased demands for accountability in the practice of mental health have required professionals to demonstrate that their services are effective. Bieber, Wroblewski, and Barber (1999) warned that unless mental health professionals can empirically demonstrate that services are beneficial, then political, financial, and other supports are likely to decrease. Accountability is thus vital to the survival of mental health service delivery.

Johnson (1995) and Bieber et al. (1999) held that, first, therapists must find new ways of incorporating outcome measures into ongoing clinical procedures, and second, they should be skilled in rapid assessment and intervention techniques. The same measurement procedures conducted in everyday clinical practices can be used to demonstrate outcomes. For example, brief assessment tools, which measure the client's symptoms and level of functioning, can be used throughout therapy as periodic indicators of client progress (Fischer & Corcoran, 1994a, 1994b). In addition, effective, ongoing outcome measures aid the therapist in determining appropriate changes during treatment and for termination (Sauber, 1996).

The days of generic therapy, in which the same treatment methods are used for most problems, are nearing an end. Speer (1998) has suggested that skepticism regarding the effectiveness of mental health interventions has arisen because little difference has been found among a variety of therapeutic interventions (Beutler & Clarkin, 1991; Garfield & Bergin, 1986) and because of discrepancies between laboratory and clinical settings (Coyle, 1996; Seligman, 1995; Weisz, Weiss, & Donenberg, 1992).

Hundreds of therapies exist, each with different terminologies and viewpoints. Different schools of thought in psychotherapy have their own terminologies, definitions of client progress, and modes of delivering services. Johnson (1995) stated that a common language is needed to assess patient progress. Otherwise, how can therapists comply with requests for outcome data?

Froyd, Lambert, and Froyd (1996) reported journal findings of 1,430 outcome measures used in assessing a wide range of client problem areas from several schools of thought. Surprisingly, 840 of the measures were used only one time across the 1,430; thus several problems in communicating outcome assessment among professionals still exist.

Dornelas, Correll, Lothstein, and Wilber (1996) warned that therapists have taken a passive role in providing clinical data to outside parties. Few practitioners are able to produce data about their patients without manually reviewing charts. A computerized data collection system can easily organize outcomes.

Clients have become increasingly more informed and cost-conscious in making medical choices. They want the most for their money—or, to put it in today's vernacular, the most bang for their buck. Even if money is not an issue, most clients are no longer willing to undergo long-term treatment. If Therapist A has a track record of providing quality services in significantly fewer sessions than Therapist B, who is also a fine therapist, Therapist A will most likely receive more referrals. That is, simple economics prevail when other variables are equal.

Psychotherapists, especially those in private practice, must realize that they are also running a business in which the appropriate use of data can lead to survival of the practice. Unfortunately, many therapists have been schooled against such a notion (Clement, 1999).

Most mental health expenditures are for inpatient, rather than outpatient, services. The proportion of mental health costs, compared to overall medical costs, has risen dramatically to approximately 25 percent of health care expenditures. Both behavioral and medical health costs are on the rise at a faster rate than inflation (Pallak & Cummings, 1994). For example, Browning and Browning (1996) reported that the consumer price index rose 63 percent from 1980 to 1993, but the cost of health care rose 193 percent in the same time period. The average company spends 45 percent of its after-tax profits for health care costs. Browning and Browning further added that 20 to 33 percent of all U.S. health care is unnecessary or inappropriate.

Today there is less of a stigma attached to the use of mental health services; therefore, more people are utilizing them. The stressors of today's fast-paced society, coupled with the paucity of outlets to relieve distress, have increased reliance on mental health professionals. With increasing costs, deductibles, and copayment amounts, mental health services are more difficult to afford than ever, yet the demand for them continues to increase.

Browning and Browning (1996) described five key trends managed care companies have battled in American health care (p. 3):

1. Unnecessary and inappropriate utilization of services
2. Virtually unlimited access to high-tech equipment and expensive procedures
3. A lack of incentives for health care providers to control costs in a predominantly fee-for-services insurance system
4. An overemphasis on ongoing treatment of diseases and disorders, rather than preventive education
5. An inordinate focus on insight, awareness, and exploratory factors, rather than goal-focused symptom reduction

Prior to managed care there were few restrictions on the use of mental health services. It was not unusual for a client to receive a few years of treatment for diagnoses such as Dysthymia or an Adjustment Disorder (in which today significantly fewer sessions are covered). Overuse and increased expenses of mental health benefits led to skyrocketing insurance premiums. Something had to be done to protect the consumer's economic interest by decreasing utilization of all types of health services.

THE CYCLICAL FEEDBACK PROCESS OF OUTCOME ASSESSMENT

There are at least three procedural levels incorporated in a typical outcome assessment. According to the Joint Commission on Accreditation of Healthcare Organizations (JCAHO) these components include (1) outcome measurement, (2) outcome monitoring, and (3) outcome management (Joint Commission on Accreditation of Healthcare Organizations [JCAHO], 1994). *Measurement* pertains to the systematic collection at a point in time of outcome data consisting of quantitative and measurable observations. *Monitoring* involves continued sampling of outcome measurement indicators. *Management* of outcomes pertains to integrating the information monitored to arrive at clinical decisions that best meet the client's best interest.

Measuring outcomes is a process, rather than simply a procedure or a final product. It serves several purposes depending on the needs and requirements of the agency. Specific measurement indices are designed to benefit the client throughout therapy by providing ongoing feedback about therapeutic progress and setbacks. The data in themselves provide little useful information, but systematic collection and analysis allows therapists to observe trends and make appropriate changes in therapeutic interventions based on outcome feedback.

Monitoring outcome indices on a regular basis can increase the effectiveness of treatment. Clients can benefit from therapy on a continual basis when outcome indicators are regularly assessed in the following areas:

- Severity of symptoms in affective, cognitive, and behavioral areas
- Severity of impairments in social, academic, occupational, and other areas of distress
- Status of client's daily functioning and activities of daily living
- Validation of diagnosis and medical necessity for continued services
- Strengths and limitations of current treatment

- Increased client satisfaction with therapy
- Prevention of excessive sessions
- Ability to obtain approval for additional sessions from insurers when needed

In addition to the client benefiting from on-target implementation of outcome indicators, the therapist, the agency, and the mental health profession can receive benefits in the following areas:

- Increasing therapeutic and agency effectiveness
- Increasing agency referrals
- Monitoring the cost-benefit ratio
- Demonstrating ethical clinical principles and practice

In outcome assessment, data are collected, analyzed, and interpreted. This process may lead to changes in therapeutic interventions. As interventions are modified, new data are subsequently collected, analyzed, and interpreted. Thus, progress is demonstrated empirically on an ongoing basis. The types and amount of data collected often vary due to different needs between agencies. However, the standardized procedures within an agency must be adhered to in order to reliably evaluate programs or individual outcomes.

CONCERNS ABOUT MANAGED CARE

The original intent of managed care was noble—effective treatment with cost-containment procedures. The current state is another story. Consumers initially applauded the competitiveness of health care premiums, but it did not take long to discover that the cost was not necessarily worth the price (i.e., limited or denied services). In fact, it is questionable whether managed care has reduced costs (Cummings, 1991, Knight, 1996, Sederer & Bennett, 1996). To remain competitive, managed care companies have (1) reduced benefits to consumers, (2) reduced the level of payment to providers, and (3) reduced the required educational level of providers. Negative publicity from congressional hearings and articles in national magazines has further lessened the public's confidence in managed care.

Managed care companies have managed costs by (1) defining patient eligibility for treatment in terms of benefits, (2) basing access to mental health services on UR (Utilization and Review) decisions that use restricted definitions of medical necessity, (3) limiting the number of authorized sessions, and (4) requiring specific documentation requirements. These procedures have become increasingly more stringent, to the point that seemingly endless complaints and lawsuits have been filed against managed care companies alleging denial of necessary treatment.

To defend their cost-containment policies, managed care companies began to cite research supporting a short-term therapy model. Studies such as that of Kiesler and Morton (1988) suggested that length of hospitalization was more predictable by exogenous variables unrelated to the patient's condition than the patient's condition itself. The classic study of Howard, Kopta, Krause, and Orlinsky (1986), which suggested that incremental gains decrease after 26 sessions, is still held up as strong evidence of the effectiveness of short-term therapy. Although a now-classic *Consumer Reports* magazine article (*Consumer Reports,* 1995) provided evidence that long-term therapy was more effective than short-term therapy, most managed care companies continue to authorize mostly short-term treatment—often fewer than 10 sessions in a 12-month period.

In a resource document critiquing managed care, Olson (1999) cited several studies suggesting problem areas in today's managed care. Table 2.1 summarizes some of Olson's findings regarding various surveys conducted nationally concerning therapists' attitudes toward managed care.

The increased role of managed care organizations in mental health services has led to more research being conducted regarding the efficacy of short-term therapy. Graduate schools have altered coursework to include training in short-term therapy techniques to meet today's requirements. Traditional clinical training without practical knowledge of the business of therapy will produce therapists inadequately prepared to practice in a managed care environment. For example, too frequently clients are denied services because of their clinicians' inability or inexperience in supplying "proper" documentation. A client may be in dire need of mental health services, but if the medical necessity is not documented sufficiently, services will be denied. Third-party reviewers have no evidence of a client's need for services other than the documentation in the client's charts or in the therapist's treatment plan submitted for authorization of services. Mental health providers may not know how to demonstrate that therapy has been effective because they may have received little training in how to document treatment.

There is no clear answer to the question, "How accountable should mental health therapists be for their work?" Answers may fall anywhere on the continuum, as depicted in Table 2.2.

Few therapists would disagree that since the onset of managed care the pendulum has shifted toward the right of the continuum of accountability. Table 2.2 also reflects therapists' decreasing level of control in clinical procedures. Some believe that things will work out on their own, while others have reacted by leaving the managed care loop and by changing the scope of their services. How does today's system affect students coming into the mental health field? To what degree are they being taught the survival strategies needed in today's managed care environment?

POSITIVE ASPECTS OF MANAGED CARE

Managed care cannot be blamed for every woe in the mental health profession. Prior to managed care, a number of accountability measures were on the rise (e.g., Medicare, diagnostic related groups [DRGs], JCAHO, peer review systems, insurance companies). Managed care companies accelerated a process that was in the making by organizing both the delivery and financing of mental health services.

Although the authors have no special allegiance to managed care, it is difficult to dispute some positive aspects it has had in upgrading accountability in the mental health profession. Shueman, Troy, and Mayhugh (1999) have asserted that managed care's positive contributions have been to raise awareness about the need for accountability and impose some structure on the previously unstructured realm of private mental health practice. Prior to managed care there was little accountability to anyone for what took place in the sessions, the course of therapy, or any outcomes. Specific procedures were not monitored, because there was generally no mechanism to determine therapeutic effectiveness.

Accountability is defined as being responsible to others. Therapists are accountable to many sources, including (1) the client, (2) the profession, (3) the therapist, (4) the third-party payer, and (5) the legal system. Accountability indices can be monitored only when specific documenta-

TABLE 2.1
Summary of Olson's (1999) Findings of Therapists' Attitudes toward Managed Care

Study	Summary of Findings
Newman and Bricklin (1991)	Survey of subscribers of *Behavior Today* 80% believed that the quality of mental health services suffered with managed care 79% noted concerns in limits or "caps" placed on the number of sessions allowed
Tucker and Lubin (1994)	Survey of 718 psychologists nationally 72% reported that managed care negatively affected the quality of treatment 79% reported dissatisfaction with utilization reviewers' knowledge and expertise 90% said that reviewers interfered with treatment plans that were in the client's best interest
Phelps, Eisman, and Kohout (1998)	Survey of 15,918 psychologists by the American Psychological Association (APA) regarding managed care 58% reported that it negatively impacted their practices 42% reported that it required excessive precertification and utilization review 49% reported that it has created ethical dilemmas
Sleek (1998)	Survey of 442 Indiana psychologists regarding managed care 70% stated that it had had a highly negative impact on practice 84% believed that it had taken control of aspects of care that should be in the hands of clinicians 80% confirmed that it imposed session limitations that interfered with treatment 75% believed it greatly compromised patients' confidentiality
Rothbaum, Bernstein, Haller, Phelps, and Kohout (1998)	Survey of 812 members of New Jersey Psychological Association; practitioners with medium to highest proportion of managed care clients reported Concerns noted in the following areas: Fewer covered sessions per client Decreases in average number of therapy sessions Greater pressure to decrease quality of care and to compromise ethics Increased workload, including paperwork Lower morale The eight highest-ranked concerns included: Being unable to get on the panel Having to go through lengthy precertification Having to fulfill lengthy screening requirements Being forced to discharge before the patient is clinically ready Having untrained personnel making patient care decisions Dealing with slow responses for approval of sessions

TABLE 2.1
(Continued)

Study	Summary of Findings
	Being allowed only a clinically inadequate number of sessions Delays due to increased paperwork
Murphy, BeBernardo, & Shoemaker (1998)	Survey of 442 APA members in independent practice 84% expressed loss of control over clinical decisions 80% noted caps on number of sessions interfering with services delivered 75% believed there was potential harm to patients from erosion of confidentiality

tion exists. Simply recording that a client is improving provides little information. It does not spell out the specific areas of improvement or the amount of improvement and it provides no information regarding what actions led to the outcome. Accurate measures of accountability not only demonstrate the results of therapy, but also provide a research base for future reference.

Accountability in mental health suggests ethics and responsibility. Although no one would argue against the need for ethical, therapeutic effectiveness, disagreement clearly exists as to how to demonstrate that need. Managed care companies, like no other third-party payers, have provided the impetus for increased research in clinical outcomes (better treatment in less time) and documentation procedures to demonstrate treatment results. Although one of the motives of managed care may be financial, the resultant benefits of its procedural changes have increased the account-

TABLE 2.2
Continuum of Accountability

No Accountability to Others	All Procedures Directed by Outside Sources
Full control by therapist	No control by therapist
No limits on number of sessions	Mandated limits on number of sessions
Fees determined by therapist	Fees determined by third party
Client selects therapist	Third party selects therapist
Therapist chooses type(s) of therapy	Third party approves which therapies may be conducted
Client initially contacts therapist for appointment	Client must initially contact gatekeeper for appointment
Minimal documentation	Documentation of all aspects of therapy
Therapist selects psychometric tests	Each psychometric test must be preapproved
For each of the preceding variables: (a) Where were we in 1980? 1990? Today? (b) Where will we be in 5 years? (c) Where does the client's best interest fit in? (d) How far will we go before we burn out?	

ability of therapists and increased research as to what produces the most effective therapy.

Prior to managed care, few controls were placed on therapists as to which assessment tools were used, how many tests were administered, and how well the assessment results matched the treatment plan. Some therapists have historically administered the same extensive battery of psychometric tests to every client, regardless of the presenting problem.

Assessing a client with a standardized battery of tests prior to the diagnostic interview is not a clinically sound procedure. In fact, most third-party payment for testing is not approved for exploratory reasons. That is, several tests should not be given for the sole purpose of ruling out various potential problem areas unless testing is the most efficient means of obtaining needed information to best benefit the client. The more knowledge a therapist has in diagnostic interviewing and psychopathology, the less the need for excessive testing.

Managed care has demanded that all services for which third-party payment is made must be both medically necessary and appropriate to the diagnosis. Ongoing confirmation of the diagnosis and impairments is required to continue receiving payment. The treatment plan must correspond to the identified problem areas, and treatment must match the objectives of the treatment. Managed care guidelines require specific documentation of changes in client functioning due to the effects of treatment. The system is intended to provide the most efficient therapeutic procedures in the least amount of time.

OUTCOME MEASURES

Procedures to monitor therapeutic effectiveness continue to be developed. Today's outcome measures go beyond global pretests and posttests. Ongoing measures conducted throughout therapy, in conjunction with global measures, are becoming the new standard of clinical effectiveness. Information obtained from ongoing assessment leads to immediate implementation of necessary changes to the treatment plan. Time is saved and treatment is correctly focused. Years of research have provided information about which interventions work best for which people and situations (Barlow, 1993; Roth & Fonagy, 1996).

DOUBLE BIND

Imagine yourself as the director of a managed care company providing mental health services. Your job requires that you obtain as many employer contracts as possible, provide quality services, and take in enough revenue to stay in business. In order to obtain contracts, you must be competitive in price. If the lowest price wins the contract, how can you afford to provide the same services as those charging a higher price for benefits? There are only so many pieces of the pie. Your choices include, but are not limited to: (1) cutting administrative expenses, (2) allowing fewer sessions of outpatient psychotherapy, (3) paying less to therapists, or (4) possibly taking a financial loss.

When administrative expenses are lowered, the quality of services decreases because of the increased time needed to handle claims. If staff is decreased to contain administrative costs, it will take longer to obtain referrals, approvals, and payment. Allowing clients fewer sessions reduces costs, although managed care companies cannot directly require therapists to conduct fewer sessions for ethical reasons. One means of subtly obtaining fewer sessions is to burden the therapist with excessive paperwork in which the results of a few sessions must clearly document the course of therapy. To compound the problem, it may take as much as a few weeks to obtain an approval after submitting a claim, and any services conducted during this waiting period are not necessarily reimbursed. Some managed care companies forbid therapists by contract to receive any private pay from their policyholders. To further hinder the process, the paperwork, based on only a few sessions, must clearly demonstrate that therapy has been helpful; however, if it has been too helpful, the client may not receive authorization for any more services. Although managed care companies do not issue a decree stating, "Cut the average number of sessions from eight down to five," they have succeeded in encumbering therapists with various procedures and paperwork that have produced the same result.

Paying less money to therapists is another means of reducing costs. Therapists who contract with managed care companies (panelists) to provide services routinely receive considerably less payment for services than they would from private pay clients for the privilege of being a provider with that company. Despite this, serving on provider panels can be extremely competitive. The lower fees paid to providers by managed care organizations are intended to be offset by increased referrals to providers by the managed care company. A clinic may benefit from a volume of referrals because, even though there may be less revenue per client, individual therapists will make more money if they are paid a percentage of fees collected (see Box 2.1).

Competition has increased among psychotherapists since the 1960s (Clement, 1999). Clinicians who demonstrate positive outcomes may have the edge needed when marketing their services. Few mental health therapists are able to provide specific written evidence of their overall therapeutic effectiveness or success rates. At this time, such evidence is not required by any outside sources, nor do most therapists know how to conduct procedures that would provide such evidence.

Simple data-recording procedures can provide readily accessible information to potential clients regarding average number of sessions, early dropout rates, client satisfaction, and clinically effective change in several areas. In addition, factors such as the therapist's experience and success with various diagnoses, age groups, and cultural backgrounds are easily recorded and can positively impact a potential client's view of the practice.

Ethical Concerns

The demand for accountability has introduced several potential ethical concerns. In order for clinical data to be evaluated, client records must be accessible. Without client records to evaluate, there is no research. In the past, mental health records were confined to the individual clinic and written in pen and paper; and, in fact, computerized records are still foreign to most private practitioners. A typical chart is composed of several handwritten notes, a treatment plan, and related information incorporated by the local clinic. When client records are requested, the usual method of relaying the information is to manually place selected records into a copy machine.

The demand for a national network of information creates an ethical dilemma. Large mental health organizations and national managed care organizations have opened the door for increased computer usage in tracking outcomes across numerous client, therapist, and clinic variables. Unlike smaller private practice agencies, larger organizations have switched to computerization of client records. When charts are requested, it is

Box 2.1

Q: If therapists in Clinic A and in Clinic B each earn a fee of 50 percent, who makes more money?
A: Therapists from Clinic A, of course.

Assume that Clinic A has four mental health therapists, each working full-time seeing an average of 25 clients per week (total of 100 clients per week). The therapists are paid a rate of 50 percent of the $100-per-hour fee. The clinic therefore grosses $10,000 per week and then pays the four therapists their 50 percent fee of $5,000 ($1,250 each).

Clinic B obtains a managed care contract in which it will average 200 clients per week at a reduced rate of $75 per hour. In order to maintain a caseload of 25 client hours per week, the clinic employs eight therapists. As in Clinic A, therapists are paid a rate of 50 percent commission of the $75 per hour fee. When paid, the clinic grosses $15,000, and then pays the eight therapists their 50 percent fee of $7,500 ($937.50 each).

Clinic A's portion of the fees is $5,000, compared to Clinic B's portion of $7,500 when given business by managed care. This scenario presents several problem areas. The obvious financial concern is that a therapist at Clinic B has an income of 25 percent less than the therapists at Clinic A. To make up for the decrease in pay, therapists from Clinic B will have to increase their client load to 33 clients per week, an arduous task when cancellations and no-shows are factored in. Managed care has been detrimental for the individual therapist in this case. It may appear that the ownership of Clinic B is benefiting from managed care, but other factors stemming from having twice as many employees, an increased number of office spaces, insurance, employee benefits, clerical help, etc., quickly narrow the margin of profit.

Suppose that both Clinic A and Clinic B do not pay therapists by commission. Instead, they pay their therapists a weekly salary of $1,250 (as in Clinic A). In the managed care situation, the economics would impact the clinic, but not the therapist. With a gross income of $7,500 per week, and eight therapists to pay (8 × $1,250 = $10,000), the gross income to the clinic would be only $5,000, minus several additional office expenses. That is, if salaries to therapists are equal, the clinic with the large managed care contract may earn significantly less profit despite having double the clients. In this case, as in the previous example, the therapists' client load would have to increase, without a raise in salary, for the clinic to benefit financially.

Box 2.1 *(Continued)*

In these situations, the best financial situation for both the therapist and the clinic is not being dependent on managed care. The combination of decreased income, increased expenses, increased client loads, and additional paperwork may not offset any benefits. But, as the percentage of clients with managed care insurance benefits increases, many therapists will opt to be panelists for managed care by default. In fact, it is difficult to remain in private practice today without managed care contracts.

now possible for those not directly involved in the case to access client records from a remote location. Procedures are being developed to safeguard misuse of data; however, if clients expect that their files will not remain confidential, how much will they disclose to mental health professionals? The therapeutic, confidential nature of the session would be compromised to the detriment of the profession.

Few would disagree that a certain amount of client information is needed by third-party payers. The debatable question is which information or how much information about the client's personal life should be shared. Without accountability to an outside paying source, there is much room for abusing the system. Historically, insurance companies have requested no more client information than the client's diagnosis and the number and length of sessions. Managed care companies and other organizations tracking treatment outcomes require more information than what was requested in the past. It is not uncommon for third parties today to access a client's entire chart. The accumulation of client information helps the mental health field in assessing the most effective forms of treatment. However, the client is generally not aware that such personal information has been disseminated.

As client records become more computerized, it will become easier for client confidentiality to be compromised. Procedures must be initiated to ensure that the only information reviewed by third parties is that which is necessary for making a decision. Perhaps a tiered system such as the one described in Table 2.3 could be employed.

Clinicians must be extremely careful in deciding which types of information to incorporate in their clients' files. Information in charts must document clients' medical need for services, diagnosis, ongoing problem areas, and response to treatment. Third parties do not ask for potentially embarrassing or damaging personal information. Many clinicians choose to put this type of information in progress notes, but do have a choice as to what personal information to include. For example, in a situation in which a client is concerned that the chart might be reviewed by others who may misuse the information, personal information must be worded carefully. Some specific personal issues or historical data may be important in the therapeutic process, but may best be referred to vaguely in progress notes that may be scrutinized by others.

Although third-party payers may initially inform clients that they have access to all client information (e.g., via the fine print in insurance contracts), most clients are not aware of this stipulation. The therapist has an obligation to

TABLE 2.3
Example of a Three-Tiered Level of Information Dissemination

Level	Types of Client Information	Purpose
1	Name, diagnosis, dates and length of services, types of services	Billing
2	Level 1, plus treatment plan, progress notes, progress reports	Requests for additional services
3	Levels 1 and 2, plus all other information in charts	Chart review Changes in therapists Court orders

explain the limits of confidentiality to the client. There are two distinct areas in clinical practice in which the therapist should receive client consent: (1) disclosure to third parties, and (2) use of data in research (including outcome assessment). The client may choose not to allow personal information to be disclosed to others. Such a decision could prevent insurance payment, but the matter is between the client and the third-party payer, not the client and the therapist. Wedding, Topolski, and McGaha (1995) review several issues in a thoughtful discussion of ethical concerns in computerized mental health outcome data. Form 1, adapted from Wiger (1999b), provides explanations of the limits of confidentiality in mental health, as well as permission to incorporate client information in outcome assessment.

In any professional field, ethical parameters are formed as confounding issues challenge practitioners. Mental health ethical guidelines exist in each of the mental health professions. Outcome assessment can pose ethical questions in clinical practice.

Outcome assessment combines the ethics guidelines of clinical and research practice. Clients must give informed consent to each of the two procedures. Clients have the right to know how data regarding them will be used. If data are not being used in research studies, rules of clinical confidentiality apply. Most universities and larger clinics have an ethics committee, a human subjects committee, or both, to provide specific guidelines. Each mental health profession (e.g., psychology, social work, marriage and family counseling) has its own ethical guidelines that therapists are required to follow.

When data are used for research purposes, clients should be given an opportunity to allow or forbid information about them to be used in research studies. The client should sign a consent form that follows the typical rules of clinical research confidentiality. In either case, the therapist must inform the client as to the extent of confidentiality of his or her records.

It may be tempting for therapists to document the course of treatment in a self-serving manner. For example, if the therapist believes that there is pressure to obtain positive results due to clinic or third-party pressures, it may be tempting to report only results that appear favorable. A clinician does not have to modify test results or blatantly misreport client progress to be involved in unethical documentation practices. Simply picking and choosing which information to report or chart, based on its potential to influence a third party in a certain way, is unethical. When the therapist incorporates multifaceted outcome measures and indicators, it is not unusual to

FORM 1 LIMITS OF CONFIDENTIALITY—USE OF CLIENT INFORMATION

Confidentiality

The contents of a counseling, intake, or assessment session are considered confidential. Verbal information and/or written records about a client cannot be shared with another party without the written consent of the client or the client's legal guardian. It is the policy of this clinic not to release any information about a client without a signed release of information. Noted exceptions are as follows in points 1–8 below.

(1) Duty to Warn and Protect

When a client discloses intentions or a plan to harm another person, the health care professional is required to warn the intended victim and report this information to legal authorities. In cases when the client discloses or implies a plan for suicide, the health care professional is required to notify legal authorities and make reasonable attempts to notify the family of the client.

(2) Abuse of Children and Vulnerable Adults

If a client states or suggests that he or she is abusing a child (or vulnerable adult) or has recently abused a child (or vulnerable adult), or a child (or vulnerable adult) is in danger of abuse, the health care professional is required to report this information to the appropriate social service and/or legal authorities.

(3) Prenatal Exposure to Controlled Substances

Health care professionals are required to report admitted prenatal exposure to controlled substances that are potentially harmful.

(4) In the Event of a Client's Death

In the event of a client's death, the spouse or parents of a deceased client have a right to access their child's or spouse's records.

(5) Professional Misconduct

Professional misconduct by a health care professional must be reported by other health care professionals. In cases in which a professional or legal disciplinary meeting is being held regarding the health care professional's actions, related records may be released in order to substantiate disciplinary concerns.

(6) Court Orders

Health care professionals are required to release client records due to a court order.

(7) Minors/Guardianship

Parents or legal guardians of nonemancipated minor clients have the right to access the client's records.

(8) Other Provisions and Procedures

When fees for services are not paid in a timely manner, collection agencies may be utilized in collecting unpaid debts. The specific content of the services (e.g., diagnosis, treatment plan, case notes, testing) is not disclosed. If a debt remains unpaid it may be reported to credit agencies, and the client's credit report may state the amount owed, the time frame, and the name of the clinic.

Insurance companies and other third-party payers are given information that they request regarding services to clients. Information that may be requested includes type of services, dates/times of services, diagnosis, treatment plan, description of impairment, progress of therapy, case notes, and summaries.

Information about clients may be disclosed in consultations with other professionals in order to provide the best possible treatment. In such cases the name of the client, or any identifying information, is not disclosed. Clinical information about the client is discussed. In some cases notes and reports are dictated/typed within the clinic or by outside sources specializing in (and held accountable for) such procedures.

When couples, groups, or families are receiving services, separate files are kept for individuals for information disclosed that is of a confidential nature. The information includes (a) testing results, (b) information given to the mental health professional not in the presence of other person(s) utilizing services, (c) information received from other sources about the client, (d) diagnosis, (e) treatment plan, (f) individual reports/summaries, and (h) information that has been requested to be kept separate. The material disclosed in conjoint family or couples sessions, in which each party discloses such information in the other's presence, is kept in each file in the form of case notes.

In the event the clinic or mental health professional must telephone the client for purposes such as appointment cancellations or reminders, or to give/receive other information, efforts are made to preserve confidentiality. Please list where we may reach you by phone and how you would like us to identify ourselves. For example, you might request that when we phone you at home or work, we do not say the name of the clinic or the nature of the call, but rather the mental health professional's first name only.

If this information is not provided to us (below), we will adhere to the following procedure when making phone calls: First we will ask to speak to the client (or guardian) without identifying the name of the clinic. If the person answering the phone asks for more identifying information we will say that it is a "personal call." We will not identify the clinic (to protect confidentiality). If we reach an answering machine or voice mail we will follow the same guidelines. It is possible that the clinic could be identified through Caller ID or similar means over which we may have no control.

Please check where you may be reached by phone. Include phone numbers and how you would like us to identify ourselves when phoning you.

__✔__ HOME   Phone number *(999)555-1313*

How should we identify ourselves? *"the clinic"*

May we say the clinic name? ____Yes __✔__No

______WORK   Phone number______________________

How should we identify ourselves?______________________

May we say the clinic name? ____Yes ____No

______OTHER   Phone number______________________

How should we identify ourselves?______________________

May we say the clinic name? ____Yes ____No

I agree to the above limits of confidentiality and understand their meanings and ramifications.

Client's name (please print) John Adams

Client's (or guardian's) signature X *John Adams* Date 3 / 15 / 2000

Use of Client Information in Outcome Research

Client information is often used to evaluate the effectiveness of types of therapy, treatment procedures, the therapist, and/or other factors in which a more careful study may help in the delivery of mental health services. Client names are not used when client information is evaluated for outcome evaluation purposes.

I agree to allow data from my record (not my name) to be used for outcome purposes.

Client's name (please print) John Adams

Client's (or guardian's) signature X *John Adams* Date 3 / 15 / 2000 obtain conflicting results. Sound ethical practice suggests integrating conflicting results, rather than ignoring that which does not fit the therapist's expectations or perceived needs.

Summary

Today, clinicians must provide specific therapeutic services that have been empirically demonstrated to produce outcomes specific to clients' specific problem areas. Generic treatment procedures are time-consuming and their helpfulness is questionable. Clients are more cost-conscious and more knowledgeable as to what to expect in the course of treatment. Outcome assessment allows for ongoing feedback in which each aspect of therapy is monitored and thus immediate revisions in the treatment plan are possible and the client's best interest is served.

Managed care has both helped and hindered the delivery of mental health services. Although it has increased therapists' accountability in the practice of mental health, it has also led to fewer services being available to consumers. Therapists must learn specific documentation techniques to demonstrate the effectiveness of their treatment and to receive authorization for additional services. Increased documentation requirements have raised several ethical issues regarding dissemination of information.

3

INDIVIDUAL AND NORMATIVE APPROACHES TO OUTCOME ASSESSMENT

Chapter 1 outlined some of the meanings and connotations of the term *outcome* in mental health clinical work and research. Much of the published work on outcome involves outcome research, or studies conducted to evaluate the effectiveness or efficacy of psychotherapeutic interventions. Although it is useful to have knowledge of what works and what doesn't in therapy, this body of research can seem distant from the day-to-day realities of clinical practice. In Chapter 2, the need for documenting outcome in the actual practice setting is explained. This chapter outlines the two major approaches to documenting outcome.

When conducting outcome assessment, clinicians are not asked to empirically demonstrate that their school of thought or treatment methods, in themselves, are efficacious. That is, they are not asked to answer the question, "Are my clients getting better under my care than they would if they weren't receiving any treatment?" The efficacy/effectiveness question can only be answered by larger-scale research studies. However, clinicians are being asked to demonstrate the progress their clients have made over the course of treatment. This requires clinicians to track outcomes for individual clients in the local clinical setting.

The starting point for outcome assessment involves what the clinicians do as a matter of course in their day-to-day work: conducting assessments and developing treatment plans. Documentation difficulties occur when the process is conducted informally and qualitatively rather than quantitatively. Informal clinical impressions are unlikely to satisfy the demands of third-party payers. Each aspect of assessment must be validated with empirical evidence.

This text describes and integrates two distinct approaches to the assessment of clinical outcomes. The first, termed *individualized outcome assessment,* emphasizes the regular assessment of progress for each client according to criteria developed specifically for the client in the individualized treatment plan. The assessment is incorporated into the client's treatment and monitored closely in the context of session-by-session treatment. The individualized approach flows most directly from the typical clinical process just described. The difference is that treatment goals are established in a more formalized and quantitative fashion than the clinician is likely used to. The goals should be based on the client's diagnosis and should be quantitative, observable, and individualized. The latter is especially important in this context. Patient-specific outcomes require patient-specific measures. One size will not fit all with this approach, since each client's goals are unique to that individual. Client progress is determined by the extent to which the client has met his or her individually set treatment goals. This approach is fundamentally ideographic in nature.

The second approach, *normative outcome assessment,* incorporates preexisting measures for which normative data are available. In the normative approach, which is nomothetic, the reference point for the determination of clinical progress is established by determining similarity to individuals with and/or without a similar diagnosis. While the focus remains on the individual client, the client's outcome is evaluated relative to the larger population. In other words, in the individualized approach the question is whether the client has improved relative to where he or she started at the beginning of treatment. In the normative approach, the question is either how the patient is doing relative to other patients with similar diagnoses or how the client compares to individuals without the diagnosis.

INDIVIDUALIZED OUTCOME ASSESSMENT

Individual outcome indicators must demonstrate specific progress of a definable behavior. The identified outcome indicators are the same behaviors as the treatment plan goals/objectives. Outcome indicators that do not clearly depict measurable client progress provide vague results in which progress is questionable. Examples of poor outcome indicators are depicted in Table 3.1.

Individual outcome indicators are specific measurable and quantifiable behaviors that are monitored throughout therapy to indicate client progress. Examples of appropriate outcome indicators are found in Table 3.2. The numbers correspond with the poor individual outcome indicators depicted in Table 3.1.

In the individualized approach, determination of a client's progress is made with reference to the individual client's specific progress session by session. Clients are not directly compared to other clients or any reference group. Baseline measures are initially taken for each outcome indicator in which subsequent treatment plan goals and objectives are set. The effectiveness of treatment is based on the client's level of progress toward the therapeutic goals.

TABLE 3.1
Poor or Vague Outcome Indicators

1. Increase amount of sleep
2. Eliminate panic attacks
3. Increase socializing
4. Achieve adequate attendance at work
5. Comply with medications
6. Reduce bedwetting
7. Get along with teacher at school
8. Do homework
9. Reduce alcohol consumption
10. Decrease compulsive behaviors
11. Eliminate purging behaviors
12. Decrease/eliminate auditory hallucinations
13. Decrease level of personal distress
14. Enhance level of functioning
15. Remain in classroom seat
16. Attend to homework assignments
17. Reduce number of temper tantrums
18. Decrease length of tantrums
19. Decrease severity of tantrums
20. Reduce crying spells

TABLE 3.2
Appropriate Outcome Indicators

Outcome Indicators	Baseline	Objective
1. Hours of uninterrupted sleep (per night)	2	6+
2. Number of panic attacks (per day)	5	0
3. Social contacts (per week)	0	4+
4. Attendance at work (hours per week)	20	40
5. Medication compliance (% of time)	20	100
6. Bedwetting (nights per week)	6	<2
7. Arguing with teacher (incidents per week)	15	<3
8. Completed homework assignments (per week)	0	4+
9. Alcohol consumption (drinks per day)	8	<3
10. Checking locked doors (per day)	40	<5
11. Purging food (times per day)	6	0
12. Auditory hallucinations (per day)	5	<2
13. Subjective level of distress (0–100)	95	<50
14. GAF score	40	60+
15. Leaving classroom seat due to hyperactivity (per day)	6	<2
16. Hours of focused study on homework (per day)	0.25	1+
17. Temper tantrums, frequency (per day)	6	<2
18. Temper tantrums, duration (minutes)	30	<5
19. Temper tantrums, severity (0–100)	90	<50
20. Crying spells (per day)	5	<2

Most individualized outcome assessment indices do not have standardized norms. For example, there is no literature available (numbers 17–19, in Table 3.2) to evaluate the national average for frequency, duration, and severity of temper tantrums. Individual outcome indicators are based on the idiosyncratic client behaviors that lead to the need for services. The baseline represents a point of comparison, while the goals represent a level at which it is expected that diagnostic symptoms and/or client distress will be sufficiently alleviated to allow adequate function.

Some outcome indicators do not clearly represent specific mental health concerns, but represent ongoing measures of general areas of functioning. For example, Global Assessment of Functioning (GAF), Subjective Units of Distress (SUDs), and similar scores (described in Chapter 4) do not represent identifiable behaviors, but provide ongoing indices of progress. Although GAF scores can be used for both individual and normative scores, they do not have norms available for specific diagnoses; percentiles are available for scores.

Hawkins, Mathews, and Hamden (1999) point out that a number of current documentation systems are based on intermittent measurement systems that use general indices of adjustment. Two problems exist in this paradigm. First, when the client progresses and setbacks are measured intermittently, clinical effectiveness may be compromised as more time lapses between measures. "The more frequent, relevant, credible, and specific the feedback, the more it 'teaches' the clinician how well s/he is doing at achieving the objective of the treatment" (p. 5). A second concern in current outcome techniques is the choice of tests. Too often, general or global tests of adjustment are used because they encompass a wide range of client problem areas. The trade-off is vague information by which outcomes are measured. (See Ogles, Lambert, & Masters, 1996, for a more detailed discussion.)

The procedure for collecting the data is as important as the data themselves. Concerns are noted due to the added time and costs of additional data collection. Dornelas, Correll, Lothstein, and Wilber (1996) suggested a shift from thinking of outcomes as an additional procedure to a part of routine clinical care contributing to the clinical care of the client. Informed consent in all procedures, especially after termination, is crucial ethically.

The individualized approach to outcome assessment utilizes measures that are tailored to a client's specific treatment needs. Global measures have their place when employed periodically as measures of overall well-being or as comparisons to normative groups, but they are not very helpful as means of measuring problem areas specific to the client. General tests cannot measure progress on specific treatment plan objectives.

The clinician must decide whether to use the outcome procedures that are designed to track client-specific concerns as identified in the treatment plan, or to employ predetermined global measures, or both. Each method measures outcomes, but the more vague or global the measurement instruments used, the more vague the interpretation of results. The more global the measure, the less specific information is known about the client's individual concerns.

Individualized outcome data may come from a variety of sources depending on the client's level of functioning, environmental supports, age, and other factors. Some procedures are standardized—that is, clients are compared to normal and clinical populations—while others measure changes within the individual. Both indices are helpful in outcome assessment.

Whether client progress is evaluated individually or normatively, clinical and behavioral improvements typically take place at varying rates. It is not unusual for progress to be exhibited in spurts, rather than in a consistent manner.

Normative Outcome Assessment

The normative approach to outcome assessment stems from the tradition of psychological testing rather than the psychotherapy tradition. As with other psychological testing, this approach requires the use of instruments for which there are some kind of normative data available. Most modern psychological tests are empirically constructed, such that a high (or sometimes low) score indicates that the individual being tested is responding similarly to a group of individuals who carry a particular diagnosis or exhibit a certain pattern of disordered behavior. In other words, the purpose of the assessment is to establish whether a particular individual client is a member of a population of individuals with a specific disorder or type of distress.

Concordant with the procedures suggested by Jacobson and Truax (1991), the normative approach to outcome assessment described in this book reverses the typical diagnostic assessment process. It is assumed that initial assessment of the client indicates the presence of a disorder. Another assessment is conducted later in treatment to determine whether the test score of an individual client is no longer typical of the population of individuals who carry a particular diagnosis. If this is the case, the data provide evidence that the client has recovered. However, other outcomes are also possible. On occasion, the evidence might imply that the client has actually deteriorated over the course of treatment. While unfortunate, such data would certainly suggest a rethinking of the treatment approach. At times the client will neither improve nor deteriorate. Under this circumstance, an argument can often be made that additional treatment is required. Similarly, a patient may show improvement, but still not score in the "normal" range. Again, if the goal of treatment is recovery, an argument could well be made in this case that additional treatment is warranted.

A wide variety of instruments are available for normative outcome assessments. Some of these, like the Beck Depression Inventory (BDI) and the Symptom Checklist 90 (SCL-90), are well known and commonly used for diagnostic assessment as well as outcome assessment. Other instruments, like the Outcome Questionnaire-45 (OQ-45) and the Behavior and Symptom Identification Scale 32 (BASIS-32), have been recently developed specifically for tracking clinical outcomes. Other instruments, like the Dyadic Adjustment Scale, the Addiction Severity Index, the Children's Depression Inventory, or the Fear Questionnaire, have been developed for use with specific diagnostic categories or treatment populations. Many of these instruments are commercially available. Some measures are in the public domain or may be used with the permission of their creators.

Aside from suitability for the treatment population being evaluated, the main requirement for a normative outcome measure is that normative data be available. The minimum requirements for normative data include: (1) a value indicating the reliability of the test scores from the instrument, (2) values for the mean and standard deviation of scores on the instrument when administered to a clinical or "dysfunctional" population, and (3) values for the mean and standard deviation of scores on the instrument when administered to a nonclinical or "functional" population. These data are typically available in the manual of published, commercially available tests. They are often also available for instruments that need not be purchased, but have been presented and described in published research articles. It is also possible for the practitioners to develop their own norms on new or untested instruments.

Normative outcome measures are usually administered at the beginning, at the end, and sometimes during the course of treatment. On occasion, the instrument may also be administered as a follow-up measure some time after treatment has ended. The goal of normative outcome assessment is to establish whether the client has recovered, improved, stayed the same, or deteriorated relative to the larger population of individuals with and without a similar disorder. In the normative approach, the reference point for the determination of clinical progress is established by comparison to individuals with a similar diagnosis and/or to a normal population. Table 3.3 provides examples of normative outcome indicators. The determination of client status is based upon a clinically significant change analysis of pre- and post-treatment scores, as described in Chapter 8. In this example, it is assumed that each indicator is from a different client.

INTEGRATING INDIVIDUALIZED AND NORMATIVE APPROACHES

The individualized and normative approaches to outcome assessment are not incompatible. Depending on specific needs, the individual clinician might elect to use the individualized approach, the normative approach, or both approaches in combination. The advantage of the

TABLE 3.3
Examples of Normative Outcome Indicators and Conclusions about Client Functioning

Outcome Indicator	Pretreatment Score	Posttreatment Score	Client Status
Beck Depression Inventory	28	12	Recovered
Beck Depression Inventory	21	35	Deteriorated
SCL-90-R (Global Severity Index)	0.72	0.64	No Change
Dyadic Adjustment Scale	74	88	Improved
Outcome Questionnaire	70	41	Recovered

individualized approach is in the way it is tailored to the individual client's unique needs. The treatment goals for one individual are seldom if ever identical to the treatment goals for another individual; therefore measurement of improvement is always client-specific.

The greatest strength of the individualized approach is also its main limitation. The reference point is always the client him- or herself. It is not possible to assess whether the client has improved or recovered relative to other individuals with similar diagnoses. The normative approach allows assessment of the extent to which the client has returned to normal functioning, or at least whether the client has shown significant improvement. In order to use this approach, it is necessary to have normative data on the assessment instruments. This consideration highlights the disadvantage of the normative approach: The assessment instruments used must be standardized. They are limited in number, and certainly not tailored to the individual client's treatment plan.

Usually, the same assessment instrument cannot be used for both individual and normative assessments. Some tests, such as the Beck Depression Inventory, are commonly used session by session; however, such tests are not individualized to specific client concerns. The difference between nomothetic (e.g., individualized) and ideographic (e.g., normative) approaches has been noted throughout the history of personality theory, psychotherapy, and psychological assessment. Table

TABLE 3.4
Comparing Individualized and Normative Outcome Assessment Approaches

Area of Strength	Individualized	Normative
Provides ongoing assessment data	Yes	Seldom
Part of ongoing treatment process	Yes	Seldom
Client participation in outcome indicators	Yes	No
Describes specific client problem areas	Yes	Sometimes
Tailored specifically to the client	Yes	No
Objective measures	Usually	Yes
Subjective measures	Sometimes	No
Standardized norms available	No	Yes
Measures are prewritten and readily available	No	Yes
Data are appropriate for program evaluation	Sometimes	Yes

3.4 lists various aspects that compare the individualized and normative approaches in assessing outcomes.

Summary

The strengths and weaknesses of individualized and normative outcome measurement approaches suggest that incorporating both types of measures will provide a well-rounded, multifaceted assessment of outcomes. Each approach complements the weakness of the other. When both approaches are incorporated, the client's mental and behavioral health can be both compared to a normative population and assessed against the identified target problem areas of the individual client.

II

INDIVIDUALIZED OUTCOME ASSESSMENT

4

MEASURING AND QUANTIFYING ONGOING BEHAVIORS

Mental health symptoms cannot be measured directly. They can be rated by various scaling systems, estimated by the myriad of tests on the market, and observed by trained collaterals; nevertheless, direct measurement is not possible. There are no specific, quantifiable means to determine how anxious, depressed, or paranoid a person becomes. Pearsall (1997) described the concept of determining the effects of psychotherapy as "maddeningly resistant to measurement by conventional scientific tools," comparing it to "measuring a balloon with yardstick . . ." (p. 599).

Standardized tests can compare the client's level of symptomology to that of a reference group, but measurement is based on theory and correlations with people with similar problem areas. The same stressor may affect two people quite differently. One person might be able to continue functioning in most activities of daily life, while the other might be incapacitated. Likewise, two people with the same score on a given standardized test may function at different levels due to their ability to cope with stressors. A character-building stressor or life event to one person could be the undoing of another.

Accurate outcome assessment requires data that can be trusted as accurate and as able to distinguish individual client differences. The less empirical the data, the poorer the assessment. Quality improvement efforts require sound data. There must be measurable and empirical outcome indices to demonstrate that improvement has taken place in any outcome system (Brown, Dreis, & Nace, 1999).

A number of outcome procedure systems rely on lengthy record keeping. Several clever forms and systems have been devised since the early days of measuring outcomes. Standardized checklists and tests are certainly helpful, but the more time-consuming and unrelated to specific treatment issues they are, the greater the therapist's dissatisfaction and noncompliance will be.

Endorsement of outcome measures that rely primarily on ipsative (existence versus nonexistence of symptoms) symptom checklists can be problematic if the degree of individual impairment is not assessed. Simply endorsing the existence or nonexistence of symptoms would lead to a quasi documentation of mental health problem areas. The clinical process of mental health diagnosis has gone beyond simple endorsement of symptoms to associating the symptoms with identifiable impairments that adversely impact daily activities. Throughout therapy, the degree, not the mere existence of, both symptoms and impairments is evaluated in confirming the diagnosis.

Strupp, Horowitz, and Lambert (1997) observed that outcome researchers are consistent in examining clients' emotional states and levels of functioning. Lambert, Salzer, and Bickman (1998) note that the client's emotional state is generally conceptualized as presence or absence of symptoms, while level of functioning is noted as adequacy in social functioning and satisfaction in interpersonal relations.

Although client emotional states and level of functioning are related concepts, they must be treated differently in data analysis aspects such as objectivity in measurement, rater perspective, and type of data analysis needed for measurement. Different types of data depict vast differences in interpretability depending on the quality or level of data obtained.

TYPES OF DATA

Traditionally, at least four types of data are used in measurement: nominal, ordinal, interval, and ratio. Ordinal data are broken down into at least two categories, each of which serves a distinct purpose in helping to measure and quantify human behavior.

Nominal Data

The most basic type of data, *nominal,* categorizes or assigns a number that is not quantitative. For example, numbers on football jerseys provide no quantitative or qualitative information about the football player. The number simply identifies the player. The player wearing jersey number 35 is not necessarily a better player than number 34 simply because of the higher jersey number. Likewise, a house with the address 200 Main Street is not necessarily of higher quality than the house at 100 Main Street.

In the mental health field, nominal data are not used in analysis other than to denote categories or the existence or nonexistence of certain traits, symptoms, or behaviors (see Box 4.1). For example, the client might endorse either being depressed or not being depressed. Other examples of nominal data may include categories or labels such as gender, race, religion, zip code, or other variables in which there are no clear quantifiable or qualitative differences.

Ordinal Data

Ordinal data go beyond nominal data in that they provide rank order. There are two types of ordinal data: ordinal categorical and ordinal metric. Both provide rank order, but ordinal metric data assume equal distance between data points. The difference between data points is not assumed to be equal in ordinal categorical data; instead, the categories ranked are in progressive order.

Ordinal Categorical Data

Most mental health checklists are ordinal categorical (see Box 4.2). The designer of the checklist must decide which adjectives or nouns best describe the data points between the extreme data points on the checklist. When using descriptive adjectives as a measure of outcomes, the clinician cannot assume equal distances between points of data or the numbers assigned. Statistically, it is difficult to analyze ordinal categorical

Box 4.1

Following are three examples of questions commonly used today that employ nominal data in collecting diagnostic information.

Example 1. Please check which symptoms you are experiencing at this time. (1) Depression (2)__Anxiety (3)__Confusion (4)__Anger problems (5)__Alcohol abuse

Example 2. Please check Yes or No as to which symptoms you are experiencing at this time.

Depression	__Yes __No
Anxiety	__Yes __No
Confusion	__Yes __No
Anger problems	__Yes __No
Alcohol abuse	__Yes __No
Hallucinations	__Yes __No
Suicidal thoughts	__Yes __No

Example 3. Please list your racial background. If mixed, describe in the blank labeled Other.

__African American __Caucasian __Hispanic __Oriental __Other__________

The nominal information in Examples 1 and 2 denotes no more than whether or not the client is experiencing some level of symptoms. Nominal data in mental health symptoms do not indicate the degree of distress or the level of functional impairment. Nominal or yes/no types of questions are helpful in the initial diagnostic interview when the clinician is ruling in and ruling out various categories of clinical syndromes. For example, if the client denies having any problems with depression, but endorses having problems with anxiety, the clinician saves time by asking more focused, anxiety-related questions to ascertain specific information needed for diagnosis, treatment planning, and outcomes. In Example 3 the client endorses one of several choices. Each category is independent from the others. None is higher or lower than the others, just different.

Box 4.2

Examples of ordinal categorical data in demographic, affective, and behavioral areas:

Age level	(1)__Infant	(2)__Toddler	(3)__Child
	(4)__Adolescent	(5)__Adult	(6)__Senior
Annual income	(1)__<$10,000	(2)__$10,001–$25,000	
	(3)__$25,001–$50,000	(4)__>$50,000	
Excessive worrying	(1)__Never	(2)__Seldom	(3)__Sometimes
	(4)__Often	(5)__Always	
Number of arrests	(1)__None	(2)__1–2	(3)__3–6
	(4)__7–12	(5)__>12	

data with any precision or level of certainty because the data points are too subjective, being based on verbal descriptions rather than equally spaced data points.

For example, the educational levels of (1) less than high school, (2) high school graduate, (3) college graduate, and (4) advanced degree are definite progressions of educational attainment, but there is not necessarily an equal amount of knowledge increments or years of education between the levels. Inferential statistics cannot be performed because ordinal data cannot be added, subtracted, or multiplied.

Grissom (1994b) warned that the chi-square test is insensitive and inappropriate for use when outcome variables are ordinal categorical. The appropriate nonparametric test is the Mann-Whitney *U* test (Grissom, 1994a; Moses, Emerson, & Hosseini, 1984).

Data analysis and interpretation of verbal descriptors are problematic, leading to, at most, tentative interpretation. Consider the example in Box 4.3. If the data in this example are to be quantified, it is not statistically sound to assign numbers to the descriptors unless ordinal data are assumed. For example, the numerical difference between Excellent and Very Good is not necessarily equal to the difference between Fair and Poor. Nevertheless, if data analysis measures are used that treat the data as if there is equal distance between numbers, results will be misleading. This is a common mistake for the nonclinician or those not trained in the use and misuse of data.

Further, if a 1- to 5-point system is used to evaluate the data, the midpoint is a 3, which is depicted as Good. Describing the midpoint as Good, in this writer's opinion, suggests a positively biased scale. It appears that three, and possibly four, of the anchor points in the preceding example suggest at least adequate functioning. Only one data point (Poor) suggests any problems.

Box 4.3

What is your overall present level of functioning throughout the day?
(1)__Excellent (2)__Very good (3)__Good (4)__Fair (5)__Poor

An interpretable analysis of change should be no more than a discussion of the descriptive responses (e.g., "The client initially described her present level of functioning as Fair. After 10 sessions, she rated it as Good."). Although this description provides more information than no description, there are more precise methods available. The client must be presented with more response options. Another example of a similar item (adapted from a popular outcome instrument) is in Box 4.4.

In this example, the numerical distance between data points is clearly uneven. The difference between responses 2 (Once or twice) and 3 (Several times), compared to 5 (Most of the time) and 6 (All of the time), is clearly discrepant. There might even be disagreement as to which of responses 3 (Several times) or 4 (Often) represents a higher frequency. Nevertheless, this example is not an uncommon outcome evaluator.

Another concern in using response sets with limited response choices is tracking degree of improvement. In the previous example there appears to be a narrow gap between responses 6 (All of the time) and 3 (Several times), then a wide gap between responses 3 (Several times) and 2 (Once or twice). That is, little behavioral or affective change is required to jump from a 6 to a 3, but getting to the next step, response 2, involves significant change. Little relative change is needed to progress to response 1. These six responses are not only confusing, but their uneven distribution leads to potentially invalid data analysis results. Remember the computer adage, GIGO (garbage in, garbage out). Imagine how someone could misinterpret the preceding data as in the following example.

Questionable Interpretation of Data

Bill has been in treatment for 10 sessions. On assessment, his initial rating of suicidal feelings was a 6. By the fifth session, he rated suicidality at a 4. Now, after the 10th session, he has progressed significantly to rating feelings at only a 3. At the present rate of change, it is predicted that his feelings of suicide will be alleviated within the next few sessions because only ratings 2 and

Box 4.4

How often do you have suicidal ideas?
(1)__Not at all
(2)__Once or twice
(3)__Several times
(4)__Often
(5)__Most of the time
(6)__All the time

1 are left. Therefore, therapy has been extremely effective.

Alternative Interpretation of the Same Data

Bill has been in treatment for 10 sessions. His ratings of suicidal feelings have been as follows:

How often do you have suicidal ideas?

Session 1: All the time
Session 5: Most of the time
Session 10: Several times

The client's subjective ratings indicate that after 10 sessions he still feels suicidal "Several times," suggesting that the present course of therapy has not been effective.

The same data were used for each scenario, but the conclusions were opposite, suggesting clear evidence of the GIGO principle when ordinal categorical data are misused. The interpretation of the numbers (i.e., 6, 4, 3) is misleading. The alternative explanation, which limits the interpretation to the categories themselves, is much more accurate. As noted earlier, inferential data analysis must be based on data with equal distances between numbers. Checklists are simply descriptive, and thus do not and cannot meet that requirement. It is much more academically and professionally honest to report results of ordinal categorical data in terms of the descriptions on the checklists used, rather than in misleading or inaccurate, quantifiable numerical terms.

When verbal descriptors are used, the clinician is cautioned to list the ratings but not to attempt to numerically convert responses as if they were a higher level of data. For example, statements such as, "Victoria began therapy rating her level of energy as 'Poor.' At this time she rates her energy level as 'Good,' " do not distort the data. Appropriate statistical analysis is crucial in ordinal data. Consider another example: If this same therapist has another client who states that his initial energy level is 4 (Fair), and later rates it as 1 (Excellent), we cannot assume that there was the same amount of effective change between the clients simply because the ratings of each increased by 3 points. *Change scores* are the net difference between pretest and posttest (or intermediate) measures. Change scores, in themselves, do not present an adequate clinical picture.

Example of Misusing Change Scores. This writer once completed a college elective course in bowling in which the grade was based primarily on change scores. In the beginning of the course, each student initially bowled a game (pretest) in which a baseline measure was taken. Throughout the course, instruction (treatment) in bowling principles was taught by the professor. At the end of the course, students were required to bowl a final game (posttest). The course grade was largely based upon how much each student improved during the term. The result was that those who entered the course with little or no bowling experience received the highest grades because they "improved the most."

Consider two students in the course. Student A had never bowled prior to the course; therefore, on the pretest, Student A bowled a very low score of 25. Student B, an accomplished bowler, scored a remarkable 250, one of her better games, in the pretest. At the end of the course, Student A bowled 75, which is still a low bowling score, but a 50-point or 100 percent improvement over the pretest score. Student B scored a 260 on the final game; therefore, her score increased by only 10 points or 4 percent. Because a change score criterion was used, Student A received a higher bowling grade than Student B, who was a clearly superior bowler. After the course grades were distributed, the students with the initial high scores protested that the grading (outcome indicators) was unfairly biased because they had less room for improvement. The next time the course was given, the graduates of the course warned the incoming students to be sure to bowl a poor game at the beginning of the course. Great improvements took place!

Comparing the Bowling Example to Change Scores in Mental Health Treatment. If the final bowling score (posttest) had been the only factor to determine the grade (outcome measurement), the course would have been unfair to the initially poor bowlers (lower functioning) who exhibited significant change, yet did not become expert bowlers (higher functioning) by the end of the course. It is difficult to imagine a beginning bowler with an initial score of 25 scoring in the 250 range in the time frame of one college semester. Initial improvement may be rapid, but as the scores increase, it takes much more time and effort to perfect the skills needed to attain high scores. That is, individual bowling scores do not consistently increase linearly (at the same rate). Several possible factors may limit a person's potential in all areas of life, including bowling and mental health functioning.

In the span of a college semester, bowling scores could be expected to increase at different rates for a beginner compared to an expert bowler. Student A would most likely demonstrate high initial progress. Student B would show a lower rate of progress, because her initial learning curve had already taken place when she originally began to bowl.

The further a bowler goes up the scale, the less improvement is possible, because the task becomes more difficult, following a typical learning curve. Thus, a curvilinear relationship exists. Realistically, the learning curve for bowling scores (for those practicing regularly) may be similar to that depicted in Figure 4.1.

Because only one bowling course is available, students cannot be placed in beginning or advanced courses. Suppose, however, that the college has three professors teaching different levels of courses in bowling. Professor A teaches Introductory Bowling 101, Professor B teaches Intermediate Bowling 201, and Professor C teaches Advanced Bowling 401. The professor (therapist) provides training or coaching (therapeutic interventions) throughout the entire term (course of therapy). If the college (clinic) rates the three professors' (therapists') effectiveness by students' (clients') change scores in bowling (psychological ratings scales), the rating system is likely to favor professors (therapists) whose bowlers (clients) have more room to change, or lower-functioning bowlers (clients).

Figure 4.1

Learning Curve for Bowling Scores

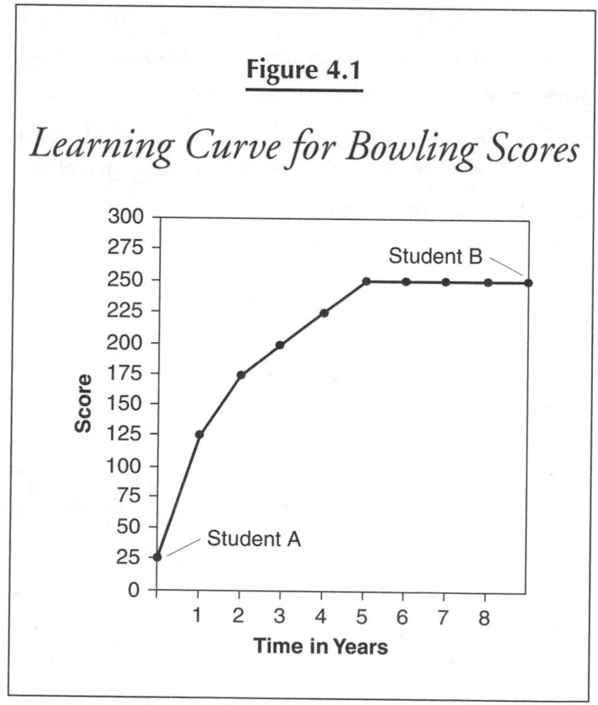

The analogy of the bowling scores to mental health functioning ratings has similarities when considering the rate of progress for lower- versus higher-functioning mental health clients. For example, lower-functioning clients are apt to receive initial intense treatment because they may be a danger to themselves or others. When they attain a minimum level of functioning, they might progressively transfer to day treatment, weekly outpatient treatment, and maintenance, then end treatment. The rate of progress gradually declines as adaptive skills are fine-tuned.

The bowling analogy is not useful when describing clinical setbacks. With practice, bowling scores tend to increase or stabilize. It is not likely that a bowler's average score will drop from a 275 to a 25; however, a major crisis in a person's life may be accompanied by a significant drop in his or her mental health rating.

This is not to imply that extremely low-functioning clients can progress to higher mental health functioning in the same manner in which bowling scores can improve. Neurological, genetic, characterological, environmental, and other therapeutic factors can impose limits on the potential benefits of therapy. The bowling example simply aids in understanding the issues in outcome assessment.

Results of data analysis can be misleading, especially to those who are not trained in the critical thinking aspects of statistics. The following two examples present different ways to analyze the same data, pointing out methodological concerns. Consider the information in Box 4.5.

Three methods of analyzing the bowling progress of Students A and B are presented in the following paragraphs. Each method yields significantly different results, but when their logic is explained, it provides a much clearer understanding of the potential problem areas and benefits of each method when incorporated in mental health outcomes.

Method 1: The Baseline Method. The first data analysis method is based on improvement possibilities determined by the relationship between the pretest and posttest. For example, Student A bowled 25 points in the pretest and 50 points in the posttest. Therefore we state that the score has doubled, or that there has been a 100 percent improvement or a 25-point change score. The baseline method of data analysis and interpretation is based on the relationship between the pretest and posttest scores. This method notes no statistical difference between improving from, for example, 10 to 20 compared with 290 to 300. Because the same change score was attained in each case, those incorporating this method

Box 4.5

Student	Initial Score	Potential Improvement (Maximum Goal)
A	25 (out of a possible 300)	275 points possible (300 – 25)
B	250 (out of a possible 300)	50 points possible (300 – 250)

assume equal improvement. Consider the example in Box 4.6.

Comparing the Bowling of Student A and Student B with Method 1. Although Student A, who began with a pretest score of 25, would need to increase his bowling score by only 3 points to raise it by 10 percent, Student B would have to increase her score by 25 points to attain a 10 percent increase. Equal increases in change scores thus do not represent equal levels of improvement. For example, if Student A increases his bowling score by 50 percent, he has added only 13 points (change score) to his score. However, if Student B increases her score by 13 points, the percentage of improvement is only 5.4 percent (5.4 percent of 250 points = 13 points).

If a grading criterion is based on change scores from the pretest as an indicator of progress, Student A does not have to progress much at all to show what appears mathematically to be significant improvement. However, in terms of bowling, the improvement is not significant. Student B must make tremendous strides to attain even minor percentages in improvement. Those who bowl at the level of Student B rarely improve beyond the pretest score. If students are rated by their percentage or amount of improvement

Box 4.6

Formulas (example from Student B's bowling scores):

(1) Posttest Score = (Pretest Score + Amount of Improvement or Change Score)
260 = 250 + 10

(2) Change Score = Posttest – Pretest
10 = 260 – 250

(3) Percentage of Improvement = Change Score / Pretest score
4% = 10 / 250

Student	Attained Score* at 10% Improvement	Attained Score at 25% Improvement	Attained Score at 50% Improvement
A	28 (25 + 3)	32 (25 + 7)	38 (25 + 13)
B	275 (250 + 25)	>300[†] (250 + 63)	>300 (250 + 125)

*Score = number of total points needed to attain the following percentages (10%, 25%, 50%) in improvement. (All fractions are rounded up because there are no fractions in bowling scores, and a partially tilted pin will most likely tip!)

[†]The highest possible bowling score is 300 points; therefore a ceiling level is reached quite early when using this method.

from their pretest score, results can be quite misleading. Even after a 50 percent improvement, Student A is still a poor bowler. Student B reaches a ceiling level (only 300 points are possible) quickly when this criterion is used.

Likewise, in mental health ratings, any system that interprets raw scores or ratings and goes no further than analyzing the change scores or percentages of improvement is utilizing an extremely biased and often invalid method of analysis. Statistically, there is a reference point (the pretest or baseline measure), but there is no standard by which to compare the baseline score in Method 1. Methods 2 and 3 provide such a standard.

Change scores, in themselves, can be helpful when used appropriately. For example, if a client is initially attending school only one day per week, and after treatment attends school an average of four days per week, the change score is quite helpful, especially when the standard of a five-day week of schooling is the normal criterion for all students. When the data are kept to an intraclient level, change scores provide an easily understood assessment technique. However, when change scores are used to compare progress between two or more clients, such as in the case of bowling students A and B, results can be biased.

The example of Students A and B demonstrates how the same change score can appear statistically significant for one client (A), but not the other client (B). However, clinically significant change may take place in one client (B), but not the other (A). Improper use of data analysis techniques can lead to results that are opposite of what takes place clinically.

Method 2: The Maximum Possible Score Method. The maximum possible score method is based on improvement possibilities determined by the pretest score compared to the maximum possible score.

The maximum possible score in bowling is 300. Student A initially bowled 25; thus there are 275 possible points of improvement. Because Student B initially bowled 250, there are only 50 possible points for improvement. When considering the students' actual amount of improvement compared to the amount of improvement that is still possible, the improvement rates are quite different than in Method 1. The analysis of data is denoted as the change score divided by the difference between the maximum score and the pretest score. The result is the percentage of the maximum possible change that has taken place since the time of the pretest.

In this example, Student A increased his bowling score by 18 percent. The calculation is based on 50 / (300 − 25) = 18%, which, in simple terms, states that Student A has progressed 18 percent of the way to bowling a 300 game. His baseline (0 percent) began at a score of 25 (his pretest score). Another way of looking at the equation is that 50 units of change out of a possible 275 (18 percent) have taken place.

Student B fared at 10 / (300 − 250) = 20%. That is, she attained 20 percent of the possible change available on the scale. Her baseline began at a bowling score of 250. Now that she has bowled a 260, she has progressed 20 percent of the way to her goal of bowling 300. Here is the formula (example from Student B's bowling scores):

$$\% \text{ Increase to Maximum Possible Score} = \frac{\textit{Change Score}}{\text{Maximum Possible Score} - \text{Baseline Score}}$$

or

$$20\% = 10 / (300 - 250)$$

Considering the amount of change that took place for each student, compared to the amount that could have taken place, Student B actually scored higher by 2 percent when considering progression toward the maximum goal of bowling a 300 game.

Box 4.7 represents the scores that would be attained for given percentages of improvement for both Students A and B. The numbers listed in parentheses in columns 2 through 4 indicate the additional number of pins needed to attain the percentage of the goal of 300 pins. The initial number in columns 2 through 4 represents the students' score when the additional pins are added to the baseline score.

Because this example may be more difficult to understand, further explanation may be helpful. Student A originally bowled a score of 25; thus he has the potential of scoring 275 additional points. For a 10 percent improvement in the 275 possible additional points, he would have to add 28 points (27.5 rounded up) to his total score. Using the same procedures, Student B would have to add only 5 points to her baseline score to attain a 10 percent improvement (based on potential improvement of a score of 300).

The major problem with the maximum possible score method is that it assumes that the individual has the potential to reach the maximum possible score in a limited time period. In mental health treatment, it is not reasonable to set the same treatment goals for two different clients. For instance Client A may be extremely dysfunctional, with a 25-year history of chronic delusions, paranoia, suicide attempts, chemical dependence, and antisocial behavior. Client B may never have experienced any significant mental health issues, but is currently seeing a counselor for help coping with the death of his grandfather. Different goal levels will be set for Clients A and B, because at this time they do not have the same possible maximum level of functioning. That is, it is not reasonable to assume that each client will attain a superior level of mental health functioning in the same time period.

Method 3, discussed in the following text, combines the strengths of Methods 1 and 2.

Method 3: The Reasonable Goal Attainment Method. The reasonable goal attainment method is based on improvement possibilities determined by the pretest score compared to a reasonable possible score.

It is not likely that bowling students A and B have the same potential score during the time period of the academic term. Neither Method 1 nor Method 2 seems fair to evaluate their grade. The reasonable goal attainment method sets specific goals for the students depending on the esti-

Box 4.7

Student	Score at 10% of Maximum Possible Score	Score at 25% of Maximum Possible Score	Score at 50% of Maximum Possible Score
A	53 (25 + 28)	94 (25 + 69)	163 (25 + 138)
B	255 (250 + 5)	263 (250 + 13)	275 (250 + 25)

mated reasonable amount of progress possible. For example, suppose that the literature on bowling progress, combined with the professor's experience in reviewing student gains, suggests that no more than 10 percent of beginning bowlers improve in their bowling scores more than 60 points in one academic term. Further, suppose that the same literature holds that an advanced bowler is not likely to increase his or her score more than 12 points in the same time period. In this case, the goals in Box 4.8 could be set for Students A and B.

The formula for determining the percent of change toward the reasonable potential is identical to that for determining progress toward the maximum possible goal. The procedure shown in Box 4.8 is similar to the maximum potential method except that the goal is individualized to fit the person's reasonable level of progress rather than the lofty goal that the lower-functioning bowler could not reach. With these changes, Student A must increase his score by 60 additional points to reach his full reasonable potential, or 100 percent of goal attainment. A 30-point gain would result in 50 percent of goal attainment. The scores in Box 4.9 represent the scores that would be attained for given percentages of individualized goal attainment. All fractions are rounded up.

Although psychotherapy has few commonalities with a course in bowling, this example provides an analogy elucidating the inherent problems of incorporating change scores as the sole evidence or a major indicator of outcomes. Change scores are helpful as one index of outcomes, but when clients are compared to others with dissimilar baseline levels of functioning at the beginning of treatment (the initial bowling scores), the outcome measures (course grades) are clearly unfair. Unfortunately, the quantification methods might appear to be sound statistical procedures, but the results are not consistent.

It could be argued that therapists see a wide range of clients, and therefore the average level of functioning of clients per therapist will be similar. This assumption is most likely untrue, however, because there are several progressive degrees of mental health services available. For example, clients would not go to a state agency where people are committed for mental health dysfunction for long periods if they are seeking counseling for personal growth. Likewise, someone with active, severe, chronic schizophrenia would not seek services solely from a beginning counselor for three sessions of talk therapy, expecting full remission of symptoms.

The reasonable goal attainment method is

Box 4.8

Student	Initial Score	Estimated Reasonable Potential Gain	Estimated Reasonable Potential Score (Individualized Goal)
A	25	60	85
B	250	12	262

Box 4.9

Student	Score at 10% of Reasonable Potential	Score at 25% of Reasonable Potential	Score at 50% of Reasonable Potential
A	31 (25 + 6)	40 (25 + 15)	55 (25 + 30)
B	252 (250 + 2)	253 (250 + 3)	256 (250 + 6)

promising in mental health documentation because the reasonable goal becomes the treatment plan goal. It is client-specific and provides a means for comparing one client's outcomes to those of others. Outcome indices and clinical procedures can be integrated and mutually beneficial.

There are cases in which the reasonable goal is the same as the maximum possible goal. In such cases, there is no difference in the calculations. For example, if a client must return to work five days per week in order to keep her job, both the reasonable and the maximum goal would be returning to work five days per week.

Specific Examples of Ordinal Categorical Procedures: Global Assessment of Functioning (GAF) Scores. Axis V of the *Diagnostic and Statistical Manual of Mental Disorders*—Fourth Edition (*DSM-IV*) (American Psychiatric Association [APA], 1994), is a single, global measure of the client's overall level of functioning that is intended for planning treatment, evaluating the impact of treatment, and predicting outcomes. The therapist, not the client or collaterals, assigns the GAF rating. The rating (1 to 100) is based on functioning at the time of the evaluation and subsequent periodic ratings. Therefore it is subject to periodic changes, aiding in therapeutic decision making. The *DSM-IV*'s suggested format for listing the GAF is to denote the GAF rating number, followed in parentheses by the time period referred to. For example, GAF = 70 (current) denotes that the client is currently experiencing mild symptoms of impairment, but is generally functioning well. Other common usages of the time descriptor include (on admission), (at discharge), and (highest level past year). For example, the Axis V evaluation for someone being discharged from the hospital might be listed as GAF = 43 (on admission), GAF = 62 (at discharge).

The GAF scale is adapted from the Global Assessment Scale (GAS) devised by Endicott, Spitzer, Fleiss, and Cohen (1976). High interrater reliability has been demonstrated with GAS ratings for psychiatric patients when raters were adequately trained (Dworkin, Friedman, Telschow, Grant, Moffic, & Sloan, 1990). The GAS creators (Endicott et al., 1976) have reported reliability coefficients of 0.61 to 0.91. Researchers generally obtained higher reliability results than clinicians (Clark & Friedman, 1983; Endicott et al., 1976; Plankun, Muller, & Burkhardt, 1987).

Although the 1-to-100 scaling system in the GAF may appear to be ordinal metric data (described in next section), it actually contains both ordinal metric and ordinal categorical properties because of the verbal descriptors that result in unequal distances between the descriptors (see Figure 4.2). However, each of the 10 data points between the descriptors is assumed to be at equal distance. The anchor points (e.g., minimal, transient, mild, moderate, serious, problems with reality testing, danger to self, etc.) may be helpful to a person filling out a rating sheet, but the data are no longer linear. Although few would disagree that the descriptors increase in severity as the GAF lowers, the data nevertheless are subject to the constraints of ordinal statistical analysis. It is quite common, however, to use the GAF scale as ordinal metric data. The authors do not advise against assessing outcomes with GAF change scores, but believe that some precision in the data may be compromised.

GAF scores are not normally distributed. That is, the majority of people have relatively high scores, with few people having low scores. A very low percentage of the population has GAF scores between 0 and 40. Most of the population has a GAF score over 70. That is, the same numbers of people do not graduate from a GAF score of 10 to 20 as graduate from 80 to 90. Statistical operations that attempt to compare the client to a normal population, using GAF scores, might consider *Z* scores, while intraclient comparisons tend to look at the GAF scores in themselves as outcome indicators.

GAF scores estimate the client's current level of global functioning, an important aspect of mental health diagnosis. However, when the scores are subject to data analysis, interpretation errors are imminent if the change scores are the sole primary means of analysis. For example, when measuring effective change, a therapist might naively and inappropriately perform the procedure in Box 4.10.

In this case, Client A and Client B are clearly functioning at different levels. Client A entered therapy with relatively few problems that were perhaps transient, depending on the level of stress present. At the end of therapy, minimal symptoms existed. Client B entered therapy being influenced by hallucinations, and still had major impairments at discharge. Simply stating that the degree of client change is equivalent provides little useful information. However, when data are analyzed as if an equal amount of change in a score is equivalent to the actual behavioral change, useless or inaccurate interpretations may take place.

The authors suggest exercising caution when

Figure 4.2

GAF Scale

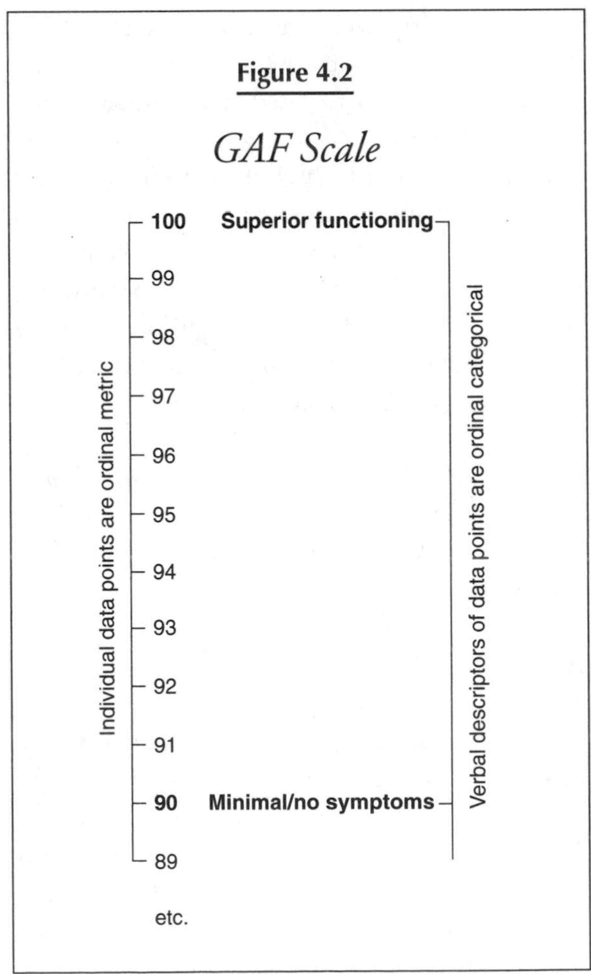

Box 4.10

	Initial GAF Score	Subsequent GAF Score	Change Score
Client A	30	40	+10
Client B	80	90	+10

using outcome assessment procedures that incorporate quantification methods not intended to go beyond categorization. The resultant change scores, in effect, provide little information as to the client's functioning level.

Incorporating Data Analysis Methods 1 through 3 into GAF Scores. The following examples of the three data analysis methods presented in the previous section demonstrate how the choice of mathematical procedures can influence the reporting of results.

Two clients, A and B, have gone through 12 weeks of psychotherapy, yielding the GAF Scores in Box 4.11.

Method 1: Baseline Method. Using Method 1, the percentages of change do not portray a clear picture of the clients' changes (see Box 4.12). From this method of analyzing the data, it appears that Client A has improved more than Client B. However, the change scores are the same, and Client B leaves treatment at a higher level of functioning than Client A. The existence of data analysis methods does not assure their accuracy.

Box 4.11

Client	Pretest	Posttest	Change
A	40	60	+20
B	60	80	+20

Comparing a client's pretest and posttest GAF scores provides some information, but little help in assessing outcomes. It simply suggests how much a client has improved, but does not tell the degree to which treatment was successful. In the case of Clients A and B, their change scores were identical, but Client B leaves therapy with a minimum of mental health problems. Client A still has a moderate amount of dysfunction and may require more sessions. However, Client A's change score is helpful in demonstrating that the amount of treatment rendered to date has brought about an increase in functioning. The percentage of improvement score, in itself, provides no useful information other than demonstrating that some improvement took place. Percentages based on change scores are not valid measures of improvement. In this case, stating that Client A improved 50 percent has no clinical meaning. The logic of using percentages in change scores is demonstrated as flawed in the

Box 4.12

Formula	Percentage of Improvement	=	Change Score	/	Pretest score
Client A	50%	=	20	/	40
Client B	33%	=	20	/	60

following example: Client A has an initial GAF score of 40. After treatment, the GAF increased to 60. The resulting change score is 20—a 50 percent increase. If this logic is used, then a 100 percent increase would suggest a GAF score of 80, which has little meaning. It further suggests that, to attain a GAF of 100, the client would have to improve over 100 percent. Percentages of ratings scores have no statistical meaning when used in this manner.

Percentages can be helpful when discussing percentage of progress toward a goal. Methods 2 and 3 incorporate this type of evaluation.

Method 2: Maximum Possible Score Method. The maximum possible GAF score is 100, which represents superior mental health functioning. When considering the maximum possible gain for Clients A and B (see Box 4.13), Client A has progressed 33 percent of the maximum possible toward the highest possible GAF (100), while Client B has attained 50 percent of the maximum possible. Results directly conflict with those obtained using Method 1. If the therapist is using Method 1, it appears that Client A has progressed more, whereas Method 2 favors the progress of Client B.

Method 3: Reasonable Goal Attainment Method. Each client is assigned a different GAF goal, based on what is reasonable for the expected duration of treatment and overall potential. The reasonable GAF goal becomes one of the treatment plan goals. Method 3 allows the therapist to

Box 4.13

Formula:	Current % Increase to Maximum Possible Score	=	Change Score	/	Maximum Possible Score	–	Baseline Score
Client A	33%	=	20	/	(100	–	40)
Client B	50%	=	20	/	(100	–	60)

measure the percentage of the goal reached to date.

The amount of reasonable change could be different for clients with the same initial baseline score. For example, a client with a chronic history of mental illness who has a baseline GAF score of 45 will not have the same reasonable potential goal as a client with the same current GAF (due to a significant stressor) but without a history of mental illness. The reasonable GAF goal for the client with chronic mental illness may be at a maintenance level, or perhaps no more than 55 to 60, while the client with an acute problem area may have the goal set to 75 to 80 for the same time period. The GAF scores and reasonable goals for the clients are set as shown in Box 4.14.

Method 3 allows for measuring the client's change score, plus the client's percentage of attainment toward the individualized goal. This method is more capable than the others of comparing the progress of clients with different levels of functioning. The goals are deemed reasonable given the client's current mental health condition. In this situation, each client leaves therapy at a different level of functioning, but it is estimated their relative progress is similar. If the reasonable goal for either client were set 5 points lower in the example in Box 4.14, goal attainment would be 100 percent.

This method is useful in that client progress is based on level of attainment of the treatment plan GAF goal. It incorporates the GAF, the treatment plan, and an outcome measure. Problems occur if the clinician sets goals too low or high. Goals set too high will not be reached; goals set too low could lead to premature termination of services. If therapists' effectiveness is partially evaluated by client goal attainment, it may be more likely that reasonable goals are set.

Other Considerations with GAF Scores. Because GAF scores are ordinal data, there are limits to

Box 4.14

Client	Baseline GAF	Posttest GAF	Change Score	Estimated Reasonable GAF Goal	Estimated Reasonable GAF Change
A	40	60	+20	65	+25
B	60	80	+20	85	+25

Formula:

	Current % in Increase to Reasonable Goal	=	Change Score	/	(Reasonable Goal	–	Baseline Score)
Client A	80%	=	20	/	(65	–	40)
Client B	80%	=	20	/	(85	–	60)

the extent to which data analysis can be performed. Clinicians may disagree as to whether GAF scores are ordinal metric or ordinal categorical. The authors suggest that ordinal metric data can be assumed, but with moderate confidence, because every 10th score has a categorical label. If GAF scores were simply rated on a scale of 1 to 100, with no verbal descriptors, they would be ordinal metric. GAF scores are not normally distributed.

Percentages cannot be used in ordinal data. For example, a person functioning at a GAF score of 40 is not 50 percent as functional as someone is with a GAF score of 80. It can be assumed, however, that if someone has a GAF goal of 80, and has increased in GAF score from 60 to 70, than the person has reached 50 percent of the GAF goal.

Problems When Solely Incorporating Change Scores in GAF Ratings. Consider the following statement in which the data are misrepresented. "Client A has been in inpatient counseling for 10 weeks due to a psychotic episode with a suicidal attempt after her daughter unexpectedly passed away. Her GAF score has now risen from 20 to 40; therefore, there has been a 100 percent increase in her mental health functioning. Due to her 100 percent increase, discharge is recommended."

It is suggested that the data be interpreted as follows: "Client A has been in inpatient counseling for 10 weeks due to a psychiatric episode with a suicidal attempt after her daughter unexpectedly passed away. Her initial GAF rating of 20 suggested that she was in some danger of harming herself upon being admitted. Her current GAF of 40 suggests major impairment in several areas of her life—she is still quite despondent and confused, and still threatens suicide at times. Due to her current level of functioning, discharge is not recommended."

Other Ordinal Categorical Measures Used in Individualized Outcome Assessment. Specific problem areas can be monitored throughout treatment if they are sufficiently quantified for measurement and are adequately and periodically monitored. Goal Attainment Scaling (GAS: Kiresuk & Sherman, 1968) sets up incremental goals prior to treatment. Each goal is broken down into increasingly more desirable outcomes that can be observed empirically. Each increasingly higher step clearly represents higher functioning. Outcomes are measured periodically throughout treatment. The client, therapist, or both may set the goals. A wide variety of behaviors may be evaluated in Goal Attainment Scaling, ranging from describing specific behaviors such as bed-wetting, hours of sleep, or alcohol consumption, to test scores.

Clement (1999) suggests the Scale of Functioning (SOF) rating for each problem area on a 1-to-10 Scale of Functioning system in which 10 separate levels of functioning for given behaviors are defined and quantified. The SOF score is similar to Axis V (the GAF) on the *DSM.* Increments of 10 are used, rather than the 1 to 100 on the GAF. The therapist charts progress on the scale throughout therapy as a measure of outcomes. Clement (1996) suggests making a master list of problem areas in which progress can be easily monitored and evaluated. Clement states that his average number of problem areas per client is more than 12. For example, if 12 client problem areas are noted and each has 10 separate behavioral definitions, based on degree of functioning, then 120 separate behavioral descriptors must be operationally defined.

Problems are apparent when considering the time involved in setting up the several incremental goals for each problem area. As treatment progresses, the predetermined goals may need several revisions, further increasing administrative time.

If Goal Attainment Scaling or Scale of Functioning procedures are used, they should be the treatment plan goals and objectives, rather than separate paperwork procedures.

Differences in the Number of Data Points. It is difficult to quantifiably document clinical changes when few data points are available. If only four to seven anchor points are available, such as in a typical rating scale, it may take a long time for a client to progress only 1 point, even when some clinical progress has taken place. Therefore, the scaling system itself can hinder accurate documentation of client change. However, a scale with 100 anchor points, such as the GAF or an SUD, requires little change to document progress. While actual clinical progress does not change due to the scale being used, the scale with more data points is more sensitive in documenting clinical changes.

Consider the example in Box 4.15 of comparing a 5-point scale to a 100-point scale. Client A's behaviors are rated on a 5-point scale, while Client B's ratings are on a 100-point scale. Each client begins therapy with significant problem areas; therefore, they are rated as Client A = 2

Box 4.15

Check how often you have problems in the following areas.

1. Depression (1)__Never (2)__Rarely (3)__Sometimes (4)__Often (5)__Always
2. Anxiety (1)__Never (2)__Rarely (3)__Sometimes (4)__Often (5)__Always
3. Confusion (1)__Never (2)__Rarely (3)__Sometimes (4)__Often (5)__Always
4. Anger (1)__Never (2)__Rarely (3)__Sometimes (4)__Often (5)__Always
5. Alcohol Abuse (1)__Never (2)__Rarely (3)__Sometimes (4)__Often (5)__Always
6. Hallucinations (1)__Never (2)__Rarely (3)__Sometimes (4)__Often (5)__Always

This example provides more specific information than nominal data, but it takes slightly more time to attain. Clients are forced to subjectively rate the degree of each symptom, rather than simply endorsing its existence or nonexistence. In these examples, clinical judgment must be exercised because the different degree of existence between symptoms has different clinical implications. For example, it may be normal for clients to state that they sometimes have problems with depression. They might not need any treatment. Perhaps from time to time they experience normal life stressors leading to predictable, reactive, acute depression. However, if the same clients answer 3 (Sometimes), when responding to Item 6 (Hallucinations), considerable concerns are noted. That is, there is a significant clinical difference between sometimes feeling depressed and sometimes experiencing hallucinations. Which is more severe, a 4 on Item 1 or a 2 on Item 6?

(out of 5), Client B = 40 (out of 100). If Client A's level of improvement increases to a 3, an equal amount of change for Client B would be at an equivalent score of 60. However, if each client's ratings improved to a lesser degree, such that Client B's score elevated to a 50, there would be no notable change in Client's A's rating. That is, in this case, the outcome indicators would yield no change for Client A, but a change can be documented for Client B.

Although numbers are assigned to the data points (1 to 5), mathematical operations such as addition and multiplication cannot be performed. There is not necessarily equal distance between the descriptors. For example, it would be absurd to add 2 (Rarely) plus 3 (Sometimes), and state that the answer is 5 (Always). The categories are simply listed in rank order, with no mathematical relationship other than rank order. Further, a rating of 3 (Sometimes) is not three units of anything. The numbers simply denote that a rating of 3 (Sometimes) is more than a rating of 2 (Rarely), but less than a rating of 4 (Often).

Progress can be shown by comparing categories. For example, if a client initially endorses using alcohol as 4 (Frequently), then, after two months of treatment, states that usage is 2 (Seldom), progress is noted, but it has not been clearly measured.

Concerns about Using Ordinal Categorical Data in Outcome Assessment. Many outcome systems use interval categorical data, but incorrectly use statistical analyses that are intended for a higher level of data. They are problematic because increases or decreases in data points in different parts of the scale are not equal to change in other parts of the scale. Results are usually misleading depending on the bias of the scales.

For example, consider the scale in Box 4.16. This example demonstrates how symptoms can be rated equally on an ordinal categorical scale, yet actually represent significantly different levels of the symptom or behavior. For example, Client A describes five weekly panic attacks as "Frequently," but Client B describes five weekly panic attacks as only "Sometimes." Whenever ordinal

Box 4.16

Frequency of panic attacks:
(1)__Never (2)__Seldom (3)__Sometimes (4)__Frequently (5)__Always

Client A's perception of the scale in terms of number of panic attacks per week:

(1)__Never	(2)__Seldom	(3)__Sometimes	(4)__Frequently	(5)__Always
0	1	2	5	7

Client B's perception of the scale in terms of number of panic attacks per week:

(1)__Never	(2)__Seldom	(3)__Sometimes	(4)__Frequently	(5)__Always
0	2	5	14	30

data can be expressed in terms of interval data, outcome assessment is more specific.

Ordinal Metric Data

The difference between ordinal categorical and ordinal metric data is that it can be assumed that there are equal distances between data points in ordinal metric data. For example, the two types of ordinal data could be graphed hypothetically on a 10-point scale as in Box 4.17.

In ordinal metric data, by definition, there are equal distances between data points. The example in Box 4.17 depicts one of several possible relationships within the ordinal categorical data. There is a linear relationship among the ordinal data. The ordinal categorical data are not linear because of the unequal distance between the data points. The nonlinear relationship within ordinal categorical data makes it difficult to measure client progress because, even if the client improves on a steady basis, the uneven data points will make progress appear to take place at the rate concordant with the distance between descriptors. Figures 4.3 and 4.4 rate a client's progress on both an ordinal metric and ordinal categorical scale as depicted in Box 4.17. If the actual client progress is linear (equally spaced), the ordinal metric data accurately represent the linear progress. However, the ordinal categorical scale would artificially depict the client's progress in a different time progression than actually took place, due to unequal data intervals. (Note: Linear progress is depicted for the sake of example. In clinical practice, progress is not expected to be linear).

Metric rating scales are designed to provide a wide range of options in rating behaviors or emotions. The end points are adjectives describing extreme levels of various behaviors, such as Always to Never. Other terms describing extremes or end points may include those such as Excellent to Poor. For example, Box 4.18 represents a metric rating scale.

In this example, we assume equal distances between numbers; therefore, for example, the progression from a 2 to a 3 is assumed to be equal to the progression from a 4 to a 5. That is, the relationship between numbers is linear. Numerical operations cannot be conducted, however. For example, a 4 is not twice as much as a 2.

Subjective Units of Distress (SUDs). SUDs are the client's subjective rating of the amount of distress being experienced due to a given stressor. SUD ratings are based on a 1-to-100 rating sys-

Box 4.17

Type of Data	Numerical Descriptors
Categorical (Unequal spacing)	1 2 3 4 5 6 7 8 9 10
Metric (Equal spacing)	1 2 3 4 5 6 7 8 9 10

Figure 4.3

Rating on Ordinal Metric Scale

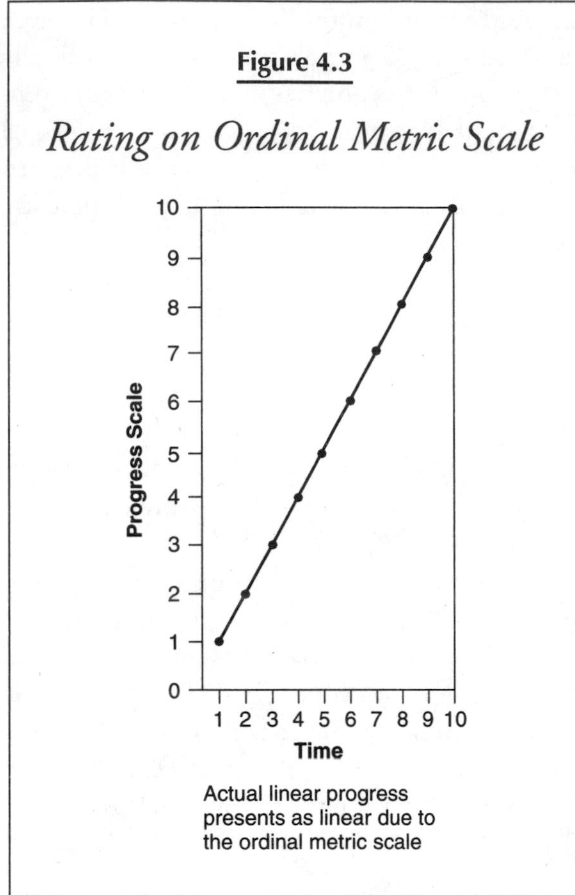

Actual linear progress presents as linear due to the ordinal metric scale

Figure 4.4

Rating on Ordinal Categorical Scale

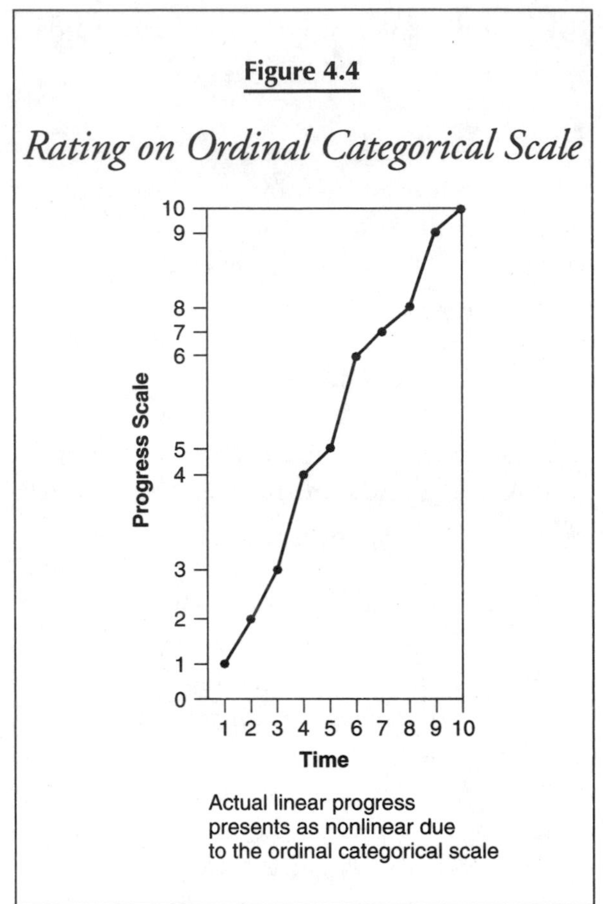

Actual linear progress presents as nonlinear due to the ordinal categorical scale

tem. For example, a client presenting with agoraphobia may be asked to rate the amount of distress he feels when he goes out in public. The therapist routinely explains that a rating of 1 represents the complete absence of distress, while a 100 represents the maximum amount of distress possible. A severely distressed client might rate his amount of distress at the beginning of therapy at a severity of 95. As therapy progresses, subsequent ratings are taken as a measure of progress. Treatment plan objectives may incorporate various desired SUD levels periodically. We can assume that a 10-point drop from 95 to 85 is similar in relative level of improvement to a 10-point drop from 75 to 65. However, we cannot assume that someone is one-third less depressed when a drop in scores from 90 to 60 takes place.

Interval and Ratio Data

Ratio data are not applicable to mental health outcome assessment. Interval data assume equal distance between data points. Numerical operations such as addition, subtraction, multiplication, and division can be performed. The numbers depicted directly represent the amount of behavior, not a rating of the behavior. Interval data best represent objective, not subjective, behavior. An example of interval data in mental health is in Box 4.19.

Box 4.18

Check your current satisfaction in your marriage.

Extremely Negative	__1	__2	__3	__4	__5	__6	__7	Extremely Positive

In this example, behaviors are easily measured and compared over time. For example, a decrease in panic attacks from six to two per day results in four fewer panic attacks per day, or a 67 percent decrease. A decrease in the average length of a panic attack from 30 minutes to 10 minutes further represents data capable of undergoing addition, subtraction, multiplication, and division. The data are therefore highly objective, measurable, and empirical.

If the data on panic attacks had been nominal, they would have been analyzed as A = Yes or B = No. They would provide no indication of the degree of panic attacks; therefore, diagnosis would be, at most, tentative.

If the previous example were listed in ordinal data, its severity could be approximated, but the amount of change due to treatment is fairly subjective and bound to the confines of the limited measurement scale. Interval data are clearly the most accurate form of measurement in outcomes.

Not all behaviors are subject to interval measurement. We cannot place an interval number on mental health constructs, but we can measure behaviors suggestive of various mental health concerns. For example, it is not appropriate to say that we have 4 units of sadness, and if 2 units of happiness are attained, there will be 50 percent more happiness. It makes more sense to say that we are engaging in 50 percent more enjoyable activities, thus the level of depression may have decreased. Examples of interval data in mental health documentation are shown in Box 4.20.

The clinical example in Box 4.21 depicts the differences in the quality of data due to the type of measurement scale chosen.

These examples demonstrate the usefulness of

Box 4.19

Frequency of panic attacks per day?

__0 __1 __2 __3 X4 __5 __6 __7 __8 . . .

Duration of panic attacks per day?

Average length of a panic attack = *15 minutes*

Box 4.20

(1) 3 auditory hallucinations per day on average
(2) Absent from school at least 12 days per month
(3) Drinks 1 liter of gin per day
(4) Disrupted class 24 times last week
(5) Started 5 fights in the past month
(6) Lost 30 pounds in the past 60 days
(7) Checks for unlocked doors an average of 60 times per day
(8) Sleeps no more than 2 hours at a time
(9) Complied with medication regime 10 days last month
(10) Leaves house an average of 12 minutes per week

each type of data. In the diagnostic interview the therapist initially questions the client as to whether symptoms (in this case, panic attacks) exist (nominal data). If the client denies the existence of a symptom, the clinician goes on to another topic or category of symptoms. But, if the client endorses that panic attacks occur, the clinician then determines the degree of panic attacks (ordinal data). In order to quantify the severity of the panic attacks, an SUD rating may be included (ordinal metric data). Finally, objective questions regarding the frequency and duration of panic attacks are included (interval data).

Although each type of data serves a different purpose, they are all important for different reasons. The frequency and duration of panic attacks (interval data), without the knowledge of the severity of panic attacks (ordinal metric data), are not sufficient to clearly document medical necessity. For example, two people might both experience three panic attacks per day that last about 15 minutes. One person may experience mild symptoms that do not significantly impair any areas of functioning, while the other person might become extremely dysfunctional both affectively and physically during panic attacks.

Are Ordinal Categorical and Ordinal Metric Data Significantly Different?

Studies comparing ordinal categorical and ordinal metric data have primarily dealt with attitude scales such as Likert (1932) scales. Today, usage of the term *Likert scale* has mixed meanings; the term *Likert-like scales* is commonly used. A Likert scale consists of ordinal data, which include an equal number of positively and negatively worded response options. It is assumed that there is equal spacing (linearity) between item descriptors, suggesting unidimensionality and assignment of consecutive integers for data analysis. The items containing an odd number of response options contain a neutral item in the middle. For example, a Likert scale might be written as follows:

(1)__Strongly Agree (2)__Agree
(3)__Neutral (4)__Disagree
(5)__Strongly Disagree

Box 4.21

Scenario: Client is experiencing an average of 4 panic attacks per day that last 20 minutes each.

Nominal Data
Typical question asked:
Do you have panic attacks?
_X_ Yes ___No

Best use: Nominal data are best used in the initial interview to determine whether or not a specific symptom is present. It takes little interview time to inquire about the several possible *DSM-IV* symptoms a client may be experiencing. Behavioral and symptom checklists filled out by a client before the initial interview often contain nominal questions in which the clinician will further probe problems that have been endorsed by the client as taking place. Nominal data provide no information as to the frequency, duration, or severity of the symptoms. When the client endorses that a symptom exists, further questions are asked (rule-in). Symptoms not endorsed by the client as taking place are part of the rule-out process. The rule-in/rule-out procedure is also referred to as a *decision tree.*

Ordinal Data
Ordinal Categorical
Typical question asked:
Severity of panic attacks?
1___ None 2___ Mild 3_X_ Moderate 4___ Severe

Best use: Ordinal categorical data provide an indication of the degree of severity, frequency, or duration of a symptom or a behavior experienced by the client. Categorical labels are easy to read and generally take little time to fill out. The categories provide a quick reference point by which comparisons and evaluations can be made.

Ordinal Metric
Typical question asked:
Severity (or SUDs) of panic attacks?
None 0 ___80___ 100 Extreme

Best use: Ordinal metric data are similar to ordinal categorical data in that a subjective rating is made. The data points are equally spaced, allowing for more accu-

(continued)

Box 4.21 *(Continued)*

rate measurement of incremental progress. The person filling out the information is not forced to make predetermined choices.

Interval Data

Typical question asked:
Frequency of panic attacks per day? *3 per day (average)*
Duration of panic attacks? *20 minutes (average)*

Best use: Interval data are best employed in providing direct measurement of various aspects of behaviors. Measurements are objective, rather than subjective. A wide range of data analysis procedures can be performed that are not available for the other types of data.

According to Chang (1997), the middle point allows for no opinion or a neutral opinion, but a number of studies have suggested that a neutral item may lead to a response bias (Bendig, 1954; Cronbach, 1950; Goldberg, 1981; Nunnally, 1967), while even-numbered response sets were more reliable (Bendig, 1954; Masters, 1974). Chang (1997) points out that the wording of the middle item in odd-numbered scales increases the difficulty of designing a scale with equally spaced intervals. It is also important that the middle term be perceived by all as truly neutral.

Chang's (1997) research further suggests that Likert-type ratings are reliable in a number of ways. When the endpoints changed from *strongly agree* and *strongly disagree* to *agree* and *disagree,* there was no difference in mean scores on a 4-point scale. Chang further found no difference between using only endpoints of *completely agree* and *completely disagree* and labeling all descriptors on a 6-point scale. Results suggest that ordinal categorical data can be similar to ordinal metric data if it is assumed that there is equal space between data points. Chang (1997) concluded that Likert-type scales can be generalized across anchoring labels and that researchers do not need to be overly concerned about the choice of verbal descriptors.

Other studies provide mixed results as to whether full labeling, no labeling, or labeling only the endpoints produces different results. Newstead and Arnold (1989) found that unlabeled scales produced the highest means. Huck and Jacko (1974) obtained the opposite results, whereas others (Dixon, Bobo & Stevick, 1984; Finn, 1972) found no differences.

Chang (1997) notes that Likert scales have received much attention in determining which verbal descriptors best suggest equally perceived distances between them (Bass, 1968; Bass, Cascio, & O'Connor, 1974; Cliff, 1959; Spector, 1976). For example, Bass (1968) demonstrated that students perceive the adjectives *always, very often, fairly often, sometimes, seldom,* and *never* as equidistant. In such cases ordinal categorical data are not differentiated from ordinal metric data

Box 4.22

(A) Good	Slight	Some	Moderate	Serious
(B) Always	Usually	Sometimes	Seldom	Never

because of equal spacing between descriptors. However, Masters (1985) warned:

> A continuous issue in the analysis of Likert data is the question of how responses to question items should be combined. Likert (1932) assigned successive integers to response categories and simply summed over the items to obtain questionnaire scores for each respondent. However, this approach has been criticized on grounds that it assumes equal distances between adjacent response categories.

Likert-like scales in outcome assessment are a commonly accepted means of evaluating attitudes. But outcome research is not about attitudes. Nevertheless, data analysis procedures that are used in Likert scales are often used in ordinal categorical data. Although Likert scales may appear to be ordinal categorical, they are actually ordinal metric because of the equidistance between rating points criteria.

Typical rating descriptors in outcomes are those in Box 4.22. Such descriptors are clearly different from the nature of Likert scales. Likert scales measure attitudes, whereas outcome measures measure behaviors. Behaviors are much more subject to change and generally represent frequencies or intensities of actions, affective responses, or evaluations. There are no neutral responses in outcome measurements, but they can take place in attitudinal research. The data analysis methods employed in Likert ratings are not applicable to outcome research unless there is equal distance between the descriptors.

SUMMARY

Mental health constructs cannot be directly measured. Problems are complicated by the various schools of thought, which view client change differently. Current standards in mental health outcome assessment attempt to provide data that are observable, measurable, and quantifiable in client symptomology and functional impairments. The various levels of data each provide important, but qualitatively different, client information. Each level of data requires different methods of analysis, which, if incorporated erroneously, will lead to misleading results.

The same data can demonstrate either effective or ineffective therapy depending on the analysis procedure. In this chapter, the problem of incorporating change scores into outcome assessment is examined. Three modes of data analysis are proposed to evaluate change scores. The clinician must be careful and ethical in selecting the most appropriate method of data analysis; therefore, some understanding of research methodology is helpful.

5

ASSESSING OUTCOME THROUGH THE *DSM-IV* INTERVIEW AND INTAKE INFORMATION

There must be a universal standard on which each system of mental health outcomes is based. Commercial or informal outcome-measuring instruments and systems may be excellent in attaining and organizing relevant information, but without a clear universal standard, results are no more than tentative. The reference point for definitions of mental health diagnoses is the *Diagnostic and Statistical Manual of Mental Disorders*—Fourth Edition (*DSM-IV*) (American Psychiatric Association [APA], 1994).

Third-party payers routinely require evidence that the *DSM-IV* Axis I diagnosis remains prevalent to approve further benefits. The diagnosis therefore must be validated regularly throughout treatment. Clement (1996) reports that in the past there was little relationship between diagnosis and treatment, whereas the contemporary trend is for providers to write treatment plans to fit the diagnosis (see Knesper, Pagnucco, & Kalter, 1986; Wiger, 1999a).

Hundreds of tests are available commercially that measure a wide range of mental health symptoms. No test is 100 percent concordant with the *DSM-IV* in providing a specific diagnosis. Typical assessment methods involve incorporating several possible procedures in which the *DSM-IV* diagnosis is both a reference point and a conclusion. The diagnosis is primarily based on *DSM-IV* criteria that have been validated by various clinical procedures. The *DSM-IV* is the constant, whereas other clinical procedures may be variable. They are designed to correlate with the *DSM-IV* but have less correlation with each other. Therefore, the *DSM-IV* must be the most valid constant in outcome measures when considering individual progress. Outcome systems (various procedures and repeated measures) are intended to most reliably represent the client's current status of mental health functioning in relation to the *DSM-IV* diagnosis. Independent systems of outcome assessment are needed to organize outcome indicators because the *DSM-IV* itself is not an outcome system. When third-party requirements are considered, outcome measurements that are not based on the *DSM-IV* are not necessary, sufficient, or helpful. Outcome assessment measures that use the *DSM-IV* as the universal standard provide therapists with a wide selection of psychometric, observational, and self-report indices to validate clients' current levels of *DSM-IV* symptomology and impairments.

Third-party payers require a *DSM-IV* Axis I diagnosis for payment. In order for the client to receive ongoing services, the *DSM-IV* diagnosis must be confirmed periodically, meaning that the therapist must consistently document evidence that the client's symptoms and impairments continue to cause dysfunction, distress, or both (see Box 5.1). When there is no longer evidence of a *DSM-IV* diagnosis, or if treatment is not effective, services are terminated. Confirmation of a mental health condition by any standard other than the *DSM-IV* may jeopardize reimbursement. For example, if an outcome measurement system confirms the need for continued services by using itself or other psychometric tests as a standard for client progress, the client may appear to be making significant strides, yet the system itself is not necessarily a valid or reliable predictor of *DSM-IV* diagnoses. The more consistent the outcome measurement system is with the *DSM-IV*, the more valid the outcome indicators will be.

DSM-IV: SYMPTOMS AND IMPAIRMENTS

In the not-so-distant past, we defined mental health diagnoses primarily by endorsing a client's symptoms. More recently, the *DSM-IV* has clarified that there are cases in which clients have mild symptoms of a diagnosis but do not demonstrate clear impairment. The *DSM-IV* describes level of impairment as the threshold by which a diagnosis is made or not made. The *DSM-IV* also allows clinicians flexibility in making a diagnosis when the client's symptomology may not exactly match *DSM-IV* standards, but the clinician's level of expertise and judgment indicate that a diagnosis is warranted.

Beutler, Goodrich, Fisher, and Williams (1999) distinguished level of impairment and subjective distress as different measures; thus outcome research would yield mixed results depending on what is being measured. (See Beutler, Wakefield, & Williams, 1994; Strupp, Horowitz, & Lambert, 1997.) Thus, test selection must include a careful examination of what is being tested (e.g., symptoms, impairments, personal distress, global func-

Box 5.1

Q: Why do you spend so much time talking about diagnoses? I thought we treated the person.

A: Therapists treat the person, not the diagnosis, but a diagnosis is a means of communicating problem areas. The diagnosis is extremely important because without it treatment will not be reimbursed, nor will there be adequate communication describing the problem areas. We treat the individual. Thus, therapists document the *DSM-IV* requirements for the diagnosis in order to be able to continue treatment.

tioning, personality). The reporting of outcomes must clearly discuss the validity of the instruments used; otherwise the GIGO (garbage in, garbage out) principle prevails.

MEDICAL NECESSITY

Although symptoms are necessary in deriving a mental health diagnosis and validating treatment outcomes, they are not sufficient. Clients may continue to exhibit mild symptoms of a disorder but experience no significant impairments (see Box 5.2). Although such clients would likely benefit from counseling, most third-party payers do not pay for services unless they are medically necessary. *Medically necessary* means that without such services, the client would most likely not improve in a reasonable time period. Thus, ongoing impairments must be clearly documented throughout treatment.

In today's managed care environment, mental health services that are not medically necessary are similar to elective medical procedures, that is, treatment that is not necessary for the client's well-being. In such cases, insurance coverage is denied. For example, certain types of counseling, including personal growth and skills training, are not considered medically necessary and are usually spelled out in provider contracts as noncovered services. Therapists must always document the medical necessity of services or they may not be reimbursed for services or may be asked to pay back the money at a later date.

Clients do not necessarily come to therapy solely because of specific symptoms or a documented mental health impairment. Many seek counseling because they have emotional prob-

Box 5.2

Examples of various *DSM-IV* symptoms

Social withdrawal	Low self-esteem	Hallucinations
Lack of pleasure	Paranoia	Sadness
Suicidal ideations	Irritability	Appetite problems
Decreased concentration	Low motivation	Stuttering

Types and examples of mental health impairments

Type	*Example*
Social	Has not contacted any friends or family members in the past year
Occupational	Work performance is 40% less than previous output
Academic	Failing all classes at school
Affective	Feels despondent over 90% of the time
Legal	In danger of arrest due to violent behavioral outbursts
Physical	Has unintentionally gained more than 10 pounds per month for the past 6 months

lems that inhibit them from functioning normally. A diagnosis is simply descriptive and does not describe the client's degree of impairment (see Box 5.3). The symptoms define a diagnosis. Impairments are the resultant behaviors, consequences, and cognitive/affective problem areas, which, if not treated, will most likely not improve or further decline. The level of impairment a client experiences is affected by the degree of stressors, symptoms, coping ability, personality factors, environmental strengths and limitations, and much more. Impairment is indicated when the client's symptoms reach a level at which they significantly interfere with daily functioning, and treatment is medically necessary for the client to return to adequate functioning.

ESSENTIAL AND ASSOCIATED SYMPTOMS IN THE *DSM-IV*

The *DSM-IV* describes each diagnosis as having at least one *essential symptom.* An essential symptom is a symptom that must exist in order for the diagnosis to be made. For example, the essential symptom of the *DSM-IV* diagnosis of Attention-Deficit/Hyperactivity Disorder (ADHD) is a persistent pattern of inattention, hyperactivity-impulsivity, or both. There are 18 other *DSM-IV* symptoms of ADHD, but without the essential symptom(s) a diagnosis cannot be made. Several diagnoses additionally require a time period in which symptoms must be prevalent to make the diagnosis. Table 5.1 briefly paraphrases essential symptoms from selected *DSM-IV* diagnoses. Keep in mind that each diagnosis includes several other requirements that also must be met. Wiger (1999a) described what the *DSM-IV* calls *the essential symptom(s)* as *the primary essential symptom,* and the other *DSM-IV* essential symptoms (in which a set number of specific symptoms must be prevalent) as *secondary essential symptoms.*

Some clients exhibit several symptoms of their diagnosis, while others exhibit few. If two clients have the same diagnosis, they each share the

Box 5.3

Q: Which of the following statements best describes a client's condition?

1. Pat drinks more alcohol than he did in the past. Everyone is worried about him.
2. Pat was fired from work due to being drunk on the job three times last month. Last week, he was arrested twice for (a) starting a fight in a bar and (b) domestic abuse.

A: Both examples 1 and 2 list the symptom as drinking alcohol. Example 2 lists three areas of impairment to investigate: occupational, legal, and domestic. In this example, it is difficult to measure or quantify symptoms, but impairments easily lend themselves to measurement. Quantification of impairments is documentable in both baseline and ongoing measures.

essential symptom(s). The other associated symptoms may vary significantly, and their degree of impairment may also differ.

The clinician must choose which aspects of treatment will serve as outcome indicators for third-party reimbursement. If the clinician charts outcomes for every symptom and impairment, the paperwork will be tremendous. The authors suggest that the problems associated with the essential symptoms are always included as outcome indicators. The client's other most salient problem areas, that is, those that demonstrate the primary need for treatment, should comprise the other indicators.

Integrating Outcome Measures and Usual Clinical Procedures

Outcome procedures do not have to be separate and burdensome paperwork tasks. Appropriate use of the collected data can be an integral part of the therapeutic process. Whatever tools or procedures are used, the necessary information includes baseline measures, ongoing measures, and termination, and may include posttermination material. Caution must be taken if the therapist decides to use any rating scales or tests that are not highly correlated with the *DSM-IV.* Reliability is preserved when the same measurement indices, rating scales, or tests are used consistently throughout treatment. Much time and effort is conserved when these same indices are used for both outcome measures and usual clinical procedures. Redundancy in paperwork is never welcomed by the therapist.

Some tests are time-consuming and expensive to administer. No third party would authorize extensive testing every session or every few sessions, nor would this benefit the client. Ongoing assessment is most efficient when the procedures aid in outcome documentation and in improving the session-by-session quality of treatment.

Standardized tests, in which the client's behaviors are compared to those of a normative population, are designed to provide diagnostic information. Traditionally, clinicians have administered lengthy tests once, in the initial assess-

TABLE 5.1
Essential Symptoms for Selected *DSM-IV* Disorders

Diagnosis	Primary Essential Symptom(s)
Substance Dependence	Continued use of substance despite significant problems
Conduct Disorder	Continued inappropriate (societal, legal) behaviors
Major Depressive Episode	Usually depressed or loss of pleasure, 2+ weeks
Dysthymic Disorder	Usually depressed, 2+ years
Manic Episode	Elevated, expansive, or irritable mood
Panic Disorder	Panic attacks
Social Phobia	Fear of social or performance situations
Generalized Anxiety Disorder	Excessive anxiety and worry
Obsessive-Compulsive Disorder	Obsessions or compulsions
Pain Disorder	Pain causes significant distress
Anorexia Nervosa	Refusal to maintain minimal normal body weight
Adjustment Disorder	Significant symptoms in response to stressor(s)

See *DSM-IV* for more complete descriptions of symptoms required for each diagnosis.

ment. Early outcome procedures incorporated the same tests in pretest and posttest measures. More current outcome procedures have added ongoing measures, some of which are standardized but most of which provide intraindividual measurement.

Comparing one outcome index to another decreases both the validity and the reliability of the construct being measured. For example, if the Minnesota Multiphasic Personality Inventory-2 (MMPI-2) is used to assess a client's level of depression in the initial evaluation and the Beck Depression Inventory-2 (BDI-II) is administered subsequently to periodically monitor the client's level of depression, the scores cannot be compared because each instrument measures different aspects of depression. Thus, the concept of depression becomes more vague. A thorough system of outcome assessment considers both normative and intraindividual measures. Normative measures answer the question, "How is the client faring compared to other people?" Intraindividual measures answer the question, "What is the client's opinion of the therapeutic progress?"

Further, the therapist must be careful in choosing outcome tools that are sensitive to client change. Any tool that purports to measure stable or enduring personality traits may not be very helpful in measuring clinical progress. Outcome measures that are sensitive to subtle changes are generally brief scales that are designed to measure specific behaviors. Tests that purport to measure enduring traits must be differentiated from those measuring transient states.

INTAKE INFORMATION

The initial interview is one of the most crucial sessions in therapy. Decisions such as whether the client needs services, the type(s) of services needed, the diagnosis, the baseline measures, and the therapist assignments stem from this meeting. Poor rapport may lead to the client not returning for future sessions. Either overengaging or underengaging the client may also prevent any future services. Eliciting too much information may be threatening to the client, but obtaining too little information may not allow the need for mental health services to be documented.

The initial interview is not intended to be a counseling session, yet can be therapeutic when the therapist remains on target diagnostically and exhibits appropriate empathy. Vague inquiries lack direction and provide few or no data by which to set specific treatment objectives. Therapists who solicit nonspecific diagnostic information may be excellent clinicians, but make it nearly impossible to measure therapeutic outcomes due to lack of outcome indicators.

A therapist well versed in the *DSM-IV* and in psychopathology will quickly rule in and rule out diagnostic categories and help pinpoint the problem. Once an accurate diagnosis is validated, specific problem areas and impairments are documented. Problem areas are subsequently translated into measurable and quantifiable objectives.

The material for the initial diagnosis comprises at least five types of information: (1) diagnostic interview, (2) personal history (biographical information), (3) clinical observations, (4) collateral information, and (5) standardized testing. Baseline measurements can be taken from any of these areas; later observations using these baselines for comparison can be helpful in assessing outcomes.

Diagnostic Interview Data

The quality of the diagnostic interview is highly proportionate to the clinician's knowledge of the *DSM-IV* and psychopathology. The information obtained is intended to be atheoretical. It is based on objective data, not idiosyncratic indices designed to back a school of thought. Ideally, the interview provides specific baseline information in several areas that will create a starting point for any type of treatment.

It would be unnecessarily time-consuming to incorporate every possible type of information in assessing outcomes. Minimally, any validators of the diagnosis such as symptoms, impairments, and personal distress should be included. The *DSM-IV* requires each of these in order to substantiate a diagnosis. As indicated earlier, endorsement of symptoms is necessary, but not sufficient, to make a diagnosis. A client who has minor but sufficient levels of *DSM-IV* symptoms but who is not significantly distressed or impaired socially, occupationally, academically, or in other areas, cannot be diagnosed with the disorder.

There is nothing unusual or pathological about feeling sad, withdrawn, or fatigued and having a decreased appetite at times. Normal life stressors lead to such symptoms, but they are not considered as requiring medically necessary treatment. Most people who exhibit mild symptoms of a disorder do not experience any loss of work or schooling and are able to maintain their social lives. In such cases it is not appropriate to make an Axis I diagnosis because no mental health disorder is evident. When the symptoms become distressing to the point that activities of daily living are negatively impacted, such as significantly decreased attendance or performance at work or school, the functional impairment or medical necessity criterion is met, and a diagnosis may be made.

Measuring Symptoms, Impairments, and Distress

There is no direct means—such as a tape measure, probe, or temperature gauge—of measuring symptoms and impairments. Measurement in mental health is more complex than simply stating that the problem exists or does not exist. Affective distress is often measured subjectively, while behavioral impairments are most often measured objectively.

Whenever mental health symptoms or impairments can be described in terms of frequency or duration, quantification for documenting progress or setbacks is not difficult. When symptoms can be measured in terms of severity, the data are somewhat more subjective, but are still of higher quality than simply stating whether or not a problem exists. For example, a rating scale of 1 to 100 is better than yes/no because the 1 to 100 scale allows 100 data points for noting the degree of distress the client is experiencing due to the problem area.

A yes/no type of rating forces the client to designate whether or not the symptom exists. A major problem with this type of measurement (ipsative) is that normal life stressors and everyday problems often lead to some degree of a number of minor mental health symptoms. Perhaps a more valid yes/no question is not whether symptoms exist, but rather, whether the problem is impairing the client's functioning. Consider the two scenarios in Box 5.4.

The SUD ratings not only note the client's subjective degree of distress from the symptoms, but also provide baseline measures. Some may hold that subjective ratings are not as empirical as objective data. Although this argument has merit, it is noted that clients usually come to therapy due to subjective distress. They enter treatment because of their subjective feelings (or they are referred to therapy due to subjective and objective observations of others). They know when their condition is worsening, and ask for treatment when a threshold level is approached. Therefore, subjective ratings are concordant with the degree of the presenting problem, not simply the existence of a symptom.

Other important diagnostic intake information, which may not directly affect outcome measures but is necessary in treatment and prognosis,

Box 5.4

Person A has a midterm exam in college tomorrow. Today, his anxiety about the test has led to the following symptoms: restless feelings, decreased appetite, increased worrying, fatigue, and social withdrawal. If no other measurements are taken other than ipsative endorsement of symptoms, Person A would appear to be suffering from an Axis I disorder. His symptoms dissipate after the test.

Person B has been anxious all of her life. She regularly misses social functions and work, and her health is declining. She cannot sit still for more than a few minutes without appearing jittery and restless. She endorses the same *DSM-IV* symptoms as Person A (restless feelings, decreased appetite, increased worrying, fatigue, and social withdrawal). If the only measuring system of her problem area is existence of symptoms, there appears to be no difference between her and Person A in the documentation material.

When Persons A and B are asked to rate their symptoms on a 1-to-100 (1 = absence of distress, 100 = extremely distressful) Subjective Units of Distress (SUDs) scale, the following information is obtained:

Symptoms Endorsed	**SUDs (1–100)**	
	Person A (Acute Anxiety)	Person B (Chronic Anxiety)
Restless feelings	40	85
Decreased appetite	35	80
Increased worrying	52	95
Fatigue	55	76
Social withdrawal	44	80

includes the history, biopsychosocial information, antecedents, and precipitating factors affecting the client's condition. The various schools of thought also include information that fits their specific theoretical foundations.

SUD ratings are used to gauge how subjectively distressing an affective response or a situation is to a client. Level of distress is difficult to determine by any other means. For example, it is not possible to directly measure how anxious someone is due to a potential job layoff. There is no test that could indicate that someone has, for example, 250 units of anxiety, the way we measure our weight. Tests such as the Beck Anxiety Inventory (BAI), in which the person is compared on a normative scale to other people with anxiety, may provide a general index of anxiety. However, the SUD rating, when directly focusing on a client-specific anxiety-provoking situation, is much more specific to the client's presenting problem.

Some *DSM-IV* symptoms are primarily affective in nature, while others are behavioral or cognitive; thus different types of measurement are needed. An SUD rating is most helpful when the client can rate the level of distress caused by the problem area. Other symptoms are not suitable for subjective ratings. Client behaviors such as being disruptive in school, missing work, avoiding people, stealing, alcohol consumption, hallucinations, lack of sleep, mania, and several others are better measured by other means because they may not be particularly distressing to the client. Nevertheless, they represent Axis I symptoms concordant with a mental health disorder. In such cases, quantifiable indices such as frequency, duration, or both are more helpful than subjective ratings.

Other symptoms or situations may cause no affective distress, but may endanger the client's life or the safety of others. Symptoms such as hallucinations, binge eating, disruptive behavior, and social withdrawal may be nonstressful, or perhaps even rewarding, to the client. Likewise, clients with poor insight or low cognitive functioning are often not aware of the extent of their need for psychological services.

Other symptoms lend themselves to both subjective and objective measurement. For example, panic attacks and their related symptoms can be measured both by SUDs and in terms of frequency and duration. The severity (mild, moderate, or severe) is similar to SUD ratings in that it suggests the intensity of symptoms. The therapist assigns *DSM-IV* severity ratings, whereas the client rates the SUDs. A good balance of documentation incorporating both subjective and objective measures will provide well-rounded outcome assessment (see Box 5.5).

Form 2 is a sample form providing initial diagnostic information about "John Adams." This form is designed to fit Joint Commission and typical third-party payer requirements. It is further designed to be used in concordance with Form 3 (described in the next section).

Much information is attained in the initial assessment, not all of which is needed for outcome assessment. Intake information is also used to increase understanding of the client's (1) previous functioning levels, (2) current supports, (3) cultural/ethnic/spiritual concerns, (4) legal issues, (5) educational background, (6) employment, (7) physical concerns, (8) chemical use history and patterns, and (9) several other possible areas depending on the outside requirements and the perspective of the therapist. Some of these variables will be incorporated into outcome indices depending on the client's most fitting outcome indicators. Information that is not part of the outcome assessment may be crucial in providing therapy.

Whatever school of thought is employed in therapy, outcome indicators should reflect the client's presenting problem using the *DSM-IV* as a reference point. Regardless of the therapist's educational and theoretical background, the outcome indicators should be similar, although the means employed to achieve the desired outcome may differ significantly.

Personal History Data

Personal history (or biographical information) is background material the client usually supplies outside of the session. Several forms are commercially available for clients to fill out either prior to the first session or shortly after this session. The information obtained complements and adds to the data received in the diagnostic interview. Because clients fill out the information at their convenience, there are no time pressures as there may be in the diagnostic interview. Although diagnostic information is certainly collected throughout the course of therapy, most third parties will pay for one to two hours of billing designated as the diagnostic interview.

Depending on the nature of the questionnaire, very specific problem area data can be obtained and further probed in the next session. Besides specific data for outcome measurements, the information elicited in a personal history form can be very helpful in the counseling process.

Box 5.5

Examples of Quantifying Various *DSM-IV* Symptoms of Depression

Different methods are employed in documenting outcome indicators depending on the type of symptom. The same measure (e.g., SUD rating scales, frequency of behavior, etc.) cannot be used for each problem area. Multiple measurement indices are needed to best describe the client's condition.

***DSM-IV* symptoms**	**Examples of possible baseline and ongoing measurements**
1. Depressed mood most of the day	Duration: depressed at least 75% of the time Frequency: daily Severity rating by client: SUD level = 90 Severity rating by therapist: severe (6 of 7) Testing: BDI Score = 28

Each of these measurements provides some information about the client's condition. The frequency and duration remarks not only validate the diagnosis but also provide baseline measures. The BDI test score is helpful for comparing progress and outcomes of several aspects of depression over time. Since the test is standardized across several people with varying types and degrees of depression, it provides little specific client information, nor does it specifically address the *DSM-IV* symptom of being depressed most of the time. Severity ratings by both the client and the therapist can be effective outcome measures of personal distress when scores or ratings are compared session by session.

2. Diminished interest or pleasure	Duration: currently involved in pleasurable activities an average of half an hour per week Frequency: average of two times per week Rating: client rates enjoyable activities as taking place at level 2 (Seldom) on a 1-to-7 scale

The duration and frequency of these behaviors easily lend themselves to documentation. Clear, measurable information such as being involved in two pleasurable activities per week is easily chartable, and specific objectives can be set to increase both the frequency and the duration of the target behavior. In this exam-

Box 5.5 *(Continued)*

ple, SUD level would not be helpful because a depressed client may or may not view lack of pleasure as particularly distressing.

3. Significant weight loss or gain	Frequency: eats no more than one meal daily Amount: from 143 to 120 pounds in the past three months

This symptom is easily measurable in amount of weight and in frequency of eating. The treatment plan objectives can incorporate specific actions and behaviors such as return to usual weight and eating at least two to three full meals per day.

Form 3 (from Wiger, 1999b) is designed to elicit such information. It follows the same format as Form 2; therefore, information from one source supplements the other.

Clinical Observation Data

Clinical observations are important for ongoing validation of the client's condition. It is not common to incorporate clinical observations from the session into outcome measures, but they nevertheless provide important clinical information to the therapist. Clinical observations are more commonly used in a manner that supports the clinician's theoretical stance. For example, it is difficult to empirically measure a client's level of insight. Nevertheless, insight has historically been highly regarded by many schools of thought as a necessary goal of treatment. Other therapists do not view client insight as sufficient to bring about client change. The *DSM-IV,* being atheoretical, does not view lack of insight as being a primary symptom of any Axis I mental health diagnosis. However, for those who view insight as a crucial therapeutic component, it is necessary in clinical observations and treatment.

There are several other clinical observations that do not follow a particular theoretical stance but are considered valuable by most clinicians. For example, consider a client who presents in the initial sessions with slumped posture, poor hygiene, and blunted affect. After several weeks of therapy, the client shows up for sessions more neatly dressed and cheerful. There is clinical significance in these observations. However, this information may not necessarily be incorporated as one of the specific documented outcome measures. For example, a client who becomes dependent or ingratiating toward the therapist might exert much energy in the sessions to please the therapist, but there is no assurance that the behaviors will generalize to the client's life the rest of the week.

Some therapist observations can be outcome indicators. Examples include behaviors such as weight loss or gain, some kinetic behaviors, certain self-injurious behaviors, and other behaviors that are not alterable due to demand characteristics from a clinical session.

FORM 2 INITIAL ASSESSMENT—ADULT

Client's name *John Adams* Date *3/15/2000*

Starting time *1:00 pm* Ending time *2:50 pm* Duration *110 min*

PART A. BIOPSYCHOSOCIAL ASSESSMENT

1. Presenting Problem

Lack of pleasure and motivation. Increased fatigue. Several current stressors (deaths of loved ones, problems at work, marital conflict, financial problems) leading to poor coping ability. Increased social withdrawal.

2. Signs and Symptoms (*DSM* based) Resulting in Impairment(s)
(Include current examples for treatment planning, e.g., social, occupational, affective, cognitive, physical)

Social: Currently avoiding all peers. Not answering phone.

Physical: Constant fatigue, low energy level.

Affective: Low motivation. Usually sad and frustrated.

Occupational: Has missed 6 of the past 10 workdays.

3. History of Presenting Problem

Events, precipitating factors, or incidents leading to need for services *History of problems coping with stress. Currently: (1) dealing with spouse's extramarital affair, (2) not being promoted at work, (3) recent financial threats from IRS. Current symptoms began "about 4 months ago."*

Frequency/duration/severity/cycling of symptoms *Depressed most of the time, mainly in the morning. Symptoms exacerbated by spouse's indifference, IRS phone calls, and increasing warning slips at work in past few months.*

Was there a clear time when symptoms worsened? *IRS notification on 5-12-2000.*

Family mental health history *No known problem areas or treatment for mental health issues.*

4. Current Family and Significant Relationships (See Personal History Form)

Strengths/support *Parents very supportive, have offered loan.*

Stressors/problems *Marital conflict, very stressful.*

Recent changes *Spouse's extramarital affair.*

Changes desired *Intact, monogamous marriage.*

Comment on family circumstances *Not sure of spouse's intentions.*

5. Childhood/Adolescent History (See Personal History Form)

(Developmental milestones, past behavioral concerns, environment abuse, school, social, mental health)

Normal developmental milestones in all areas. Maintained childhood friendships. Average school attendance and grades. Denies any childhood mental or physical health problems.

6. Social Relationships (See Personal History Form)

Strengths/support *One close friend. Time available for activities.*

Stressors/problems *Shy most of life. Perceives self as socially inferior.*

Recent changes *Avoiding most people for past few months.*

Changes desired *Increased social activities, more time with best friend.*

7. Cultural/Ethnic (See Personal History Form)

Strengths/support *"My parents taught me to be proud of my race."*

Stressors/problems *Frustrated because of prejudice in the world.*

Beliefs/practices to incorporate into therapy *No*

8. Spiritual/Religious (See Personal History Form)

Strengths/support *Raised with strong religious and ethical beliefs.*

Stressors/problems *Feels "abandoned by God."*

Beliefs/practices to incorporate into therapy *Positive faith, optimism.*

Recent changes *No longer attending church services or activities.*

Changes desired *Return to former belief system.*

9. Legal (See Personal History Form)

No history of current problem areas.

Status/impact/stressors

10. Education (See Personal History Form)

Strengths *High school grades "good." Enjoys learning.*

Weaknesses *None known.*

11. Employment/Vocational (See Personal History Form)

Strengths/support *History of being an excellent mechanic.*

Stressors/problems *Not promoted in a timely manner, frustrated.*

12. Military (See Personal History Form)

Viewed army as a positive experience: "I grew up."

Current impact *"I learned to respect others."*

13. Leisure/Recreational (See Personal History Form)

Strengths/support *History of several physical activities.*

Recent changes *No activities at this time.*

Changes desired *Resume activities, "just no motivation."*

14. Physical Health (See Personal History Form)

History of good health. Currently fatigued and tired for past 3 months. Gained 25 pounds in past 3 months.

Physical factors affecting mental condition *None known*

15. Chemical Use History (See Personal History Form)

No history of CD issues.

Patient's perception of problem *NA*

16. Counseling/Prior Treatment History (See Personal History Form)

Marital counseling in 1997, believes it was helpful at the time.

Benefits of previous treatment *Spent more time with spouse.*

Setbacks of previous treatment *Spouse's current extramarital affair.*

PART B. DIAGNOSTIC INTERVIEW

Mood

Common mood disorders listed below (rule in and rule out signs and symptoms: validate with *DSM*)

Predominant mood during interview *Dysphoric, frustrated*

Current Concerns (give examples of impairments, severity [s], frequency [f], duration [d])

Adjustment Disorder

(within 3 mo of identified stressor, symptoms persist <6 mo after stressor, marked distress)

___Depressed ___Anxiety ___Mixed anxiety and depression ___Conduct

___Emotions and conduct ___Unspecified

Specify disturbance ___Acute (<6 mo) ___Chronic (>6 mo) ___________

See Major Depression

Impairment(s) ___Social ___Occupational/educational ___Affective ___Cognitive ___Other

Examples of impairment(s) ___________

Major Depression (2 or more wks) ___Usually depressed or ___Anhedonia (4+ of following)

✔ Weight +/(–) 5%/mo ✔ Appetite +/(–) ✔ Sleep +/(–) ✔ Psychomotor +/(–)

✔ Fatigue ✔ Worthlessness/guilt ___Concentration ___Death/suicidal ideation

Other ✔ Crying spells ✔ Withdrawal ___Additional symptoms ___________

Impairment(s) ✔ Social ✔ Occupational/educational ✔ Affective ___Cognitive ___Other

Examples of impairment(s) *Avoiding all friends, missing 2 days of work per week, always sad, despondent.*

Dysthymia (2 or more years) ___Depressed most of time (2+ of following)

___Low/high appetite or eating ___In-/hypersomnia ___Low energy/fatigue ___Low self-esteem

___Low concentration/decisions ___Hopelessness ___Other ___________

No

Impairment(s) ___Social ___Occupational/educational ___Affective ___Cognitive ___Other

Examples of impairment(s) ___________

Mania (3+)

___Grandiosity ___Low sleep ___Talkativeness ___Flight of ideas ___Distractibility

___Goals/agitation ___Excessive pleasure

No

Impairment(s) ___Social ___Occupational/educational ___Affective ___Cognitive ___Other

Examples of impairment(s) ___________

Panic Attacks (4+, abrupt development of)

___Palpitations ___Sweating ___Trembling ___Shortness of breath ___Feeling of choking

___Chest pain ___Nausea ___Dizziness ___Light-headedness ___Derealization

___Fear of losing control ___Fear of dying ___Numbness ___Chills/hot flashes

No

Impairment(s) ___Social ___Occupational/educational ___Affective ___Cognitive ___Other

Examples of impairment(s) ______________________________

____

Anxiety (GAD 3+, most of time, 6 mo)

___Restlessness ___Easily fatigued ___Concentration ___Irritability

___Muscle tension ___Sleep disturbance

No

Impairment(s) ___Social ___Occupational/educational ___Affective ___Cognitive ___Other

Examples of impairment(s) ______________________________

____

Other Diagnostic Concerns or Behavioral Issues

(e.g., _*N*_Dissociation _*N*_Eating _*N*_Sleep _*N*_Impulse control _*N*_Thought disorders _*N*_Anger

_*N*_Relationships _*N*_Cognitive _*N*_Phobias _*N*_Substance abuse _*N*_Medical conditions

_*N*_Somatization _*N*_Sexual PTSD, etc.)

____

Impairment(s) ___Social ___Occupational/educational ___Affective ___Cognitive ___Other

Examples of impairment(s) *See Major Depression*

____

USE ADDITIONAL PAPER AS NECESSARY

Mental Status

(Check appropriate level of impairment: N/A or OK signifies no known impairment. Comment on significant areas of impairment.)

Appearance	N/A or OK	Slight	Moderate	Severe
Unkempt, disheveled	(___)	(___)	(✔)	(___)
Clothing dirty, atypical	(✔)	(___)	(___)	(___)
Odd physical characteristics	(✔)	(___)	(___)	(___)
Body odor	(___)	(✔)	(___)	(___)
Appears unhealthy	(___)	(✔)	(___)	(___)

Posture	N/A or OK	Slight	Moderate	Severe
Slumped	(___)	(___)	(✔)	(___)
Rigid, tense	(___)	(___)	(✔)	(___)
Body Movements	N/A or OK	Slight	Moderate	Severe
Accelerated, quick	(✔)	(___)	(___)	(___)
Decreased, slowed	(___)	(___)	(___)	(✔)
Restlessness, fidgety	(✔)	(___)	(___)	(___)
Atypical, unusual	(✔)	(___)	(___)	(___)
Speech	N/A or OK	Slight	Moderate	Severe
Rapid	(✔)	(___)	(___)	(___)
Slow	(___)	(___)	(✔)	(___)
Loud	(✔)	(___)	(___)	(___)
Soft	(___)	(___)	(✔)	(___)
Mute	(✔)	(___)	(___)	(___)
Atypical (e.g., slurring)	(✔)	(___)	(___)	(___)
Attitude	N/A or OK	Slight	Moderate	Severe
Domineering, controlling	(✔)	(___)	(___)	(___)
Submissive, dependent	(___)	(___)	(___)	(✔)
Hostile, challenging	(✔)	(___)	(___)	(___)
Guarded, suspicious	(✔)	(___)	(___)	(___)
Uncooperative	(✔)	(___)	(___)	(___)
Affect	N/A or OK	Slight	Moderate	Severe
Inappropriate to thought	(✔)	(___)	(___)	(___)
Increased lability	(✔)	(___)	(✔)	(✔)
Blunted, dull, flat	(___)	(___)	(___)	(___)
Euphoria, elation	(✔)	(___)	(___)	(___)
Anger, hostility	(___)	(✔)	(___)	(___)
Depression, sadness	(___)	(___)	(✔)	(✔)
Anxiety	(✔)	(___)	(___)	(___)
Irritability	(___)	(___)	(___)	(___)
Perception	N/A or OK	Slight	Moderate	Severe
Illusions	(✔)	(___)	(___)	(___)
Auditory hallucinations	(✔)	(___)	(___)	(___)

Visual hallucinations	(✔)	(__)	(__)	(__)
Other hallucinations	(✔)	(__)	(__)	(__)
Cognitive	N/A or OK	Slight	Moderate	Severe
Alertness	(__)	(✔)	(__)	(__)
Attention span, distractibility	(__)	(✔)	(__)	(__)
Short-term memory	(__)	(✔)	(__)	(__)
Long-term memory	(__)	(✔)	(__)	(__)
Judgment	N/A or OK	Slight	Moderate	Severe
Decision making	(__)	(__)	(✔)	(__)
Impulsivity	(✔)	(__)	(__)	(__)
Thought Content	N/A or OK	Slight	Moderate	Severe
Obsessions/compulsions	(✔)	(__)	(__)	(__)
Phobic	(✔)	(__)	(__)	(__)
Depersonalization	(✔)	(__)	(__)	(__)
Suicidal ideation	(__)	(✔)	(__)	(__)
Homicidal ideation	(✔)	(__)	(__)	(__)
Delusions	(✔)	(__)	(__)	(__)

Estimated level of intelligence *Average intelligence*

Orientation ✔ Time ✔ Place ✔ Person

Able to hold normal conversation? ✔ Yes ___No

Eye contact *Normal*

Level of insight

___Complete denial

✔ Blames others

___Intellectual insight, but few changes likely

___Emotional insight, understanding, change can occur

___Slight awareness

___Blames self

Client's view of actions needed to change *"Go on with life . . . try harder."*

Comments

Appeared depressed the entire interview. Under much stress from several sources. Current symptoms suggest major depression. Very low self-esteem. Believes that all in life is going against him. He wants things to improve, but low motivation.

PART C. DIAGNOSIS VALIDATION

Diagnosis 1 *Major Depression, Moderate, Single Episode* Code *296.32*

DSM criteria

Depressed most of the time past 3–4 months. No pleasure, lost 20 pounds in past 2 months, low appetite, low sleep, psychomotor retardation, feels worthless, avoiding most people.

Examples of impairment/dysfunction *Social: avoids almost all social activities or social contact. Occupational: missing 2 days of work per week. In danger of being fired. Affective: constantly sad, little motivation. Decreased self-esteem.*

Additional validation (e.g., testing, previous records, self-report) ________

MMPI-2 scale 2 (Depression) T = 90, significant depression

BDI-2 score = 28, severe depression.

Diagnosis 2 *Partner relationship problems* Code ________

DSM criteria

Severe marital discord. Currently living with spouse, but not speaking to each other.

Examples of impairment/dysfunction *Marital problems significantly affecting self-esteem and depression.*

Additional validation (e.g., testing, previous records, self-report) ________

Diagnosis 3 ________ Code ________

DSM criteria

Examples of impairment/dysfunction ________

____

____

Additional validation (e.g., testing, previous records, self-report)____________________

____

____

____

		Diagnosis	Code
Axis I	1	*Major Depressive Episode, Moderate*	*296.32*
	2	*Partner Relationship Problems*	*V61.1*
	3		
Axis II	1	*No Diagnosis*	*799.99*
	2		
Axis III		*Defer to physician*	
Axis IV		*Occupational, social, marital distress*	

Axis V Current GAF = *50* Highest GAF past year = *75*

Prognosis ___Poor ___Marginal ___Guarded ___Moderate ✔ Good ___Excellent

Qualifiers to prognosis *R/O* Med compliance ___Treatment compliance ✔ Home environment

✔ Activity changes ___Behavioral changes ___Attitudinal changes ___Education/training

Other ____________________________________

Treatment Considerations

Is the patient appropriate for treatment? ✔ Yes ___No

If no, explain and indicate referral made ______________________________

Treatment modality ✔ Individual ✔ Conjoint ___Family ___Collateral ___Group

Frequency *Weekly* *2X/month* ________ ________ ________

If conjoint, family, or collateral, specify with whom *Spouse*

Adjunctive Services Needed

✔ Physical exam ___School records (specify)____________________

___Laboratory tests (specify)____________________

___Patient records (specify) ____________________

Therapist's Questions/Concerns/Comments ✔ Psychiatric evaluation ✔ Psychological testing

Personality testing suggested

____

____

Therapist's signature/credentials ______________________________ Date ____/____/______

Supervisor's Remarks

Agree with diagnosis. Set up testing and med eval.

Supervisor's signature/credentials ______________________________ Date ____/____/______

Therapist's Response to Supervisor's Remarks

Therapist's signature/credentials ______________________________ Date ____/____/______

FORM 3 PERSONAL HISTORY—ADULT

Client's name *John Adams* Date *3-15-2000*

Gender ___F ✔ M Date of birth *12-19-59* Age *40*

Form completed by (if someone other than client) ________

Address *789 10th Ave.* City *Bear Lake* State *NJ* Zip *76513*

Phone (home) *(999)555-6565* (work) *(999)555-5656* ext *654*

If you need any more space for any of the questions, please use the back of the sheet.

Primary reason(s) for seeking services

___Anger management ___Anxiety ✔ Coping ✔ Depression

___Eating disorder ___Fear/phobias ___Mental confusion ___Sexual concerns

✔ Sleeping problems ___Addictive behaviors ___Alcohol/drugs

___Other mental health concerns (specify) ________

Family Information

Relationship	Name	Age	Living Yes	Living No	Living with you Yes	Living with you No
Mother	*Sarah Adams*	*65*	✔			✔
Father	*Quincy Adams*	*65*	✔			✔
Spouse	*Cynthia Adams*	*40*	✔		✔	
Children						

Significant others (brothers, sisters, grandparents, step-relatives, half-relatives—please specify relationship)

Relationship	Name	Age	Living Yes	Living No	Living with you Yes	Living with you No
Brother	*Don Adams*	*42*	✔			✔
Sister	*Debra Adams*	*38*	✔			✔

Marital Status (more than 1 answer may apply)

___Single

___Divorce in process
Length of time ______

___Unmarried, living together
Length of time ______

✔ Legally married
Length of time 6 years

___Separated
Length of time ______

___Divorced
Length of time ______

___Widowed
Length of time ______

___Annulment
Length of time ______

Total number of marriages ______

Assessment of current relationship (if applicable) ___Good ___Fair ✔ Poor

Parental Information

✔ Parents legally married

___Parents have ever been separated

___Parents ever divorced

___Mother remarried (number of times)______________

___Father remarried (number of times) ______________

Special circumstances (e.g., raised by person other than parents, information about spouse/children not living with you, etc.) None

Development

Are there special, unusual, or traumatic circumstances that affected your development? ___Yes ✔ No

If yes, please describe ______________________________

Has there been a history of child abuse? ___Yes ✔ No

If yes, which type(s)? ___Sexual ___Physical ___Verbal

If yes, the abuse was as a ___Victim ___Perpetrator

Other childhood issues ___Neglect ___Inadequate nutrition ___Other (please specify)_______

Comments regarding childhood development______________________________

____

Social Relationships

Check how you have related to or gotten along with other people most of your life (check all that apply)

___Affectionate ___Aggressive ___Avoidant ___Fight/argue often ___Follower

✔ Friendly ___Leader ___Outgoing ___Shy/withdrawn ___Submissive

___Other (specify) No problems

Have your social relationships changed recently? ✔ Yes ___No

If yes, describe I avoid everybody.

Sexual orientation Heterosexual Comments ______________

Sexual dysfunctions? ___Yes ✔ No

If yes, describe______________________________

Any current or history of being a sexual perpetrator? ___Yes ___No

If yes, describe________________

Cultural/Ethnic

To which cultural or ethnic group do you belong? *African American*

Are you experiencing any problems due to cultural or ethnic issues? ✔ Yes ___No

If yes, describe *My race has held me back from being promoted.*

Other cultural/ethnic information ________________

Spiritual/Religious

How important to you are spiritual matters? ___Not ___Little ✔ Moderate ___Much

Are you affiliated with a spiritual or religious group? ✔ Yes ___No

If yes, describe *Sometimes I attend a Baptist church.*

Were you raised within a spiritual or religious group? ✔ Yes ___No

If yes, describe *Went to church weekly with parents.*

Would you like your spiritual/religious beliefs incorporated into the counseling? ✔ Yes ___No

If yes, describe *Please don't violate my beliefs and morals.*

Legal

Current Status

Are you involved in any active cases (traffic, civil, criminal)? ___Yes ✔ No

If yes, please describe and indicate the court and hearing/trial dates and charges________________

Are you presently on probation or parole? ___Yes ✔ No

If yes, please describe ________________

Past History

Traffic violations	___Yes	✔ No	DWI, DUI, etc.	___Yes	___No
Criminal involvement	___Yes	✔ No	Civil involvement	___Yes	___No

If you responded yes to any of the above, please fill in the following information.

Charges	Date	Where (city)	Results

Education

Fill in all that apply. Years of education __14__ Currently enrolled in school? ___Yes __✔__No

__✔__High school grad/GED

__✔__Vocational Number of years __2__ Graduated __✔__Yes ___No Major __Auto mechanics__

___College Number of years ___ Graduated ___Yes ___No Major ________

___Graduate Number of years ___ Graduated ___Yes ___No Major ________

Other training ________

Special circumstances (e.g., learning disabilities, gifted) ________

Employment

Beginning with most recent job, list job history.

Employer	Dates	Title	Reason for leaving	How often do you miss work?
Seymores	4/96–present	Mechanic		Lately 2x/week
A-1	2/94–3/96	Mechanic	Better job	None
Carco	1/83–2/94	Mechanic	Bored	None

Currently __FT __PT __Temp __Laid off __Disabled __Retired __Soc. Sec. __Student

Other (describe) ________

Military

Military experience? __✔__Yes ___No Combat experience? ___Yes ___No

Where __Fort Summer__

Branch __Army__ Discharge date __7-21-82__

Date drafted ________ Type of discharge __Honorable__

Date enlisted __7-18-78__ Rank at discharge __E-3__

Leisure/Recreational

Describe special areas of interest or hobbies (e.g., art, books, crafts, physical fitness, sports, outdoor activities, church activities, walking, exercising, diet/health, hunting, fishing, bowling, traveling, etc.)

Activity	How often now?	How often in the past?
Reading	None	1 hour/day
Sports	None	4 hours/week
Church	None	1 service/week
Exercise	None	1/2 hour/day

Medical/Physical Health

___AIDS
___Alcoholism
___Abdominal pain
___Abortion
___Allergies
___Anemia
___Appendicitis
___Arthritis
___Asthma
___Bronchitis
___Bed-wetting
___Cancer
___Chest pain
___Chronic pain
___Colds/coughs
___Constipation
___Chicken pox
___Dental problems
___Diabetes
___Diarrhea
___Dizziness
___Drug abuse
___Epilepsy
___Ear infections
___Eating problems
___Fainting
✔ Fatigue
___Frequent urination
___Headaches
___Hearing problems
___Hepatitis
___High blood pressure
___Kidney problems
___Measles
___Mononucleosis
___Mumps
___Menstrual pain
___Miscarriages
___Neurological disorders
___Nausea
___Nosebleeds
___Pneumonia
___Rheumatic fever
___Sexually transmitted diseases
___Sleeping disorders
___Sore throat
___Scarlet fever
___Sinusitis
___Small pox
___Stroke
___Sexual problems
___Tonsillitis
___Tuberculosis
___Toothache
___Thyroid problems
___Vision problems
___Vomiting
___Whooping cough
___Other (describe) ________________

List any current health concerns *History of good health*

List any recent health or physical changes ________________

Nutrition

Meal	How often (times per week)	Typical foods eaten	Typical amount of food eaten			
Breakfast	5 /week	*Cereal, toast*	___No	___Low	✔ Med	___High
Lunch	3 /week	*Sandwich*	___No	✔ Low	___Med	___High
Dinner	7 /week	*Full meals*	___No	___Low	✔ Med	___High
Snacks	10 /week	*Candy, chips*	___No	___Low	✔ Med	___High

Comments ________________

Current prescribed medications	Dose	Dates	Purpose	Side effects
None				

Current over-the-counter meds	Dose	Dates	Purpose	Side effects
None				

Are you allergic to any medications or drugs? ___Yes ___No

If yes, describe________________________________

	Date	Reason	Results
Last physical exam	8/99	Checkup	OK
Last doctor's visit	2/00	Sore throat	OK
Last dental exam	6/99	Cavity	Filled
Most recent surgery	None		
Other surgery	None		
Upcoming surgery	None		

Family history of medical problems Father had diabetes

Please check if there have been any recent changes in the following

✔ Sleep patterns ___Eating patterns ___Behavior ✔ Energy level

✔ Physical activity level ___General disposition ✔ Weight ___Nervousness/tension

Describe changes in areas you checked above I wake up too early. Low energy. Gained 25 pounds in past few months.

Chemical Use History

	Amount	Frequency of use	Age of first use	Age of last use	Used in last 48 hours? Yes	No	Used in last 30 days? Yes	No
Alcohol	________	________	______	_____	___	___	___	___
Barbiturates	________	________	______	_____	___	___	___	___
Valium/Librium	________	________	______	_____	___	___	___	___
Cocaine/crack	________	________	______	_____	___	___	___	___
Heroin/opiates	________	________	______	_____	___	___	___	___
Marijuana	________	________	______	_____	___	___	___	___
PCP/LSD/mescaline	________	________	______	_____	___	___	___	___
Inhalants	________	________	______	_____	___	___	___	___
Caffeine	________	________	______	_____	___	___	___	___
Nicotine	________	________	______	_____	___	___	___	___
Over-the-counter drugs	________	________	______	_____	___	___	___	___
Prescription drugs	________	________	______	_____	___	___	___	___
Other drugs	________	________	______	_____	___	___	___	___

Substance(s) of preference

1 ______________________________ 3 ______________________________

2 ______________________________ 4 ______________________________

Substance Abuse Questions

Describe when and where you typically use substances ______________________________

____

Describe any changes in your use patterns______________________________________

____

Describe how your use has affected your family or friends (include their perceptions of your use)_____

____

Reason(s) for use

___Addicted ___Build confidence ___Escape ___Self-medication

___Socialization ___Taste ___Other (specify)

How do you believe your substance use affects your life?______________________________

Who or what has helped you in stopping or limiting your use? ___________________________

Does/has someone in your family present/past have/had a problem with drugs or alcohol?

___Yes ___No If yes, describe ______________________________

Have you had withdrawal symptoms when trying to stop using drugs or alcohol? ___Yes ___No

If yes, describe____________________

Have you had adverse reactions or overdose to drugs or alcohol? (describe)____________________

____

Does your body temperature change when you drink? ___Yes ___No

If yes, describe____________________

Have drugs or alcohol created a problem for your job? ___Yes ___No

If yes, describe____________________

Counseling/Prior Treatment History

Information about client (past and present)

	Yes	No	When	Where	Your reaction to overall experience
Counseling/psychiatric treatment	✔		1987	XYZ Clinic	OK
Suicidal thoughts/attempts		✔			
Drug/alcohol treatment		✔			
Hospitalizations		✔			
Involvement with self-help groups (e.g., AA, Al-Anon, NA, Overeaters Anonymous)		✔			

Information about family/significant others (past and present)

	Yes	No	When	Where	Your reaction to overall experience
Counseling/psychiatric treatment		✔			
Suicidal thoughts/attempts		✔			
Drug/alcohol treatment		✔			
Hospitalizations		✔			
Involvement with self-help groups (e.g., AA, Al-Anon, NA, Overeaters Anonymous)		✔			

Please check behaviors and symptoms that occur more often than you would like.

___Aggression	___Elevated mood	___Phobias/fears
___Alcohol dependence	✔ Fatigue	___Recurring thoughts
___Anger	___Gambling	___Sexual addiction
___Antisocial behavior	___Hallucinations	___Sexual difficulties
___Anxiety	___Heart palpitations	___Sick often
✔ Avoiding people	___High blood pressure	✔ Sleeping problems
___Chest pain	✔ Hopelessness	___Speech problems
___Cyber addiction	___Impulsivity	✔ Suicidal thoughts
___Depression	___Irritability	___Thoughts disorganized
___Disorientation	___Judgment errors	___Trembling
___Distractibility	___Loneliness	✔ Withdrawing
___Dizziness	___Memory impairment	___Worrying
___Drug dependence	___Mood shifts	___Other (specify)
___Eating disorder	___Panic attacks	________________

Comments ____

Briefly discuss how the above symptoms impair your ability to function effectively

I don't feel like doing anything anymore. I miss so much work I might get fired. I avoid everybody. I used to like sports and other outside activities. Now I do nothing. I'm always tired. No one really wants me. I'm a failure.

Any additional information that would assist us in understanding your concerns or problems

In the past few months my life has fallen apart. I feel like hiding. In the past several months (1) my best friend passed away, (2) I didn't get promoted at work, (3) my wife had an affair, and (4) the IRS said I owe them $10,000 in back taxes.

____

____

What are your goals for therapy? *I want to be involved in activities like I used to. I want to feel alive again. I want my self-esteem back. I want my marriage back. I want respect.*

Do you feel suicidal at this time? ___Yes ✔ No

If yes, explain *But I think of it a lot.*

For Staff Use

Therapist's signature/credentials ____________________ Date ____/____/____

Supervisor's comments ______________________________

____________________ Physical exam ___Required ___Not required

Supervisor's signature/credentials ____________________ Date ____/____/____

(Certifies case assignment, level of care and need for exam)

Collateral Information Data

Collateral information is any material about the client that is observed, described, or rated by others. It includes observations of people who are in regular contact with the client, plus information provided by other professionals. Generally, the lower the client's level of insight into the problem, the higher the need for ongoing observations and specific, current information.

Collaterals are especially helpful when the client is a child or a lower-functioning adult. Collaterals may include family members, friends, employers, parents, teachers, or any others who can observe client behaviors objectively. Initial diagnostic collateral information is usually in the form of baseline measures; collaterals will be part of the therapeutic process in documenting progress and setbacks throughout the treatment process. Information on the use of collateral information throughout the course of therapy is provided in Chapter 7.

Standardized Testing Data

Psychological testing provides standardized measures of the client's condition in a number of variables. Tests are available to compare the client's level of functioning in areas such as mood, personality characteristics, cognition, memory, IQ, academic areas, thought processes, and behavioral issues. Standardized testing compares the client's test scores to those of a normative population; diagnostic and therapeutic decisions can be made with the aid of this information. Standardized tests are especially helpful for diagnostic reasons; pre- and posttests are given to compare the client's level of functioning compared to that of others and to assess intraindividual changes.

If standardized tests are the sole determinant of outcomes, much information is lost regarding problem areas in the client's life that are not specifically measured on such tests. For example, a standardized test can yield the information that a client's level of depression is at the 99th percentile, but an individualized outcome measure can rate the client's level of distress from a specific stressor in his or her life that is causing depression. Use of normative standardized outcome measures is described in Chapter 7.

SUMMARY

Third-party payers require a *DSM-IV* Axis I diagnosis for clients to receive and continue receiving funds for mental health services. Likewise, outcome measures should be based on the *DSM-IV.* An Axis I diagnosis requires endorsement of relevant symptoms and/or significant personal distress and related functional impairments. Third-party payers further require that treatment be medically necessary, meaning that treatment is needed in order for improvements to take place in a timely manner. Because clients with the same diagnosis can have very different levels of functioning, it is crucial to document the level of a client's specific areas of concern. Data to validate intake may come from a variety of objective and subjective sources, each of which can later be incorporated into treatment.

The client's problem areas, symptoms, and impairments are best documented by quantifying aspects of behavior in terms such as frequency, duration, and intensity. The initial interview provides baseline measures for each area of concern. Baseline measures may be taken from any type of data, but the ongoing measurement of behaviors throughout treatment must be consistent with the initial form of measurement.

6

ASSESSING OUTCOME USING THE TREATMENT PLAN

There is a positive relationship between treatment plan compliance and success of treatment (Edelman & Chambless, 1993). Compliance by both the client and the therapist is crucial for successful outcomes. Including more specific information in a treatment plan leads to more opportunities to evaluate treatment outcomes. For example, Persons, Burns, and Perloff (1988) documented that clients diagnosed with depression improved three times as much when they complied with homework assignments as when they did not.

A treatment plan is similar to a blueprint used in building a house. It provides a detailed written plan of what is desired after the work is finished and how the goal will be accomplished. Changes to the treatment plan must be documented and approved. When it is finished, it is reviewed by an outside source—usually the third-party payer—for approval.

The treatment plan is the primary standard by which outcome documentation and assessment are monitored. It describes the problem areas, how they will be treated, and how progress will be measured. Without a specific treatment plan based on *Diagnostic and Statistical Manual of Mental Disorders*—Fourth Edition (*DSM-IV*) criteria, outcome measurement cannot be individualized or accurately assessed. That is, without measures of client-specific outcome indicators, outcome measurements are simply normative (based on tests comparing the client to other people). Commercially available treatment plans, which are not tailored to specific client needs, may save time for the therapist, but are not necessarily good outcome indicators. Client progress can and should be measured on an ongoing basis as depicted in the individualized treatment plan. Outcome indicators become part of the treatment, rather than simply adjunctive information.

The treatment plan and subsequent progress notes are the means of regularly monitoring progress in identified problem areas. Some writers uphold keeping a separate problem list that is monitored session by session. However, this type of monitoring can become excessive and burdensome and may encumber the clinical process. Too much information is not of added value and results in diminishing returns (i.e., time wasted). The authors suggest using the treatment plan itself as the means of monitoring outcome, rather than having separate, time-consuming outcome forms and procedures. When the identified problem areas are excessive (i.e., too many to include in a typical treatment plan), the most salient problem areas should be identified in the treatment plan. Other objectives may be added as the original objectives are met. Nothing prevents problem areas that are not included in the treatment plan from being addressed in treatment.

To illustrate, let's consider football statistics as an example. Hundreds of possible "stats" are available for each football player. Some information is crucial in forming an opinion of the player's effectiveness (e.g., percentage of passes completed, number of touchdowns, running yards). Other readily available information is far less crucial (e.g., number of games played against a particular defensive coach). When most people discuss football players, they talk about the important stats, not the minor trivia. Likewise, not all information about the psychiatric client is necessary in outcome assessment. Only the information that most adeptly defines outcome in the problem areas that lead to client impairments is essential. Overdocumenting could lead to overpathologizing, excessive numbers of sessions, and excessive paperwork. As stated earlier, focusing the treatment plan (outcome assessment) on problem areas that clearly represent functional impairment preserves the medical necessity criterion for treatment and saves the therapist from documenting minor problem areas that are not the focus of treatment.

Overview of Treatment Plan Writing

A treatment plan is based on diagnostic information in which specific problem area goals are set. Goals are set by the client in collaboration with the therapist, rather than solely by the therapist. Treatment progress is based on the client's level of goal attainment. It is therefore crucial that the goals and objectives adequately and specifically represent what is needed for client improvement. Outcome depends on the extent to which goal attainment is related to the client's functional improvement. Vague goals and objectives lead to vague outcomes, which may lead insurers to refuse reimbursement. Specific client goals and objectives lead to specific outcome results and appropriate allocation of resources.

Although treatment plans may be written in a number of formats, the most common elements include (1) problem areas, (2) goals/objectives, and (3) treatment strategies. Each area is interrelated and must be clearly written to ensure an objective evaluation.

Problem Areas

The problem area portion of the treatment plan is related to giving the diagnosis and defining the symptoms, impairments, and level of distress. It serves three important purposes: (1) It defines the most salient areas of dysfunction experienced by the client, (2) it validates the diagnosis, and (3) it provides baseline measures by which outcomes of therapy can be measured. This part of the plan should clearly define, or at least summarize, the client's various problem areas using information already documented in the initial intake data and ongoing progress notes. A baseline measure denoting the specific level of the problem at the time of the assessment should be noted in order to measure ongoing progress.

Although it is not crucial to list every problem area in the client's life in the treatment plan, those that will receive the most attention and that will be treated and monitored throughout therapy as evidence of outcomes should be included. Problem areas should validate the diagnosis and illustrate why the person is in treatment (concordant with the diagnosis). For example, if a client's diagnosis is a depressive disorder and the problem areas focus on treating marital problems or anxiety, there is lack of concordance between the diagnosis and the treatment plan (to put it in the verbiage of third-party payers).

The problem portion of the treatment plan goes far beyond simply listing symptoms or the diagnosis. Identifying a client as suffering from depression provides some information about the client, but it will be difficult or impossible to measure or demonstrate clear behavioral progress or outcomes for that client. Instead, the documented problem areas should list distinct aspects in the client's life that are impaired or distressed due to depression. The *DSM-IV* requires that the client must experience significant impairment or distress as a result of the disorder for treatment to be classified as medically necessary. Other problem areas that are not the focus of treatment may be monitored but are not included in the treatment plan. Such concerns may be amended into the treatment plan if the client and therapist decide they will be treated in later sessions.

Each problem area should include a baseline measure. Note the difference between stating (1) "the client is suicidal" versus (2) "the client threatens suicide at least twice per day, resulting in affective and potential physical impairment." The latter statement provides a baseline measure by which objectives can be set. It further defines the level of suicidality (i.e., ideas, threats, attempts) and lists the impairments suffered by the client, thus meeting *DSM-IV* criteria for treatment.

Goals and Objectives

Goals and objectives are interrelated: *goals* are desired end points in therapy, and *objectives* are incremental and observable steps by which progress toward goals is measured. While the problem area section of the treatment plan defines the client's areas of concern, the goals and objectives section provides quantified information by which outcomes will be evaluated. The treatment plan objectives evaluate ongoing progress in specific problem areas. Objectives may be revised to some degree session by session as changes occur. For example, if one of the client's goals is to return to work full-time, five days per week, and the client is currently averaging two days of work per week, an initial objective may be to return three days per week. After this interim objective has been met, it may be revised to four and then five days per week. Once the last objective has been met, the goal is attained.

Treatment plan goals provide a summative statement of the direction and end points of change desired. Goal statements may be framed as the opposite of the problem area. For example, if the client's problem area is bed-wetting four nights per week, the goal may be to eliminate bed-wetting. It is important that the goals set in therapy are realistic, attainable, and set by the client. The client's premorbid functioning is the most common level of goal attainment. In cases such as organicity or other factors in which the client will not likely return to premorbid functioning, reasonable goals should be set. Goals for clients with chronic dysfunction, when premorbid functioning may not be known, should also be set at a reasonable level.

Treatment plan objectives are by definition measurable, observable, or quantifiable. Without a means of measurement, progress cannot be gauged objectively. While goals for problem areas generally remain constant, objectives are revised periodically as the client progresses toward the goals. Third parties generally require each treatment plan objective to have a time frame by which it is evaluated and revised. It is a common clinical practice to have approximately three objectives per goal. The incremental level between objectives should not be too small or too large. For example, an objective that attempts to increase a client's number of days getting out of bed from 12 to 13 days per month within a 60-day period may seem trivial and thus nonmotivating to the client. Likewise, excessively high objectives such as increasing the number of days of getting out of bed from 13 to 30 per month in a 7-day period may be unrealistic and overwhelming to the client. Therapists and clients should construct objectives that have a high probability of success, yet continue to challenge the client throughout treatment.

Examples of Documenting Measurable Problem Areas, Goals, and Objectives

Example 1

Vague or Unrealistic

Problem area: Conduct problems

Goal: Eliminate negative behaviors

Objectives:
1. Stop stealing
2. Attend religious functions more often
3. Become more honest

Specific and Attainable

Problem area: Client steals from classmates' desks an average of four times per week, resulting in social and legal impairment

Goal: Stop stealing from classmates

Objectives:
1. No incidents of stealing from classmates by November 4
2. Repay at least 50 percent of items stolen by November 4
3. Volunteer after school a total of 10 hours by November 4

Example 2

Vague or Unrealistic

Problem area: Anxiety

Goal: Eliminate anxiety

Objectives:
1. Worry less often
2. Increase income to a level of not having to worry
3. Learn money management techniques

Measurable and Realistic

Problem area: Client reports excessive worrying each time monetary concerns are mentioned, resulting in affective distress (Baseline Subjective Units of Distress [SUDs=90])

Goal: Reduce level of anxiety due to distress from monetary problems to a level of 40

Objectives:
1. Reduce SUD level to 70 by March 6
2. Set up appointment with financial advisor by April 16
3. Learn and implement three relaxation techniques by April 30

Example 3

Vague or Unrealistic

Problem area	Sleeping problems
Goal	Attain adequate sleep
Objectives	1. Increase amount of sleep 2. Feel more refreshed

Measurable and Realistic

Problem area	Client is currently sleeping no more than three hours per night, resulting in physical and cognitive impairment (constant fatigue, decreased concentration)
Goal	Increase amount of sleep to eight hours per night
Objectives	1. Make appointment for physical checkup by January 17 2. Learn and implement at least two means of stress reduction to incorporate prior to sleeping by February 12 3. Sleep at least five hours per night by February 12

Example 4

Vague or Unrealistic

Problem area	Social problems
Goal	Increase socialization
Objectives	1. Spend more time with people 2. Get out of the house more often 3. Decrease social anxiety

Measurable and Realistic

Problem area	Due to social anxiety, client has left her house no more than one time in the past month, resulting in social impairment
Goal	Increase ability to socialize outside of the house
Objectives	1. Invite three friends to home for picnic by August 4 2. Plan and complete one social activity by August 16 3. Visit psychiatrist for medication evaluation by September 16

Example 5

Vague or Unrealistic

Problem area	Sadness
Goal	Attain happiness
Objectives	1. Spend more time in enjoyable activities 2. Don't dwell on past failures 3. Alleviate depressive symptoms

Measurable and Realistic

Problem area	Client reports overwhelming dysphoric mood at least 90 percent of the time, resulting in affective impairment
Goal	Increase euthymic level until SUDs lower to 30
Objectives	1. Report overwhelming dysphoric mood no

more than 50 percent of the time by November 12
2. Beck Depression Inventory (BDI) scores to 20 or less by November 12 (current score=28)
3. Decrease SUD level to 60 by November 19 (current SUDs=80)

Example 6

Vague or Unrealistic

Problem area	Sexual problems
Goal	Eliminate sexual problems
Objectives	1. Increase sexual pleasure 2. Decrease level of pain from sexual intercourse

Measurable and Realistic

Problem area	Client reports painful intercourse 100 percent of the time, resulting in physical/sexual impairment
Goal	Attain nonpainful sexual intercourse 100 percent of the time
Objectives	1. Experience nonpainful intercourse at least 50 percent of the time by May 14 2. Make appointment with medical doctor for evaluation by April 5

The following case studies are examples of how to document problem areas, goals, and objectives appropriately. The objectives will serve as outcome indicators that the therapist will track throughout the course of therapy.

Scenario 1: Child's Behavior Problems and Dealing with Parental Arguing

Over the past three months, Billy's parents have increasingly argued and have decided to separate. Every time he hears them arguing he cries and becomes quite frustrated and angry and may have tantrums, demonstrating few, if any, adaptive coping skills. He has told his school counselor that he is afraid that the separation is his fault and he believes that when parents divorce children go into foster care. In the past month, he has initiated at least three physical fights per week in school (previously there were no concerns in this area). He teacher states that he has been quite withdrawn, showing little interest in academics or friendships. He no longer plays with children on the playground as he had previously enjoyed doing every day.

Academic, Social, and Affective Impairment

Problem Area 1

Vague documentation of problem area:	School grades have dropped
Quantifiable definition of problem area:	School grades have dropped from B average to D– average Baseline: average grades: D–

Vague objective: Raise school grades

Quantifiable objective: Increase school grades from current D– average to B (previous level) in the next marking period (March 12)

Problem Area 2

Vague documentation of problem area: Fighting in school

Quantifiable definition of problem area: Has initiated an average of three fights in school per week during the past month

Baseline: initiating three fights per week in school

Vague objective: Decrease physical aggression

Quantifiable objective: No initiation of physical fighting in school by April 13

Problem Area 3

Vague documentation of problem area: No close friends

Quantifiable definition of problem area: Initiating no social interactions on playground at school

Baseline: no positive social behaviors during school playtime

Vague objective: Play with other children

Quantifiable objective: Initiate and maintain positive social interactions with peers at least two days per week (e.g., school playground) by April 13

Problem Area 4

Vague documentation of problem area: Becomes fearful when parents argue

Quantifiable definition of problem area: Becomes fearful of future 100 percent of time when parents argue, resulting in SUD fear response rating of 95

Vague objective: Reduce negative affect

Quantifiable objective: Reduce SUD level of fear response to 60 or less by April 27

Problem Area 5

Vague documentation of problem area: Cries often

Quantifiable definition of problem area: Cries (sadness, frustration) an average of one hour per day when stressed by parents' arguing and potential separation, demonstrating no significant coping skills

	Baseline: no identifiable positive coping skills for dealing with parents' separation
Vague objective:	Reduce crying
Quantifiable objective:	Learn and implement at least two helpful adaptive coping skills by April 1

Scenario 2: Adult with Panic Attacks

Sally recently graduated from college and started a new job (high stress, high pay) several miles from her family. During college she never had a panic attack, but she has always been fairly avoidant and socially anxious. Historically she has avoided being around people she does not know because she believes she is socially inept and has nothing to say. She has never been involved in any significant social activities. During her initial job orientation training, she seemed to learn the tasks adequately, but since ending the training program and being placed in a stressful work environment she has become increasingly more overwhelmed by the multiple tasks, social contacts, deadlines, and other work pressures. Two months ago, she developed chest pains at work and was sent to the emergency room. She was diagnosed with a panic disorder. After discharge, she returned to work but has had an average of two panic attacks per day, usually lasting about 20 minutes. Even with medication, she rates the severity of panic attacks at 85 (on an SUD scale of 0 to 100). Since the onset of panic attacks, she has missed an average of 16 hours of work per week due to panic symptoms. Previously she missed little or no time from work. Her performance at work is 60 percent of that of the average worker in the same position and time on the job. She wants to keep her job, but has been warned that she will be on probation at work if her productivity and attendance do not increase.

Occupational and Social Impairment

Problem Area 1

Vague documentation of problem area:	Panic attacks at work
Quantifiable definition of problem area:	Average of two panic attacks daily at work lasting an average of 20 minutes, with severity of 85 (SUDs)
Vague objective:	Decrease panic attacks
Quantifiable objective:	1. Decrease number of panic attacks to one or less per day by June 14 2. Decrease duration of panic attacks to less than 10 minutes by June 14 3. Decrease panic attack SUD level to less than 70 by June 14

Problem Area 2

Vague documentation of problem area:	Missing work
Quantifiable definition of problem area:	Missing an average of 16 hours of work due to panic symptoms; danger of losing job; on probation at work Baseline: attending work average of 24 hours per week (of 40 possible hours)
Vague objective:	Increase time at work
Quantifiable objective:	Attend work an average of at least 38 hours per week by June 21

Problem Area 3

Vague documentation of problem area:	Not meeting quota at work
Quantifiable definition of problem area:	Work performance is at 60 percent of expectation due to lost time and decreased efficiency Baseline: work performance is at 60 percent, resulting in probation at work
Vague objective:	Increase work performance
Quantifiable objective:	Increase work performance to at least 80 percent of expectations by June 28

Problem Area 4

Vague documentation of problem area:	Social anxiety
Quantifiable definition of problem area:	Becomes anxious in social situations, resulting in feeling inept; believes has nothing important to say (involved in social situations only as necessary) Baseline: attends no non-work-related social function per week Baseline: social anxiety SUDs = 90 Baseline: Beck Anxiety Inventory score = 23
Vague objective:	Increase level of ease in social situations
Quantifiable objective:	1. Learn at least three positive social interaction methods/behaviors to be implemented at least one time per week by June 21 2. Reduce social anxiety SUDs to 75 by June 21 3. Reduce Beck Anxiety Inventory score to less than 10 by June 14

Scenario 3: Adult with Chronic Pain and Alcohol Abuse

Roger has consumed increasing amounts of alcoholic beverages for the past five years. He began drinking about two years after an automobile accident in which he ruptured three discs. He describes his pain as excruciating and chronic (scaled at 9 out of 10). Initially he tried physical therapy and underwent various operations that he stated worsened his condition. At present, he is drinking one-half of a case of beer and a fifth of vodka every day. He often binges and has blackouts. He becomes intoxicated every evening. He is currently unemployed, receiving disability payments due to his back problems. He has been married for 25 years, but his wife is threatening to leave him if he does not quit drinking alcohol. His wife states that when he drinks alcohol he regularly becomes verbally abusive (belittling, sarcasm, physical threats) an average of five times per day. Currently he makes zero to one positive remark(s) to his spouse daily (usually when he wants something from her). No physical abuse is reported. He denies symptoms of depression or anxiety.

Occupational, Physical, and Familial Impairment

Problem Area 1

Vague documentation of problem area:	Alcohol abuse
Quantifiable definition of problem area:	Drunkenness every evening with periodic blackouts and binges Baseline: daily drunkenness Baseline: one-half case of beer and one fifth of vodka daily
Vague objective:	(1) Decrease alcohol consumption or (2) abstinence from alcohol
Quantifiable objective:	1. Decrease alcohol consumption to less than 25 percent of the current amount by September 6 or 2. Remain abstinent from alcohol for at least the next 30 days

Problem Area 2

Vague documentation of problem area:	Pain
Quantifiable definition of problem area:	Chronic pain described by client as excruciating Baseline: pain scale rating of 9 out of 10
Vague objective:	Decrease pain level
Quantifiable objective:	Set up appointment for physical therapy evaluation by August 1 Defer objectives to physical therapist

Problem Area 3

Vague documentation of problem area:	Abuses wife
Quantifiable definition of problem area:	Verbal abuse toward spouse when drinking heavily Baseline: average of five incidents of verbal abuse (belittling, sarcasm, physical threats) daily Baseline: current one or less positive statement (i.e., compliments) to his spouse daily
Vague objective:	Decrease/eliminate abusive statements toward spouse
Quantifiable objective:	1. Cease verbally abusive statements toward spouse 2. Make at least three positive statements (i.e., sincere compliments) to spouse daily.

Scenario 4: Adult with Depressed Mood

Victoria, age 36, was recently dismissed from her job as an attorney. During her first few years as a lawyer, she was quite successful by most measures. Two years ago, she lost a major case in which she had invested several months of time and great effort. In addition, she was cited for an ethics violation by the bar for misconduct during the case. The incident led to a rejection in becoming a partner in the firm. Since that time she has become increasingly discouraged. Additional stressors have included the deaths of three loved ones, a breakup with her fiancé two months ago, and losing her house due to foreclosure. Since losing her job, she has not contacted any friends (nor responded to invitations) with whom she previously socialized at least once per week. She is not motivated to seek any employment. When she is alone she dwells on suicidal thoughts. Currently she sleeps at least 12 hours per day; previously she slept about 7 hours per day. Her appetite has significantly decreased and she has unintentionally lost 26 pounds (now underweight) in the past few months. She states that she is always fatigued, whereas she used to have sufficient energy. Her previous weight was within normal limits.

Physical, Social, and Occupational/Financial Impairment

Problem Area 1

Vague documentation of problem area:	Fatigue
Quantifiable definition of problem area:	Decreased physical energy with symptoms of weight loss, low appetite, and excessive sleep Baseline: current weight 94 pounds (lost 26 pounds)

	Baseline: sleeping 12 hours per night (previously 7 hours)
Vague objective:	Increase weight Decrease sleep
Quantifiable objective:	1. Attain healthy weight (as per physician's approval and recommendations) 2. Decrease amount of sleep to under nine hours per night by October 7
Problem Area 2	
Vague documentation of problem area:	Social problems
Quantifiable definition of problem area:	Avoiding friends with whom she previously socialized at least weekly Baseline: spending no time at all with friends
Vague objective:	Spend more time with friends
Quantifiable objective:	Socialize with friends at least one time per week by November 30 or Socialize with friends at least one hour per week by November 30 or Invite at least one friend for an enjoyable activity (dinner, movie, dance) per week by November 30
Problem Area 3	
Vague documentation of problem area:	Financial stress
Quantifiable definition of problem area:	Unemployed, leading to financial difficulties Baseline: applying for zero jobs per week
Vague objective:	Increase finances
Quantifiable objective:	1. Update resume by November 23 2. Register with employment service by December 7 3. Apply for suitable employment at least twice per week by December 14

Scenario 5: Teen with Oppositional Defiant Disorder

Molly, age 15, is currently grounded at home for talking back to her parents. She is suspended from classes an average four times per week. Both her parents and teachers say they are fed up with her disruptive behaviors. At home, she refuses to do chores at least 80 percent of the time. Her parents further state that she argues with them at least five times per day. They can recall few or no positive statements she makes about anyone. She tantrums for about 30 minutes, at least five times per day, about 90 percent of the time when she doesn't get her way. She refuses to do any homework or school tasks unless she has "an ulterior motive." Her teachers and parents agree that she is compliant about 5 percent of the time in academics. She is now failing three subjects and has a report card average of D. Her parents and teachers agree that she has no significant coping strategies to deal with her frustration.

Social and Academic Impairment

Problem Area 1

Vague documentation of problem area:	Behavior problems
Quantifiable definition of problem area:	Refuses to do any tasks at home Baseline: compliant an average of 20 percent of the time when asked by parents Baseline: complies in an average of one task per day when asked by parents
Vague objective:	Increase positive behaviors
Quantifiable objective:	1. Increase task compliance at home to at least 50 percent by November 8 2. Comply in at least three tasks at home by November 8

Problem Area 2

Vague documentation of problem area:	Argumentative
Quantifiable definition of problem area:	Argues with parents Baseline: argues with parents average of five times per day Baseline: positive discussion with parents an average of 20 percent of the time
Vague objective:	Do not argue with parents
Quantifiable objective:	Reduce arguing with parents to one time or less per day by November 29 Increase positive discussions with parents to at least 60 percent of the time by November 29

Problem Area 3

Vague documentation of problem area:	Uncooperative
Quantifiable definition of problem area:	Refuses to participate in any academic work Baseline: suspended from classes an average of four times per week

Baseline: completes homework assignments an average of 5 percent of the time
Baseline: currently failing three subjects in school
Baseline: current average grade in school is D

Vague objective: Cooperate

Quantifiable objective:

1. Reduce number of suspensions to less than two per week by November 21
2. Complete at least 75 percent of homework assignments by November 21
3. Increase grades to no failures by November 21
4. Increase average grade to C by November 21

Problem Area 4

Vague documentation of problem area: Temper tantrums

Quantifiable definition of problem area: Temper tantrums when she does not get her own way
Baseline: Average of five temper tantrums per day
Baseline: Has tantrums 90 percent of the time when not getting her own way
Baseline: Temper tantrums last an average of 30 minutes
Baseline: Currently no known positive means of coping when not getting her own way

Vague objective: Decrease temper tantrums

Quantifiable objective:

1. Reduce temper tantrums to less than two per day by November 29 or
   Reduce number of temper tantrums to less than 30 percent of the time when she does not get her own way by November 29 or
   Reduce average duration of tantrums to less than 10 minutes by November 29
2. Learn and implement three new means of coping when frustrated due to not getting her own way by November 29

FORM 4 INDIVIDUAL TREATMENT PLAN

Client *John Adams* Chart # *JA32200-1* Date *3-21-2000*
Diagnosis(es) *Major Depression* Therapist *JB*
Estimated # of sessions Individual *15* Group *0* Family *0* Other *Couples* *6*
Impairments ____Social ____Occupational ____Academic ____Physical ____Affective distress
___Other ______

Initial GAF *55* Target GAF *75*

Normative Outcome Measures

Test #1 *Symptoms Checklist-90 (SCL-90)*

Subscale	Baseline score	Target score	Subscale	Baseline score	Target score
GSI	*1.21*	*0.47*			
SOM	*1.01*	*0.62*			
INT	*1.24*	*0.56*			
DEP	*2.11*	*0.49*			
ANX	*0.99*	*0.47*			

Test #2 *Beck Depression Inventory-2 (BDI-2)*

Subscale	Baseline score	Target score	Subscale	Baseline score	Target score
Entire test	*30*	*12*			

TP Problem #1 *Dysphoric mood most of the time, no motivation to change.*

Frequency *Daily* Duration *80+% of the time* Severity *Moderate; SUD=90*

Goal 1 *Attain euthymic mood most of the time*

Objective 1a *Feelings of sadness <50% of the time* Target date ______

Objective 1b *Attain BDI score of <20* Target date ______

Objective 1c *Attain SUD score of <70* Target date ______

Treatment strategies *Cognitive-behavioral. Examine dysfunctional thoughts.*

TP Problem #2 *In danger of losing job. Production down to 50% of quota.*

Frequency *Missing work 2 days/wk* Duration *Working 24 hrs/wk* Severity *SUD=85*

Goal 2 *Return to full-functioning premorbid level at work*

- Objective 2a *Attain 75% of work quota* Target date *4-11-00*
- Objective 2b *Attain >32 hours per week* Target date *4-11-00*
- Objective 2c *Decrease SUD level to <60* Target date *4-4-00*

Treatment strategies *Organize tasks into meaningful units. Self-reward system.*

TP Problem #3 *Avoiding all friends and social supports.*

Frequency *No time with peers* Duration *0 social contacts* Severity *NA*

Goal 3 *Resume premorbid social functioning of 8 hours per week*

- Objective 3a *Spend 2+ hours per week socially* Target date *4-18-00*
- Objective 3b *Return phone calls 50+% of the time* Target date *4-4-00*
- Objective 3c *Plan and attend 2+ social functions weekly* Target date *4-11-00*

Treatment strategies *Role playing. Examine negative thoughts and fears.*

TP Problem #4 *Constantly tired and fatigued.*

Frequency *80% of the time* Duration *2 three-hour naps/day* Severity *NA*

Goal 4 *Return to premorbid level of physical energy*

- Objective 4a *Make an appointment for physical evaluation* Target date *3-28-00*
- Objective 4b *No more than 1 nap/day* Target date *4-18-00*
- Objective 4c *Exercise daily as per physician's approval and regimen* Target date *4-4-00*

Treatment strategies *MD referral*

TP Problem #5 ______

Frequency ______ Duration ______ Severity ______

Goal 5 ______

Objective 5a ______________________ Target date ______
Objective 5b ______________________ Target date ______
Objective 5c ______________________ Target date ______
Treatment strategies ______________________
____

TP Problem #6 ______________________
____

Frequency__________ Duration __________ Severity __________
Goal 6______________________
Objective 6a ______________________ Target date ______
Objective 6b ______________________ Target date ______
Objective 6c ______________________ Target date ______
Treatment strategies ______________________
____

(Use additional sheets as needed for more problem areas.)

I have discussed the above information, various treatment strategies, and their possible outcomes. I have received and/or read my copy of my rights as a client and procedures for reporting grievances. I concur with the above diagnosis and treatment plan.

Client's signature *John Adams* Date *3-22-00*

Guardian's signature ______________________ Date ______

Therapist's signature *Jessie Brown, PhD* Date *3-22-00*

Supervisor's signature *Pat Montana, MD* Date *3-23-00*

Treatment Strategies

The third component of a treatment plan is treatment strategies, which describe the means by which therapeutic objectives will be accomplished. Strategies such as type of therapy, school of thought, specific techniques, homework assignments, referrals, and estimated number of sessions are included. The treatment strategies reflect the therapeutic school of thought and the procedures that will take place in therapy.

Listing specific treatment strategies for each objective is important because it may provide evidence of the effectiveness or ineffectiveness of the treatment strategies. That is, decisions must be made as to whether to modify or change a treatment strategy if objectives are not being met. Many third-party payers' contracts specifically state that therapy that is experimental or not considered effective is not covered by payment.

INCORPORATING THE TREATMENT PLAN IN OUTCOME ASSESSMENT

As we have noted, the treatment plan summarizes what is intended to take place in therapy and provides specific points of reference and direction for the therapist, client, and insurer. Treatment plan data serve two purposes: highlighting therapeutic interventions and providing objectives by which outcomes may be monitored. The same data-collecting procedures can be used for monitoring intraindividual progress for both the treatment plan and outcome measures; thus no extra time is required for conducting separate procedures to chart the individual progress. When normative measures are periodically used to compare the client's progress to that of a reference group, additional time is required.

Form 4 is a sample treatment plan in which the objectives serve as outcome measures. Each objective is measurable with outcome indicators subject to data analysis as described in Chapter 4.

SUMMARY

The individual treatment plan is similar to a contract between the therapist and the client and describes the specific plans for treatment. The more focused the treatment plan, the more easy it is to evaluate its objectives. The specific treatment plan goals and objectives also serve as outcome indicators. Initial treatment plan information is taken directly from the diagnostic interview. The plan is tailored to the client's individual needs. The client's most salient problem areas are included, rather than every concern of the client. Likewise, not all treatment plan goals and objectives are necessarily incorporated into outcome measures, especially if additional forms are used for outcome assessment.

7

ASSESSING OUTCOME USING PROGRESS NOTES AND ONGOING CHARTING

Well-written progress notes provide up-to-date, ongoing outcome measures. They are designed to follow the session-by-session progress of treatment plan objectives. Standard progress note formats such as Subjective, Objective, Assessment, Plan (SOAP) and Data, Assessment, Plan (DAP) help organize information. Each portion of the progress notes has a specific purpose for which current data and comparisons from previous data are listed. In addition, a section is allowed for planning to aid in future interventions.

Overview of Progress Note Writing

Progress notes serve several purposes. First, they record the content of the session. This information helps the therapist recall what took place in previous sessions. It would be extremely difficult to remember the details of every client session without keeping progress notes, especially when a therapist may see 20 or more clients per week.

Second, progress notes are the only documentation of the course of treatment. Each session should have specific treatment plan objectives. The progress notes provide evidence that the targeted problems in the treatment plan were treated. Specific, quantified evidence of adherence to the treatment plan is crucial in today's managed care mandates. Progress notes provide ongoing validation of the diagnosis and demonstrate the benefits of treatment. Without detailed observations and specific data, outcome measures are not accurate.

There are several other uses of progress notes. State boards may request progress notes during ethical inquiries. The court may subpoena them for legal reasons. Other professionals may request the notes for collateral information. At the most basic level, progress notes are needed as evidence that a session took place for billing reasons.

Although the focus of this text is not how to write progress notes or treatment plans, it is necessary to understand the importance of providing appropriate and accurate progress notes and what should be included in them. The DAP format will be used for the sake of example.

DAP Part 1: Data

The data section of progress notes provides both objective and subjective data. Examples of objective data are specific frequencies and durations of behaviors, test results, and clinical observations. Subjective data include any data that may vary depending on point of view, such as Subjective Units of Distress (SUDs) and other client ratings and self-reports.

The information that the clinician writes in the data section is a record of the content of the session and ongoing data. The written flow of information does not have to be interrelated, nor does it have to be written in full sentences. Phrases and brief notations are acceptable. The data are extremely important because they are the primary written evidence of outcomes. Any ongoing measures of progress or outcomes are initially written in the data section. Table 7.1 provides examples of the types of data used in assessing outcomes in progress notes.

Other types of data statements that may or may not directly refer to outcomes are shown in Table 7.2

Such types of data may be helpful in assessing outcomes if they are incorporated into the treatment plan and provide helpful measurable data. Examples of incorporating collateral information are shown in Table 7.3.

DAP PART 2: ASSESSMENT

Progress notes contain much more than a description of session content. The data must be organized into consistent, meaningful units so that they can be interpreted. The assessment section of progress notes contains clinical judgments based on the data. Therefore, therapeutic decisions are made after every session because new clinical data are being assessed. In essence, revised outcome information is available session by session.

The assessment section of progress notes provides an evaluation in areas such as the progress of the sessions to date, the current session, therapeutic interventions, and any other aspects of treatment to date. The decisions that result from the assessment lead to future decisions. Assessment is not data; it evaluates the data, summarizing outcomes to date. Examples of statements written in the assessment section are shown in Table 7.4.

TABLE 7.1
Progress Note Data Used to Assess Outcomes

Type of Data Statement	Example of Progress Note Data Statement
Status of objectives	Objective: less than 2 suicidal threats per week. Past week: 0 suicidal threats.
Subjective ratings	Level of distress from guilt of previous abusive behaviors toward family: baseline SUDs = 95, current = 70, objective by November 4 = 60.*
Test results	Baseline Beck Depression Inventory (BDI) score = 32, current = 20, previous week = 23.†
Ratings by therapists	Baseline Global Assessment of Functioning (GAF), session 1 = 32, current GAF, session 8 = 50.
Addendum material	Addendum material may include homework samples, ongoing progress charts, or any other data that plot therapeutic progress and setbacks.

*It is not necessary to include the objective and baseline scores in every progress note.
†It is not necessary to include the previous and baseline scores in every progress note.

TABLE 7.2
Other Types of Progress Note Data

Type of Data Statement	Example of Progress Note Data Statement
Current progress	Reports increasing marital satisfaction.
Current setbacks	Car was repossessed this week.
Increase in symptoms	Increasing use of alcohol. Previously intoxicated an average of 1 time per week. Past 3 weeks, intoxicated an average of 4 times per week.
Decrease in symptoms	Reports 2 physical aggressions this week. Baseline was 8 per week.
Current stressors	Must find new apartment within 1 week, leading to increased frustration and decreased motivation.
Current supports	Has joined AA and found a sponsor. Attending 2–3 times per week.
Homework results	Completed homework. Contacted children to apologize. Will continue discussions with family.
Observations	Appeared frustrated, perplexed, and dysphoric the entire session.
Interventions	Analyzed dysfunctional thoughts. Confronted irrational beliefs.
Legal aspects	Reviewed previous suicide contract. No current plan or ideations.
Client quotes	Client states, "I can't stand living like this any longer . . . I want to go to the hospital."

DAP PART 3: PLAN

The plan section of the DAP progress notes contains future decisions or plans for future sessions or client actions. The plan is based on the assessment (Part 2 of the plan) of the data (Part 1 of the plan). As treatment plan objectives are achieved and performance is raised to more closely meet the treatment plan goals, the changes are listed in the plan section. Examples of material written in the plan section are shown in Table 7.5.

The therapist may choose to chart outcome

TABLE 7.3
Incorporating Information into the Treatment Plan

Situation	Useful information
Hyperactive child	Schoolteacher tallies number of times child gets out of seat during class time in a given time period. (Or, if stated in positive terms, schoolteacher tallies amount or percentage of time child spends in on-task behavior.)
Defiant child	Parent monitors proportion or number of times child refuses to do chores. (Or, if stated in positive terms, parent monitors number of compliant behaviors.)
Alcohol abuse	Spouse monitors number of times per week client comes home from work late due to use of alcohol. (Or, if stated in positive terms, spouse monitors number of times per week client comes home from work on time, sober.)
Decreased job performance	Job supervisor monitors daily production.

TABLE 7.4
Sample Statements in Assessment Section

Area	Example of Assessment Comments in Progress Notes
Ongoing ratings	SUD ratings since the initial assessment indicate significant progress in reducing paranoid behaviors. GAF scores suggest a return to premorbid functioning.
Observations	Client appears much more dysphoric than in initial sessions.
Behaviors	Disruptive behaviors in the classroom have decreased significantly.
Treatment	Client-centered techniques have been helpful in increasing trust toward others.
Testing	Increase in BDI-II scores suggests increased depression.

indicators on a regular basis using the data provided from the individual progress notes. Form 5 provides an example of filled-out progress notes.

KEEPING TRACK OF THE DATA

Poorly organized or unreliable data are misleading and confusing and can be detrimental to treatment. Simply listing data in progress notes will not support accurate outcome assessment. The data must be systematically organized and integrated on an ongoing basis. The more carefully and periodically the data are studied, the more direction there is in providing on-target treatment. The data gathered during the individual sessions can be meaningfully recorded to verify treatment plan progress.

Both standardized and nonstandardized data are helpful in assessing outcomes. Nonstandardized data, such as rating scales, SUDs, and behavioral information such as frequency and duration, are intraindividual measurements that do not have normative data. The ratings are important because they compare the client's subjective level of distress and various baseline behaviors in which measurable objectives have been set. Standardized tests allow the therapist to compare the client to others from a normal population, those who have similar diagnoses, or both.

TABLE 7.5
Sample Statements in Plan Section

Area	Example of Plan Comments in Progress Notes
Treatment	Continue training in relaxation techniques.
Treatment plan objectives	Revise objective 2c (days attending work per week): baseline = 3, current = 4, new objective = 5.
Behaviors	Homework assignment of contacting siblings to discuss previous behaviors leading to current resentments.
Termination	Discontinue treatment after 2 more sessions.
Referrals	Referred for medical evaluation to Dr. Smith.

FORM 5 PROGRESS NOTES

Client *John Adams* Chart # *JA032200* Session # *5* Date *4-11-2000*

Diagnosis *Major Depression*

Outcome indicators measured prior to session *See Treatment Plan Progress Chart*

Treatment plan objectives for this session *1 a,b,c 3 a,b,c*

D Completed homework assignment of phoning 2 friends to meet for lunch. Reports initial difficulties in motivation, but felt much better when speaking to friends. Reports a desire to spend more time with best friend. Role-played initiating a conversation with a new neighbor. Several difficulties being spontaneous. Often stated that his spouse calls him a "loser." Challenged his belief that he is not able to be liked by other people by having him list several people who have phoned him over the past two months. Listed five alternate positive behaviors to consider when he is feeling dysphoric or bored. Role-played phoning a close friend who may provide social support and encouragement. Toward the end of the session he discussed significant marital stressors. Reports several problems focusing on positive thoughts when spouse is not home, stating, "I don't trust her. . . . Where is she when she isn't at work? . . . Will she come back?" Believes he will soon return to work full-time. States that employer is supportive.

A Notable improvements in motivation to return to premorbid functioning in social time spent with friends. Spending more time in pleasurable activities, rather than dwelling on negative thoughts. Increased stress and distrust for spouse may lead to relapse in low level of self esteem, dysphoric mood, and negative thought processes.

P Homework assignment of identifying antecedents of arguments with spouse. Will phone best friend on Thursday evening. Schedule conjoint session with spouse, if possible. Practice assertiveness skills next session.

Time started *2:00 PM* Time finished *2:52 PM* Duration *52"* Next appt. *4/18/00* @ *2:00 PM*

Procedure *90844* Therapist's signature/credentials *Jessie Brown, PhD*

Some clinicians choose to incorporate repeated measures of standardized tests as an indication of outcomes. Lengthy tests such as the California Psychological Inventory (CPI) or the Rorschach Inkblot Test may be helpful as pretests and possibly posttests, but are not time-efficient as ongoing measures. Older types of outcome measures primarily relied upon pre- and posttests but did not adequately incorporate ongoing measures.

Progress in treatment plan objectives should be charted regularly. Some objectives will be met quickly and need no further revisions when the client is no longer experiencing significant impairment. Others will be modified periodically to incrementally meet the stated treatment plan goals.

Progress Charts

Progress notes document the content of individual sessions. Progress charts provide a graphic representation of treatment plan objectives. We have demonstrated that, when carefully written and planned, treatment plan objectives can also be used as outcome indicators. The various types of data must be charted carefully to avoid misinterpretation of results. For example, charting ordinal categorical data as if they are interval data could be misleading. Session-by-session progress ratings are helpful to both the client and therapist.

It is not possible for the therapist to chart all information about the client. Behavioral observations from collaterals such as family members, teachers, staff members, and others interested in the client's well-being provide additional perspectives of the client's level of functioning. Nevertheless, the information provided must be consistent, objective, atheoretical, and measurable. A baseline score is needed to provide an objective basis for evaluating progress.

The information provided from collaterals can and should be the same data described in the treatment plan goals and objectives. Empirical data of behavioral observations, rather than subjective opinions, provide information that can be evaluated by an outside source. Compare the statements in Box 7.1.

Form 6 systematically charts three possible observations of a target behavior, including frequency, duration, and severity. It allows for a wide range of collaterals such as teachers, family members, staff, or others who are in a position to make objective observations in the client's environment. Depending on the behavior, the client may choose to self-monitor. The form allows collaterals or the client to observe and report a specific behavior on a daily basis for an entire week. The baseline measurement of the behavior corresponds with the treatment plan baseline. The data are more easily monitored by the clinician when they are summarized according to the aver-

Box 7.1

Which of the following statements from collaterals provides the most useful outcome information?
Statement A: "Susan's behaviors in school have improved."
Statement B: "Since February 12, Susan's aggressive behaviors in school have decreased from an average of 12 disruptive behaviors per day to less than 4 per day. On-task behavior has increased from 60% to 85%."

age occurrence of the behavior. For example, if the client sees the therapist once per week, the data might be best depicted as the total number of occurrences per week or the average times per day during the week.

Such data are helpful in treatment planning and individual outcome assessment because they evaluate and monitor specific problem areas that cause significant impairment or distress for the client. A few examples follow.

Example 1

Baseline: Client disrupts class at school an average of 12 times per day, lasting an average of 60 seconds. Average severity of 3 (severe).

On February 10, the teacher rates the frequency, duration, and severity of the client's disruptive behaviors in class, with the following results.

Date/Day	(A) Frequency (Tally)	(B) Duration (Xsec __min __hr)	(C) Severity (1 [Mild]–3 [Severe])	Comments
February 10/	/ / / / /	30, 20, 45, 50, 60	2,1,2,3,3	Decreased duration with
Monday	/ / / / /	20, 30, 45, 60, 70	1,2,2,3,3	one-on-one attention in class-
	Total = 10	Average = 43 sec	Average = 2.2	room and after taking meds

Each day the teacher fills out a daily portion of Form 6. At the end of each week, results are shared with the therapist. As treatment progresses, the therapist, in collaboration with the teacher, monitors each aspect of the disruptive behavior (e.g., frequency, duration, and severity). The specific aspects of the problem behaviors are included in the treatment plan. For example, in the preceding situation, the treatment plan may have been as follows:

TP problem 1: Several behavioral disruptions in school class daily, leading to academic and social impairment
Frequency: Average 12 per day Duration: Average 60 sec each Severity: Usually severe
Goal 1: Increase time spent in class performing nondisruptive behavior
Objective 1a: Less than 8 disruptive behaviors per day at school Target date: February 20
Objective 1b: Disruptive behaviors last average of less than 30 sec Target date: February 27
Objective 1c: Rated intensity of behaviors at mild-moderate Target date: February 27
Treatment strategies: Reward system set up with parents based on teacher reports. Play therapy incorporating family dynamics. Role-play coping strategies.

Example 2

Baseline: Client smokes at least three packs of cigarettes per day (there are 18 hours per day in which he smokes). His physician has told him that his level of smoking is a serious potential threat to his health. The client does not view this as stressful, but wants to quit due to perceived social pressure. One of his treatment plan areas follows form 6:

Example 2 *(Continued)*

TP problem 1: Smoking 3 packs of cigarettes per day, resulting in potential physical impairment
Frequency: 3+ packs/day Duration: 18 hr Severity: None perceived by client
Goal 1: Quit smoking cigarettes
Objective 1a: Less than 1½ packs of cigarettes daily Target date: January 12
Objective 1b: Less than 8-hr period per day using cigarettes Target date: January 12
Objective 1c: Visit MD for medication evaluation Target date: December 15
Treatment strategies: Learn (1) relaxation techniques, (2) alternate behaviors. Med referral.

On December 18 the client fills out the following information regarding the number of packs of cigarettes smoked that day.

Date/Day	(A) Frequency (Packs/Day)	(B) Duration (Hours Smoked)	(C) Severity Comments	
December 18/ Tuesday	/ /	Began 6:00 A.M. Ended 8:00 P.M.	Not applicable	Smoking 1 less pack per per day. Less time smoking. Significant cravings.
	Total = 10	Total = 14 hr		

At times, behaviors are noted on an hourly basis. Form 7 is helpful in doing this. Consistency of behavioral observations is the most important element of charting the data. There must be a strong commitment from the observer to provide objective data that best meet the client's best interest. Caution must be used if the collateral providing the information could benefit from increases or decreases in the client's behaviors.

CHARTING ORDINAL AND INTERVAL DATA

Forms 8 and 9 provide examples of monitoring treatment plan objectives using ordinal or interval data. Form 8 allows for tracking all of the objectives on one sheet of paper. There is no room for comments or graphically charting the material, but little paperwork is needed. Form 9 requires a separate sheet for each objective, but specific comments and regular graphing over time are helpful in describing progress on the objectives. Therapists generally choose one of the two forms to best fit their needs.

The information for Forms 8 and 9 is taken directly from progress notes. Some therapists prefer to make a brief notation in the progress notes that data have been placed in the chart. Others write down the specific data in each progress note and also maintain separate graphs and charts of progress. The authors suggest writing treatment plan objectives data in progress notes when they are part of the content of the session. When the treatment plan objective is not a session topic, the data should be entered directly onto the form for each objective being monitored. Thus, any ongoing charting of client progress is, in effect, an extension of the progress notes.

The horizontal axis (i.e., x axis or ordinate) is a function of time, such as day number, week number, or session number. The vertical axis (i.e., y axis or abscissa) represents the behavior (e.g., frequency, duration, rating, level of distress)

FORM 6 BEHAVIORAL OBSERVATIONS: WEEKLY TALLY SHEET

Name of person observed *John Adams* Observation date(s) *3/25–3/29, 2000*

Observed by *Helen Lockery* Relationship *employer*

Behavior observed/tallied *Number of widgets produced daily*

How will the observations take place? *Work records and observations*

Check which aspects of the behavior will be observed and tallied.

(A) ✔ Frequency (how often does the behavior take place in each time period?)

(For example: January 13; 3 anger outbursts took place)

(B) ___Duration (how long it takes place) ___Sec ___Min ___Hr ___Other (specify)______

(For example: January 13; anger outbursts lasted 15, 18, and 12 minutes)

(C) ___Severity (describe severity scale used, such as SUD, Mild/Moderate/Severe, or other descriptors)

(For example: January 13; the severity [IRS] of anger outbursts was 80, 85, and 70)

Example (from the above data)

5-Mon	(A) Frequency	(B) Duration	(C) Severity	Comments
July 7	Total 3	Average 15	Average 83.3	Decreased duration when ignored

Average = Sum or durations or severities/Frequency—for example: Average duration = (15 + 18 + 12)/3 = 15

Day Date	(A) Frequency # *of widgets*	(B) Duration __Sec__Min__Hr *N/A*	(C) Severity ______ *N/A*	Comments *Quota = 20 per day*
1 ______	______	______	______	______
______	Total ______	Average ______	Average ______	______
2 ______	______	______	______	______
______	Total ______	Average ______	Average ______	______
3 ______	______	______	______	*Arrived to work 3 hours late*
______	Total ______	Average ______	Average ______	*due to Dr. appt.*
4 ______	______	______	______	*Left early due to phone call*
______	Total ______	Average ______	Average ______	*from spouse*
5 ______	______	______	______	*Excellent job*
______	Total ______	Average ______	Average ______	*cooperated well*

6 ______ ____________ ____________ ____________ ________________________

______ Total ________ Average ______ Average______ ________________________

7 ______ ____________ ____________ ____________ ________________________

______ Total ________ Average ______ Average______ ________________________

Average frequency per day = Total of averages/Number of days listed 70 / 5 = 14

Weekly average of daily averages = Total of average scores/Number of days measured

Duration weekly average = _______/ _______=_______

Severity weekly average = _______/ _______=_______

FORM 7 HOURLY BEHAVIORAL OBSERVATION TALLY SHEET

Name of person observed *John Adams* Observation dates *9/24–9/30*

Observed by *Cynthia Adams* Relationship *Spouse*

Behavior(s) observed/tallied *Negative comments to spouse*

Time period	Sun	Mon	Tue	Wed	Thu	Fri	Sat	Total	# Days	Daily hourly average
6:00–7:00 A.M.		2	3	2	4	5		16	5	3.2
7:00–8:00 A.M.		3	2	4	2	4		15	5	3.0
8:00–9:00 A.M.	7						5	12	2	6.0
9:00–10:00 A.M.	4						5	9	2	4.5
10:00–11:00 A.M.	5						8	13	2	6.5
11:00–12:00 A.M.	4						7	11	2	5.5
12:00–1:00 P.M.	3						4	7	2	3.5
1:00–2:00 P.M.	4						5	9	2	4.5
2:00–3:00 P.M.	3						6	9	2	4.5
3:00–4:00 P.M.	2						5	7	2	4.5
4:00–5:00 P.M.	5						3	8	2	5.0
5:00–6:00 P.M.	7						6	13	2	6.5
6:00–7:00 P.M.	7	8	3	6	5	4	5	38	7	5.4
7:00–8:00 P.M.	4	5	6	7	4	6	6	38	7	5.4
8:00–9:00 P.M.	5	4	9	9	6	6	6	45	7	6.4
9:00–10:00 P.M.	5	5	2	3	0	1	3	19	7	2.7
10:00–11:00 P.M.										
11:00–12:00 P.M.										
12:00–1:00 A.M.										
1:00–2:00 A.M.										
2:00–3:00 A.M.										
3:00–4:00 A.M.										
4:00–5:00 A.M.										
5:00–6:00 A.M.										

									Weekly
Daily totals	65	27	25	31	21	26	74		269
# of Observations	14	6	6	6	6	6	14		58
*Daily averages	4.6	4.5	4.2	5.2	3.5	4.3	5.3	***Total hourly average	4.6

*Daily average = Daily total/# of observations

Note: Daily averages should be based on the number of hours the behavior was observed, not 24 hours, unless it is observed 24 hours per day.

**Daily hourly average = Hourly total/# of observations for time period

***Total hourly average = Weekly total/Total # of observations for week

Remarks *Baseline from session 3 was average 7.1 per hour. Continued concerns on Saturdays and later evenings.*

FORM 8 TREATMENT PLAN OBJECTIVES PROGRESS CHART

Client *John Adams* Chart # *JA0332200* Intake date *3-22-00*

Objective # *1a* Describe *Feelings of sadness 80% of time*

Initial objective level *<50%* Revisions in level of objective *5/16: <25%*

Date	3/15	3/22	3/29	4/4	4/11	4/18	4/25	5/2	5/9	5/16	5/23	5/30	6/6	6/13	6/20	6/27	Date completed
Data	80	80	75	75	65	70	55	55	50	50	45	45	30	25	20	20	6-27

Objective # *1b* Describe *Beck Depression Inventory score of 30*

Initial objective level *Score 20* Revisions in level of objective *5/2: <16 6/13: <12*

Date	3/15	3/22	3/29	4/4	4/11	4/18	4/25	5/2	5/9	5/16	5/23	5/30	6/6	6/13	6/20	6/27	Date completed
Data	30	30	28	26	22	21	20	20	18	18	17	16	14	12	12	12	6-27

Objective # *1c* Describe *SUD score of 90 for depressed mood*

Initial objective level *<70* Revisions in level of objective *5/16: 45*

Date	3/15	3/22	3/29	4/4	4/11	4/18	4/25	5/2	5/9	5/16	5/23	5/30	6/6	6/13	6/20	6/27	Date completed
Data	90	90	85	85	80	90	85	80	80	70	65	55	60	55	50	50	Not completed

Objective # *2a* Describe *Work production at 50% of quota*

Initial objective level *>75%* Revisions in level of objective *4/11: >90%*

Date	3/15	3/22	3/29	4/4	4/11	4/18	4/25	5/2	5/9	5/16	5/23	5/30	6/6	6/13	6/20	6/27	Date completed
Data	50	60	75	85	90	90	95	100	100	100							5/16

Objective # *2b* Describe *Attending work 24 out of 40 hours*

Initial objective level *>32 hours* Revisions in level of objective *4/25: >36 hours*

Date	3/15	3/22	3/29	4/4	4/11	4/18	4/25	5/2	5/9	5/16	5/23	5/30	6/6	6/13	6/20	6/27	Date completed
Data	24	22	20	22	25	28	33	35	30	32	34	36	40	38	40	40	6-20

Objective # *2c* Describe *SUD score of 90 for level of distress on job*

Initial objective level *60* Revisions in level of objective *4/25: <40 5/16: <25*

Date	3/15	3/22	3/29	4/4	4/11	4/18	4/25	5/2	5/9	5/16	5/23	5/30	6/6	6/13	6/20	6/27	Date completed
Data	90	85	75	65	55	45	40	40	40	25	20	20					5/30

Objective # *3a* Describe *Spending only 0 hours/week with friends/family/peers*

Initial objective level *2 +hrs/week* Revisions in level of objective *5/16: 4 hrs*

Date	3/15	3/22	3/29	4/4	4/11	4/18	4/25	5/2	5/9	5/16	5/23	5/30	6/6	6/13	6/20	6/27	Date completed
Data	0	0	0.25	0.5	0.25	1.0	.75	1.0	2.0	2.0	2.5	2.5	2.0	3.0	3.0	3.5	Not completed

Objective # 3b Describe *Returning 0 phone calls*

Initial objective level 50+% Revisions in level of objective 4/4: >75%

Date	3/15	3/22	3/29	4/4	4/11	4/18	4/25	5/2	5/9	5/16	5/23	5/30	6/6	6/13	6/20	6/27	Date completed
Data	0	25	50	50	75	100	100	100									5/2

Objective # 3c Describe *Attending 0 social functions weekly*

Initial objective level 2+ Revisions in level of objective 4/25: <40 5/16: <25

Date	3/15	3/22	3/29	4/4	4/11	4/18	4/25	5/2	5/9	5/16	5/23	5/30	6/6	6/13	6/20	6/27	Date completed
Data	0	0	1	1	0	1	2	0	1	1	1	0	1	2	1	1	Not completed

Use additional sheets as necessary.

FORM 9 TREATMENT PLAN OBJECTIVES PROGRESS CHART—INDIVIDUAL OBJECTIVES

Client *John Adams* Chart # *JA032200* Intake date *3-22-00*

Presenting problem *Depressed mood, social withdrawal* Therapist *JB*

Objective (A) *X* Increase __Decrease (*B) __Duration *X* Frequency ___Rating __Test score __Other__

Outcome description of objective (*C) *Hours spent on job (out of 40)*

(*D) Baseline measurement (number or descriptor) *24*, is based on ___Average or *X* Total per (time period)

(E) Charted below as *X* Session number *X* Weekly __2 Weeks __Dates as listed __Other ______

Use one form for each treatment plan objective used as an outcome indicator.

Treatment plan objective # *26* Remarks (i.e., factors affecting objectives; include dates)

3/21 Received reprimand at work due to poor attendance

4/17 Noted improvements due to reconciliation with spouse 7/2 1st full week at work

8/12 Termination: Goal achieved (2 consecutive weeks of 40 hours at work)

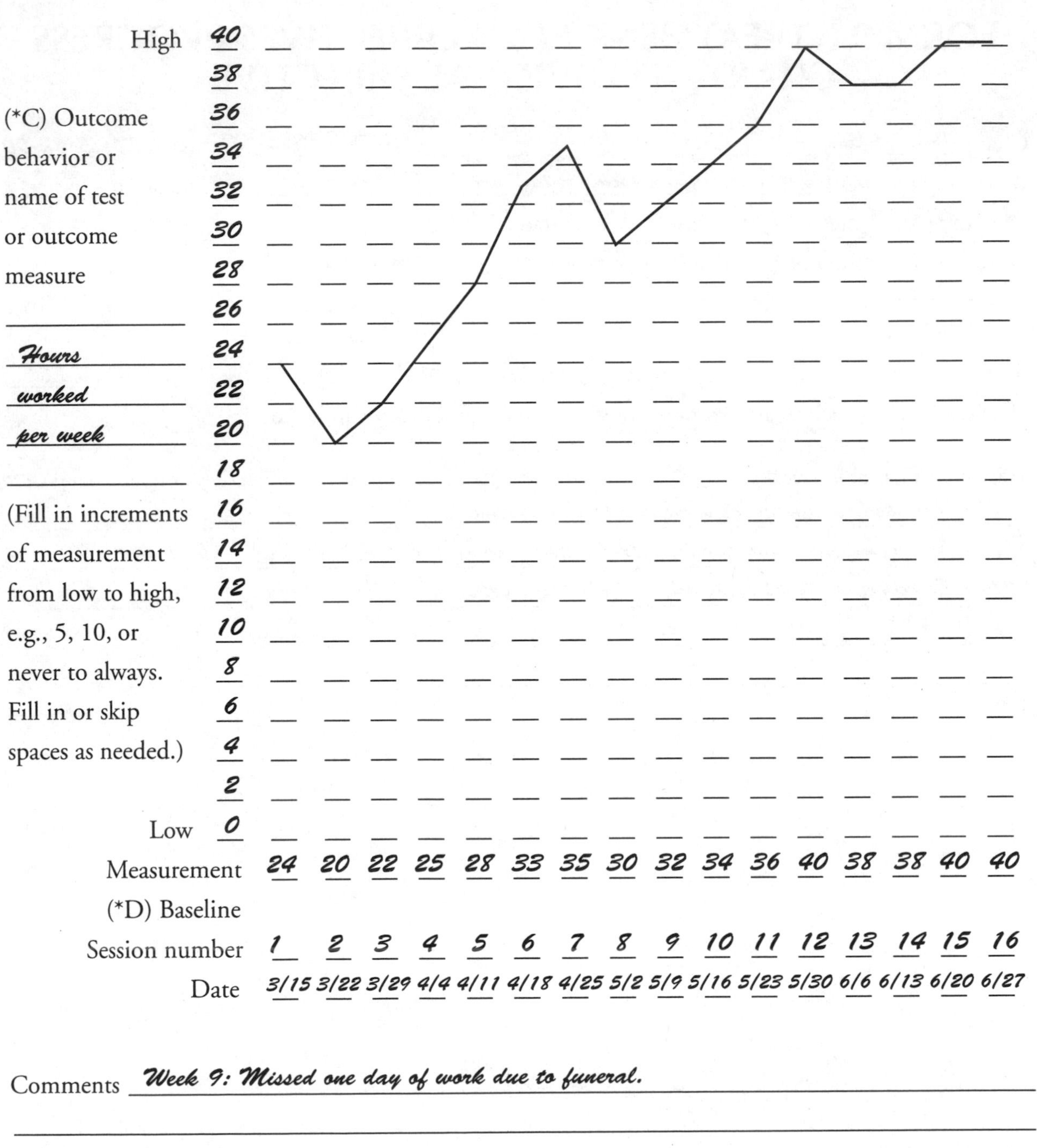

Measurement	24	20	22	25	28	33	35	30	32	34	36	40	38	38	40	40
(*D) Baseline																
Session number	1	2	3	4	5	6	7	8	9	10	11	12	13	14	15	16
Date	3/15	3/22	3/29	4/4	4/11	4/18	4/25	5/2	5/9	5/16	5/23	5/30	6/6	6/13	6/20	6/27

Comments *Week 9: Missed one day of work due to funeral.*

being measured. The level of the behavior is compared against the baseline behavior established in the initial sessions to gauge the effects of treatment over time.

Summary

Each progress note provides up-to-date evidence and assessment of outcomes. Progress notes can be written in various formats that help organize the information. (The authors recommend using the DAP format.) Progress charts, which are filled out by collaterals or clients between sessions, provide evidence of behavioral progress regarding various treatment plan objectives.

This section describes individual outcome assessment in which typical clinical procedures are adapted to outcome assessment. Both objective and subjective means of evaluation are used.

III

NORMATIVE OUTCOME ASSESSMENT

8

DEFINING CLINICALLY SIGNIFICANT CHANGE

In this section we shift our attention from assessing outcomes of individual clients to comparing clients with a normative group. In *individualized* assessment, diagnoses are made, treatment goals are set, and outcome indicators are developed with reference to the client at hand. Improvement is indicated by clients' progress relative to their own baseline behavior and distress level at the beginning of treatment. *Normative* assessment compares clients' functioning to that of a normative group using standardized measures, or at least measures for which normative data are available. There are two types of normative groups: (1) functional or nondistressed groups and (2) dysfunctional or distressed groups. Thus, in normative assessment, the client's behavior or distress level is compared against the typical level of distress or kind of behavior in the appropriate normative group. The baseline is a population baseline, not an individual baseline.

Intake Assessment versus Outcome Assessment

If a clinician is asked to conduct an assessment, the task that comes immediately to mind for most therapists involves conducting interviews, interpreting psychological tests, and gathering additional information useful to the conceptualization of the case at hand. Often this assessment process results in assignment of a diagnosis. At the very least, the assessment should result in a relatively unambiguous decision as to whether or not the client is facing issues that warrant further treatment, and some understanding of the nature of the presenting problem. A critical element of the initial assessment process involves direct observation and questioning of the client. In other words, the assessment is individualized as described in Part II of this book.

However, initial assessment may also involve

the use of standardized assessment instruments to obtain normative data about a client. Such instruments allow the comparison of the responses of the presenting client with the responses of identified populations. Here, of course, the reference is to the use of empirically constructed tests like the Minnesota Multiphasic Personality Inventory (MMPI), the Wechslar Adult Intelligence Scale (WAIS), the Strong Interest Inventory, or the Beck Depression Inventory (BDI). Tests used for diagnostic purposes are useful because they differentiate between responses that are typical of a population with a particular disorder or dysfunction and a population that does not possess that disorder or dysfunction. The initial assumption is that the client does not have a particular disorder. As with the null hypothesis in statistics, the clinician expects to reject that assumption if he or she suspects the presence of a particular disorder. If the client's test score is above a certain cutoff, the indication is that the client is responding on the test in a manner similar to individuals who are known to have an identified disorder. The logic of empirical criteria for interpreting test scores was first popularized with the MMPI. Since then a host of tests have been developed for various diagnostic purposes, including such popularly used instruments as the Beck Depression Inventory, the Millon Scales, and the Rorschach Inkblot Test. The important point here is that the logic of using such tests is always the same. The usefulness of the instrument is established by collecting normative data on known populations. To the extent that the measure differentiates between functional and dysfunctional populations, it is deemed a useful (e.g., valid) instrument for diagnostic purposes.

Although the discussion so far may seem like a review of basic assessment principles most clinicians learned early in graduate school, the relevance to outcome assessment becomes clear when we realize that the task facing the clinician when assessing outcome is the opposite of what the clinician faces when conducting an assessment for diagnostic purposes. In other words, at intake, the assessment instrument is used to determine whether the individual client is responding to the test in a manner consistent with an identified dysfunctional population. For outcome assessment, the question is whether the client is responding to the test instrument in a manner consistent with an identified functional population. We can assume that the client started out as dysfunctional (or why would the client be in need of treatment!). The outcome question is whether the patient has improved, and if so, by how much. The ideal outcome would be one in which the client not only has improved, but also has improved to the point where his or her responses are indistinguishable from those of the functional population.

Almost without exception, training and texts in psychological assessment are geared toward answering the intake assessment question. Normative data and interpretive procedures are laid out in detail to aid the clinician in determining whether the client is in need of treatment. Unfortunately, the outcome question is largely ignored in the typical text or training program on assessment. How can the clinician use testing to help determine whether the client is no longer in need of treatment?

APPROACHES TO ASSESSING CLIENT CHANGE

The outcome question is really about change. Assuming that the client began treatment in a dysfunctional state, has the client changed for the better over the course of treatment? In other words, has the client shown significant change over the course of therapy? Traditionally, the question of whether change is "significant" has been framed in statistical terms. The question of whether there was a significant change in a group of clients from before to after treatment, or whether there was a significant difference between a group of clients who received treatment and a comparable group who did not receive treatment, was considered a statistical question. A difference was presumed to be shown if there was a statistically significant difference between scores before and after treatment or between the scores of those who received treatment and those who did not. Despite the emphasis that the idea of statistical significance usually receives in graduate statistics courses, there are many conceptual and practical difficulties with the concept. Many authors have questioned the usefulness of traditional significance tests in research settings (e.g., Cohen, 1990; Schmidt, 1996; Wilkinson, 1999). The problem is that the determination of statistical significance simply yields information as to the likelihood that chance provides a reasonable explanation for any differences observed in the data. A conclusion that a statistically significant change has occurred provides no information about the magnitude of the change. Consequently, information about statistical significance in an outcome study is not particularly useful for the clinician.

In contrast to asking whether change in client functioning over treatment is *statistically* significant, the more important question is whether such change is *clinically* significant. This is not a strictly statistical question. The determination of clinically significant change involves such questions as whether or not treatment goals have been met, whether client functioning has notably improved, and whether symptoms have been reduced to the point that they no longer are of concern to the client. Most often, determinations of clinically significant change are made on a case-by-case basis for each client. Procedures for documenting such change on an individual basis are explained in Part II. As in diagnosis, there is no substitute for the careful observation of the individual client to ascertain the degree of progress being made over the course of treatment. However, as described in Chapter 4, there are times when it is useful to include normative as well as individual assessment. Just as a standardized instrument like the MMPI-2 may be useful for intake assessment, the inclusion of standardized measures can also be useful for outcome assessment. Individualized assessment answers the question of how clients are doing relative to where they were when they started treatment. Normative outcome assessment answers the question of how clients are doing relative to the larger population of individuals who have (or do not have) a similar dysfunction.

CLINICALLY SIGNIFICANT CHANGE

Normative outcome assessment is by necessity statistical in that comparisons must be made between individual scores and normative descriptive data. However, as discussed previously, the clinically important question is not one of statistical significance. What is needed is a way to look at changes in clients' scores over the course of treatment, which provides information about clinical as opposed to statistical significance. Such an approach has been suggested by Jacobson and colleagues (Jacobson, Follette, & Ravenstorf, 1984; Jacobson, Roberts, Berns, & McGlinchey, 1999; Jacobson & Truax, 1991). The development of a framework for evaluating clinical significance was initially motivated by the need for more precise ways to assess outcome in research designed to test the efficacy of psychotherapeutic interventions. Neither traditional tests of statistical significance nor measures of effect size provide clinically relevant or definitive answers to the question of whether clients receiving psychotherapy are better off after treatment than patients assigned to a control group who do not receive therapy. The problem is that such purely statistical criteria do not necessarily assess whether the goals of treatment have been met. Just because a treatment effect is shown to be statistically significant does not mean that the effect is clinically significant. As stated by Jacobson and Truax (1991):

> In contrast to criteria based on statistical significance, judgments regarding clinical significance are based on external standards provided by interested parties in the community. Consumers, clinicians, and researchers all expect psychotherapy to accomplish particular goals, and it is the extent to which psychotherapy succeeds in accomplishing these goals that determines whether or not it is effective or beneficial. The clinical significance of a treatment refers to its ability to meet standards of efficacy set by consumers, clinicians, and researchers (p. 12).

In other words, the determination of whether a client has shown significant change over the course of therapy is a clinical question and cannot be answered solely on statistical grounds. If this is true for efficacy research studies, it is also clearly applicable in the case of assessing individual client progress from the beginning to the end of treatment. Consequently, the criteria suggested by Jacobson and colleagues for assessing clinical significance have applications in clinical outcome assessment as well as in the analysis of more formal outcome research.

Two fundamental criteria are suggested by Jacobson for the determination of clinically significant change (Jacobson, Roberts, Berns, & McGlinchey, 1999; Jacobson & Truax, 1991).

1. The magnitude of the change must be statistically reliable.
2. The change must be such that the client has returned to normal functioning.

These two criteria are critical since they form the basis of the procedures laid out in the following chapters for using normative data to assess client outcome.

The first criterion—that the magnitude of change must be reliable—simply reflects the reality that all measurements are imprecise and subject to error. The amount of measurement error inherent in a given test score is calculated by finding the inverse of the reliability coefficient of the test. In other words, if an instrument is shown to have a reliability coefficient of 0.90, the assumption is that 10 percent (e.g., 1.00 minus 0.9) of the variability in the test scores is attributable to random errors of measurement. For most psychological tests, reliabilities of 0.8 or higher are considered acceptable. For the present purposes, to be considered reliable, the change in the client's score on the outcome assessment instrument from before to after treatment must be of sufficient magnitude that measurement error is an unlikely explanation of the change. In other words, relatively small changes in test scores from before to after treatment may well be explained as chance events that do not represent real change. In order to establish a criterion for reliable change, a minimum number of points of change in the test score must be set such that change greater than the minimum is considered reliable. As is shown in the next section, three parameters must be determined in order to establish this criterion: (1) A reliability coefficient for scores on the test must be available, (2) the standard deviation of scores on the test must be available, and (3) a degree of confidence or certainty must be arbitrarily established. The first two pieces of information can generally be obtained in test manuals or articles describing the psychometric properties of the test instrument. The degree of confidence in a statistical outcome is traditionally set at 95 percent. An example of how to establish an index for reliable change in a test score is provided in the next section.

The second criterion for clinical significance—that the client has returned to normal functioning—is both more controversial and more difficult to establish than the first criterion (that the change must be reliable). However, in many cases a return to normal functioning is clearly the overriding treatment goal. Assume that a client enters treatment presenting with severe anxiety and depression. These symptoms show up as elevated scores on standardized tests like the MMPI-2 and the BDI. In addition, the client reports disruption in his or her interpersonal relationships and serious difficulties at work, including lowered productivity and excessive absenteeism. After appropriate treatment, many of these problems are alleviated. The client reports improvement in relationships with friends and family. Work is also going much better for the client. Although some elements of depression and anxiety remain, these are considered to be manageable, and both the client and the therapist are satisfied with the result as the therapy is terminated. This is the kind of "success story" therapists like to see in their practice (but perhaps see all too seldom in reality). Clearly, in this case the goal of return to normal functioning has been met, and it would be fair to describe the client as recovered. We would expect that the positive outcome in this case would be reflected in improved test scores. For example, if the BDI were readministered to this client at the termination of therapy, we would reasonably expect that the previously elevated score would now be much lower. In fact, given the large degree of improvement in the client's functioning, it is likely that the posttreatment BDI score would be in the "normal" range. In other words, at the beginning of treatment the client's test scores were more characteristic of the population of individuals who are distressed or dysfunctional. However, after successful treatment, the test scores are now characteristic of the population of individuals who are not distressed.

It is immediately evident that defining successful therapy as a return to normal functioning is problematic in some settings. For example, if a therapist works with a population suffering from severe and persistent mental illness, the chances that the therapist's clients will end treatment indistinguishable from the functional population are remote. Success for these clients must be described in terms of meeting more immediate treatment goals. It is also possible that a patient who improves over the course of treatment, but still exhibits some dysfunction, might be considered a success. For example, an individual in treatment for severe alcohol dependence may succeed in obtaining a job and re-establishing important interpersonal relationships even though he or she still engages in occasional binge drinking. While clearly not "recovered," this individual has improved over the course of treatment. The implication is that the standard of return to normal functioning as a criterion for clinically significant change over the course of treatment must be evaluated for each treatment setting. In some settings, successful treatment is defined in terms of meeting treatment goals that fall short of returning to the functional population but nonetheless represent meaningful improvement in the client's condition.

The more technical difficulty in setting a criterion for return to normal functioning lies in establishing a cutoff that marks the boundary between the "functional" and the "dysfunctional" populations. Again note that the assumption is that the client begins treatment with a degree of distress characteristic of the population of individuals seeking treatment. It is likely the case that the individual client meets the criteria for one or more *Diagnostic and Statistical Manual of Mental Disorders*—Fourth Edition (*DSM-IV*) diagnoses and shows clearly elevated scores on standardized testing instruments designed to measure psychopathology and psychological distress. At the end of successful treatment, it is assumed that the client now shows a degree of distress that is indistinguishable from that of the functional population. The client no longer meets *DSM-IV* criteria (at least for Axis I disorders) and the test scores have dropped into the normal range on measures of psychopathology. The question is, Where do we draw the line between the dysfunctional population and the functional population? Although any cutoff score marking the transition between these two populations will necessarily be an arbitrary one, setting such a cutoff is necessary to establish clinically significant change according to this criterion.

Jacobson and Truax (1991) suggest three approaches to defining the point of transition from the dysfunctional population to the functional population on an outcome measure. The first possible criterion (Cutoff a) defines clinically significant change as a movement of the test score out of the typical range of scores of the dysfunctional population. According to this criterion, clinically significant change is defined relative to the mean score of the distressed or dysfunctional population. An arbitrary cutoff is set relative to the mean of the dysfunctional population, usually at one or two standard deviations from the mean (in the direction of functionality, of course). Clients are considered recovered when their scores exceed this cutoff, with the assumption that they are now not typical members of the distressed population. Depending on the characteristics of the test, this criterion is often a fairly conservative one that makes it more difficult to show clinically significant change. The second proposed criterion (Cutoff b) defines clinically significant change relative to the functional population. According to this criterion, clients are recovered when their test scores are indistinguishable from the scores of individuals who are functional or "normal." Again, an arbitrary statistical cutoff is set, usually one or two standard deviations from the mean of the functional population (in the direction of dysfunctionality). Depending on the test, this cutoff is often more liberal than cutoff a, making it easier to show clinically significant change. The third possible criterion (Cutoff c) sets the cutoff such that the client's score is closer to the mean of the functional population than the dysfunctional population. Using cutoff c often results in a cutoff that is intermediate between cutoffs a and b.

A Hypothetical Example Illustrating Clinically Significant Change Criteria

The concepts outlined in the previous section are illustrated in the following example. To make the example easier to follow, a hypothetical test with simplified characteristics is used. The same principles are illustrated in subsequent chapters using actual assessment instruments.

Assume that a test has been developed to assess symptoms of general psychological distress. The questions focus primarily on immediate symptoms of anxiety and depression, and the test is scaled such that the higher the score, the greater the degree of distress. We will call the instrument the Psychological Distress Scale (PDS). Further assume that extensive psychometric research has been reported on the PDS. In order to establish normative data, assume that the PDS has been administered to a large community sample. Individuals currently in treatment for psychological disorders were excluded from the sample, so it is reasonable to assume that the community sample represents the distribution of scores of a normal or functional population. Scores for the community sample are approximately normally distributed with a mean score of 15 and a standard deviation of 8. The test has also been given to a sample of individuals prior to treatment for anxiety disorders or depression. Since all of these individuals met *DSM-IV* criteria for an Axis I disorder, it may be assumed that their scores represent those of the dysfunctional population. Scores for the clinical sample had a mean score of 35 and a standard deviation of 8. Finally, assume that the PDS has been determined to have an internal consistency reliability coefficient of 0.85.

The previous paragraph gives the essential normative data necessary to conduct an analysis of clinically significant change according to the procedure outlined. For convenience, these data are summarized in Table 8.1. The same information is provided in graphic form in Figure 8.1, where boxes representing the distribution of scores for both the functional and dysfunctional populations are plotted on the same axis. Understanding the information in Table 8.1 and Figure 8.1 is essential in order to follow the analysis described.

Before proceeding, a brief explanation of the schematic representation of the functional and dysfunctional populations in Figure 8.1 is in order. These two distributions are usually diagrammed as two slightly overlapping normal curves. A different schematic is consistently utilized in this text, consisting of a dot to represent the mean, a three-dimensional box extending one standard deviation on either side of the mean, and a line extending an additional standard deviation from the ends of the box. If the distributions are normal, approximately 95 percent of the scores are expected to fall between the end points of the lines, and 67 percent of the scores are expected to fall within the box itself. The traditional normal curves are not used in this text for two reasons. First, scores on outcome measures are seldom normally distributed. Rather, they tend to have a pronounced skew in the direction of greater distress. The use of boxes and lines is meant to indicate that the true shape of the distribution is not being represented in the graph. Second, the authors believe that the use of boxes and lines is conceptually clearer than overlapping normal curves.

TABLE 8.1
Summary of Statistical Parameters Necessary for a Clinically Significant Change Analysis Using the Hypothetical Instrument Called the Psychological Distress Scale (PDS)

Reliability coefficient:
Alpha = 0.85
Characteristics of the functional population:
Mean = 15
Standard deviation = 8
Characteristics of the dysfunctional population:
Mean = 35
Standard deviation = 8

Consider four hypothetical clients who were given the PDS both at intake (prior to treatment) and at the termination of treatment. (Do not be concerned with differences in the characteristics of the clients, their presenting problems, or how many sessions of treatment they received.) Scores for these hypothetical clients are given in Table 8.2. An explanation of how the outcome decision was arrived at for each of these clients is given in the following sections.

Figure 8.1

Illustration of the distribution of scores for the functional and dysfunctional populations for the hypothetical PDS measure. The boxes extend to one standard deviation on either side of the mean. The lines extend from the ends of the boxes an additional standard deviation on either side of the mean.

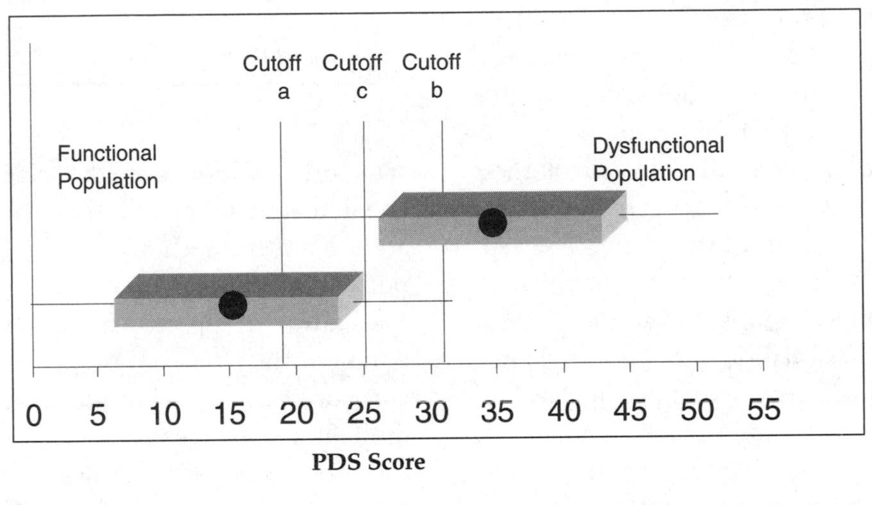

PDS Score

Determination of Reliable Change

The purpose of this calculation is to determine whether the difference between the pretreatment and posttreatment scores of an individual client is outside of the bounds of differences that might reasonably be attributed to measurement error. This calculation is based on the standard error of the difference between two scores, which is in turn related to the reliability of the test itself. The standard error of the difference gives the standard deviation of differences due to chance or measurement error. As is traditional in setting confidence intervals, cutoffs are set at two standard deviations on either side of the mean to establish a 95 percent confidence interval. This is based on the fact that in the normal distribution roughly 95 percent of all scores fall plus or minus two standard deviations from the mean.

A reliable change index (RCI) based on a 95 percent confidence interval can be established using the following formula (adapted from Jacobson & Truax, 1991):

$$RCI = 1.96\sqrt{2S^2\,(1 - r_{tt})}$$

Where 1.96 represents the Z score for a 95 percent confidence interval, S is the standard deviation of the scores on the test, and r_{tt} is the reliability coefficient for the test. Since the standard deviation and reliability coefficient were provided previously for this test (see Table 8.1),

TABLE 8.2
Scores and Outcome Decisions for Four Hypothetical Clients Who Were Administered the PDS before and after Treatment

Client	Pretreatment Score	Posttreatment Score	Difference	Outcome
Janet Doe	41	18	23	Recovered
James Doe	36	32	4	No change
John Doe	25	37	−12	Deteriorated
Jane Doe	49	33	16	Improved

the RCI for 95 percent confidence can be calculated as follows:

$$\text{RCI} = 1.96\sqrt{(2)(8^2)\,(1 - 0.85)} = 9.9$$

Rounding off the RCI to 10, we can conclude that any difference of 10 points or more between pre- and posttreatment scores is statistically reliable. That is, we are 95 percent confident that random measurement error is an unlikely explanation for differences of 10 points or more on the PDS.

Referring to Table 8.2, we can see that three of the four clients showed reliable change over the course of treatment. Only James Doe, who showed a very slight improvement of only 4 points from before to after treatment, failed to show reliable change. Of the remaining clients, we are most concerned about John Doe. His change was reliable, but unfortunately in the wrong direction. John Doe reported significantly more distress as measured by the PDS after treatment than he did before treatment. The necessary conclusion is that John Doe experienced reliable deterioration over the course of treatment. Hopefully relatively few clients will exhibit this pattern. The remaining two clients (Janet and Jane Doe) both showed reliable improvement of 23 and 16 points, respectively, over the course of treatment. The question is whether the change is clinically significant (e.g., consistent with a return to normal functioning).

Determination of Clinically Significant Change

Remember that Jacobson and Truax (1991) suggested three possible cutoff points for establishing return to normal functioning. The first, Cutoff a, is set with respect to the mean of the dysfunctional population. Assume that we establish Cutoff a as a score two standard deviations from the mean of the dysfunctional population. Since the mean of the dysfunctional population is equal to 35, and the standard deviation is equal to 8, a score two standard deviations below the mean would be at 35 − 16 or 19. This point is marked as Cutoff a in Figure 8.1. The second possible cutoff point (Cutoff b) is defined relative to the functional population. If we assume that return to normal functioning is suggested by a score within two standard deviations of the mean of the functional population, Cutoff b would be set at 15 + 16 or 31. Note that in this example Cutoff a sets a much more conservative criterion for establishing clinical significance than does Cutoff b. In other words, in many situations it is easier to demonstrate that an individual is indistinguishable from the functional population than it is to demonstrate that the individual is clearly no longer a member of the dysfunctional population. The third possible cutoff placement point (Cutoff c) is midway between the means of the functional and dysfunctional populations. In this example, the point midway between the functional mean of 15 and the dysfunctional mean of 35 is a score of 25. This point is marked as Cutoff c in Figure 8.1. It represents the most reasonable choice for a cutoff in this example.

The obvious problem facing the clinician is which cutoff to choose. There is no formula that produces a ready answer to this question. At least two factors must be taken into consideration in setting a cutoff for defining return to normal functioning. The first and most important has to do with the demands of the specific clinical setting. The choice of a more liberal or a more conservative cutoff point is ultimately a clinical, not a statistical, question. The second factor has to do with the relative separation and the shapes of the distributions of scores in the functional and dysfunctional populations. As will be pointed out later, certain problems arise if there is little or no overlap between the two distributions. In that case, just because an individual can be shown to be out of the dysfunctional population does not necessarily imply that he or she is now in the functional population. A related issue has to do with the availability of normative data in the first place. Some measures have not been systematically tested on a functional or normal population, and thus it is not possible to establish Cutoff b since data are not available. These and other details concerning the establishment of clinical significance are considered in subsequent chapters.

We will conclude this exercise demonstrating the concept of clinical significance by returning to our four hypothetical patients from Table 8.2. Recall that we have already established that James Doe improved by only a few points from before to after treatment, a change too small to be considered reliable. John Doe deteriorated over the course of treatment. Janet Doe showed the greatest improvement, and her posttreatment score of 18 clearly places her in the functional population even according to the most conservative Cutoff a criterion of 19. Consequently, Janet Doe is classified as being recovered. Jane Doe also showed reliable improvement. However, her posttreatment score of 33 leaves her in the dysfunctional population even according to the most liberal Cutoff b criterion of 31. Consequently, she is classified as improved. Hopefully, further treatment will move Jane Doe into the recovered category.

GRAPHIC ANALYSIS OF THE CLINICALLY SIGNIFICANT CHANGE MODEL

The concepts outlined in this chapter have been summarized by Jacobson and Truax (1991). To illustrate this application, let us add several additional hypothetical cases to our hypothetical outcome measure. Pre- and posttest scores for these clients are listed in Table 8.3. The first four scores are the same as those used in the previous example. The remaining scores are new.

The first step in graphing a clinically significant change analysis involves constructing a scatter plot of the pre- and posttest scores. Such a scatter plot has been constructed in Figure 8.2. Pretest scores are given along the horizontal axis and posttest scores are given along the vertical axis. Note that each axis of the graph begins and ends at the same data point. Each axis starts at a score of 0 and ends at a score of 60. For an accurate graph it is essential that this be the case. This is an important point to emphasize, because many spreadsheet and statistical programs automatically scale the axes of a graph (as did the software used to produce this graph). It is necessary

TABLE 8.3
Pre- and Posttreatment Scores on the PDS for the Four Clients from the Previous Example and Six Additional Clients

Client	Pretreatment Score	Posttreatment Score
1	41	18
2	36	32
3	25	37
4	49	33
5	25	12
6	27	29
7	47	33
8	39	15
9	18	10
10	37	25

to override the automatic scaling to produce a graph with identical scaling on each axis.

Each of the 10 clients is represented by a dot on the scatter plot. For example, we can identify the dot representing Client 1 by going up from the horizontal axis at a score of 41 (this client's pretreatment score) and reading over from the vertical axis at a score of 18 (this client's posttreatment score). The remaining clients can be identified in the same manner.

Figure 8.2

Initial scatter plot in graphing a clinically significant change analysis. Dots represent the pre- and posttreatment scores of individual clients.

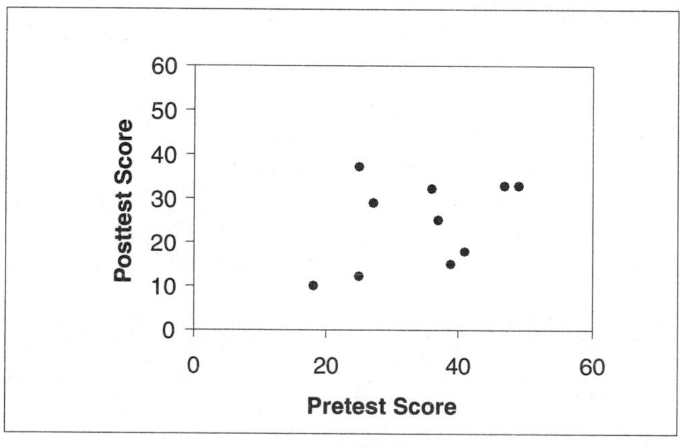

In Figure 8.3, a line has been drawn along the diagonal of the graph. This line represents no change from pre- to posttreatment. (It is not a regression line.) If a client received identical scores of 40 on the pre- and posttreatment measures, the score would fall on the diagonal. The same would be true if a client scored 20 or 30 on both tests. A client whose scores fall directly on the diagonal is showing absolutely no change from before to after treatment.

Clients whose scores fall in the area above the diagonal are scoring higher on the posttest than on the pretest. Since on this scale a higher score indicates greater psychological distress, such clients are apparently getting worse over the course of treatment. Conversely, clients whose scores fall below the diagonal are showing a reduction in measured distress over the course of treatment. In this example the vast majority of clients are showing improvement.

The last step in constructing a graphic representation of clinically significant change involves marking (1) a band to represent change that is not reliable and (2) a cutoff line to represent return to normal functioning. These lines are shown in Figure 8.4. The two dashed lines parallel to the diagonal mark a band within which any observed change may not be reliable. Recall that the reliable change margin at 95 percent confidence was approximately 10 points; thus the two dashed diagonal lines were established by moving 10 points above and below the center diagonal. These dashed lines represent the area within which change cannot be deemed reliable. In other words, change within the bounds of the diagonal may be due to measurement error. Note that in this example there were three clients (2, 6, and 9) who did not show reliable change over the course of treatment.

The area above the area of no change represents reliable deterioration. Clients whose scores

Figure 8.3

Graph from Figure 8.2, with a diagonal line added. Clients who fall above the line showed deterioration over the course of treatment; those who fall below the line showed improvement.

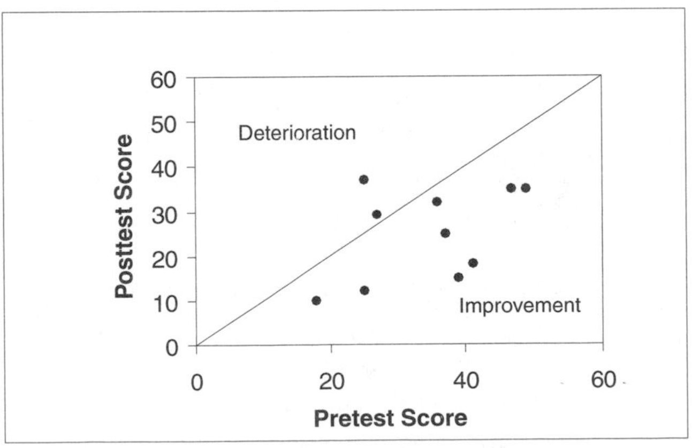

Figure 8.4

Graph from Figure 8.3, with two diagonal dashed lines added based on the reliable change index. Scores falling between the dashed lines did not show a reliable change over the course of treatment. A horizontal line has also been added to mark the cutoff for clinically significant change. Client scores that fall below the cutoff are judged to be in the range of the functional population.

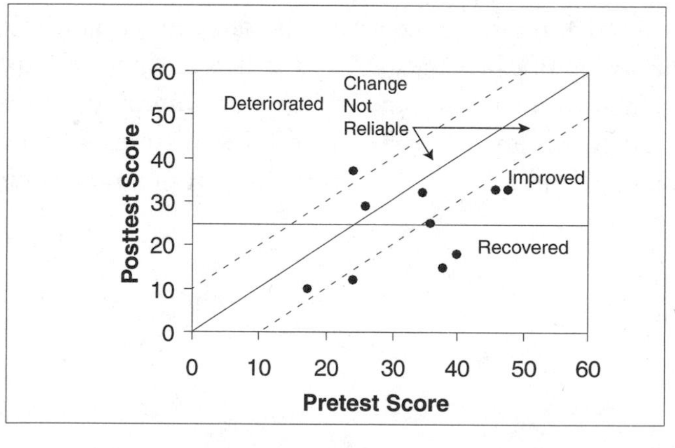

fall in this area are showing greater distress at the end of treatment than they were at the beginning of treatment. Fortunately, only a single client (Client 3) falls into this category in this example.

The other line added in Figure 8.4 is a horizontal line going across the graph at a score of 25. The is the line marking return to normal functioning. Recall the earlier discussion in which several procedures for setting this cutoff were described. An intermediate cutoff score of 25 was chosen as most reasonable for this analysis.

Clients who show reliable improvement, but whose posttreatment scores remain higher than the cutoff of 25, have gotten better but have not returned to normal functioning in terms of their level of distress. These clients can be labeled improved (but not recovered). There are two such clients in this example (Clients 4 and 7). The remaining area of the graph, at or below both the reliable change line and the cutoff for return to normal functioning, represents clients who can be said to have recovered. There are four such clients in this example (Clients 1, 5, 8, and 10). However, it should be noted that one of these clients (Client 5) was not scoring especially high on the measure at the onset of treatment, and that another (Client 10) scored exactly at the cutoff on the posttest.

SUMMARY

The graphic illustration of the clinically significant change model utilized in this book is useful in two ways. First, it provides a clear illustration of the conceptual framework of the model. Second, it is a useful way to summarize outcome data from a variety of clients. As opposed to a test of statistical significance, which would simply compare the mean scores from pre- to posttest, the analysis of clinically significant change shows the outcome for each client. This is a much more clinically useful approach than aggregate statistical comparisons that lose track of the individual client.

It is not necessary to construct a graph as illustrated in Figures 8.2 through 8.4 in order to conduct an analysis of clinically significant change. Once the necessary parameters are set for the boundaries for reliable change and for clinically significant change, an outcome decision can be made about a single client or a series of individual clients. This information complements the individual outcome assessment data recommended in Part II of this book. Spaces to fill in values for an analysis of clinically significant change are provided as appropriate in the sample forms used to illustrate the procedures recommended in this text. A graphic summary of the clients with a particular presenting problem, as in Figures 8.2 through 8.4, is particularly useful when conducting a program evaluation or effectiveness study. By placing a group of clients on the same graph and calculating the percentages that fall into the various outcome categories (no change, improved, recovered, or deteriorated), a detailed picture of the overall effectiveness of the treatment program can be obtained.

9

NORMATIVE DATA AND EXAMPLES FOR FOUR COMMON OUTCOME MEASURES

Chapter 8 gives a general description of the approach to determining clinically significant change. In this chapter we provide detailed illustrations of how to apply this approach using the following four different outcome measures:

- *Outcome Questionnaire-45 (OQ-45).* This is a short (45-item) measure designed specifically for outcome assessment. The scale measures a range of areas of concern, including psychological distress, interpersonal functioning, and social role functioning. The instrument is probably best suited for a moderately disturbed outpatient population.
- *Symptom Checklist-90-Revised (SCL-90-R).* This widely used instrument assesses a broad range of symptoms on a self-report basis. It is suitable for use in a wide variety of clinical settings.
- *Beck Depression Inventory (BDI).* This widely used instrument provides a short, reliable indicator of current level of depression.
- *Behavior and Symptom Identification Scale-32 (BASIS-32).* This instrument is a 32-item scale originally designed for use in an inpatient setting. It assesses psychosis, daily living skills, interpersonal functioning, impulsive/addictive behaviors, and depression.

The decision to include a detailed analysis of these particular instruments was guided by several factors. First, the instruments are suitable for a wide variety of clinical settings. Consequently they will be of use for a relatively large percentage of the audience for this book. It is not assumed that the small number of instruments covered in this chapter will meet the needs of all clinicians. Often, more specific measures are required for specific populations or practice settings. Suggestions for finding and using these more specific measures are provided in the next chapter. Second, the tests meet many or most of the criteria for selecting a normative outcome measure as outlined in the next chapter. In other words, they tend to be easily administered and scored, to be sensitive to short-term change in client functioning, to be relatively inexpensive, and to have normative data available.

A final caveat regarding the analyses that follow should also be made. All of the instruments reviewed (except the BDI) contain several subscales as well as a measure of overall functioning. The detailed examples that follow involve analysis of only a single measure of overall functioning for each instrument. Analysis of clinically significant change could also be conducted on selected subscales of the instrument. References are provided for finding normative data for change analysis of subscale scores, should that be desired for a particular practice setting.

Descriptions of each instrument follow the same general format. Following a general description of the instrument, details of available normative data are described. These data are drawn from a variety of published sources. Although certainly not exhaustive, for each instrument information is provided about reliability, typical scores among a functional population, and typical scores in a dysfunctional population. Detailed information about cost and how to obtain the instruments is also provided. Please note that vendor phone numbers, post office addresses, and Web site names can change over time. Thus, some information may change after publication of this book.

After the general description of the instrument, a specific example of calculating clinically significant change is laid out in detail. We have made every effort to describe the process in sufficient detail so that the reader can follow each step of the procedure. The basis for selecting normative parameters for the analysis is explained clearly. These examples will provide models for using the selected instruments in conducting analyses of clinically significant change.

THE OQ-45

General Description

The OQ-45 is a 45-item scale designed to track global symptomology and functioning in adults. The instrument was designed as an outcome measure and is very sensitive to changes in client functioning and symptomology. It was also designed to be used in the context of the Jacobson and Truax (1991) model of clinically significant change. Consequently, the manual is especially helpful in describing appropriate normative samples and makes specific recommendations for where to set the clinical significance cutoff score and for defining the reliable change index (RCI).

The OQ-45 assesses three domains: (1) subjective discomfort (mostly depression and anxiety), (2) interpersonal functioning and relationships, and (3) social role performance (especially school and work). Subscale scores are calculated for each of these areas. However, the subscale scores tend to be highly correlated, and a single total score assessing overall functioning is often used. The instrument does not assess severe psychopathology. It is designed to be used across a variety of diagnostic categories and populations.

In addition to the full 45-item questionnaire described in this chapter, a very brief 10-item questionnaire (the OQ-10.2) is also available. A version of the OQ suitable for children aged 4 to 17 has also been developed. The youth version of the OQ comes in both a parent-report version (Y-OQ-2.01) and a self-report version (Y-OQ-SR 2.0).

Administration and Scoring

The OQ-45 is self-administered in 10 minutes or less. Scoring is easy and straightforward. A computerized version is available for use on either a Windows or Web-based platform.

Scales

The OQ-45 is most often used with the total score, that is, the overall score based on all 45 items. Subscales assess symptoms distress, interpersonal relations, and social role.

Source and Cost

A great effort has been made to make the OQ-45 affordable. Unlike many instruments that require a per-use fee, a one-time licensing fee is charged for unlimited use of the OQ-45. Once the site license has been acquired, unlimited copies may be made of the instrument for use at that site. Currently examples of these one-time fees are $40 for an individual practice, $90 for a small (2 to 5 persons) practice, $500 for a large group (15 to 50 persons) practice, and $1,000 for an entire facility (e.g., a hospital). The OQ-45 is available through the American Professional Credentialing Services. A site license application form can be downloaded from the Web site.

Vendor:	American Professional Credentialing Services
Telephone:	1-888-MH-SCORE
Fax:	1-973-366-8665
Postal address:	P.O. Box 477, Wharton, NJ 07885-0477
E-mail:	apcs@erols.com
Web site:	www.oqfamily.com

Normative Data

The OQ-45 has been shown to have reasonable reliability. Measures of internal consistency (coefficient alpha) yielded values of 0.93 for the total score, 0.92 for the symptoms distress subscale, 0.74 for the interpersonal relations subscale, and 0.70 for the social role functioning subscale. Test-retest reliability was 0.85 for the total score (Lambert, Burlingame, et al., 1996).

Selected normative data for the total score on the OQ-45 are listed in Table 9.1. It should be noted that the OQ-45 does not show consistent gender differences in either patient or normal samples, making the use of separate norms for males and females unnecessary. The OQ-45 also does not seem to change as a function of age (Lambert & Finch, 1999).

Where to Find Additional Information

The manual for the OQ-45 provides complete information about the administration, scoring, and interpretation of the instrument (Lambert, Hansen, et al., 1996). A recent and comprehensive review of the OQ-45 can be found in Lambert and Finch (1999), which includes detailed information about using the clinically significant change procedure with the OQ-45 as well as additional normative data. A complete example of using the OQ-45 to analyze clinically signifi-

TABLE 9.1
Normative Data for the Total Score on the OQ-45

	Community Sample	Counseling Center	Community Clinic	Inpatient Unit
Mean	42.5	67.5	80.8	99.9
SD	17.3	20.7	26.5	28.7
N	210	53	106	24

Source: Umphres, Lambert, Smart, Barlow, and Clouse (1997)

cant change can be found in Lambert, Okiishi, Finch, and Johnson (1998). It should be noted that this example uses slightly older values for the RCI and clinically significant change cutoff than recommended in more recent publications (e.g., Lambert & Finch, 1999). Studies that evaluate the psychometric properties of the OQ-45 or provide normative data or both include Lambert, Burlingame, et al. (1996), Umphres, Lambert, Smart, Barlow, and Clouse (1997), and Mueller, Lambert, and Burlingame (1998).

Analysis of Clinically Significant Change Using the OQ-45

1. Assemble the Data to Be Analyzed

The OQ-45 was routinely administered on a voluntary basis to clients at intake in a community mental health center as part of a research project. Clients who consented to participate in the project also consented to repeat the OQ-45 approximately every five visits. Table 9.2 lists the intake scores and last scores for 22 individuals who participated in this study. It should be noted that since the OQ-45 was only administered every five sessions, the last score obtained on the OQ-45 may not be from the same day as the last therapy session. Most clients in the sample completed from 5 to 10 sessions, although a few completed 15 to 20 sessions. The clients were seen by 7 of the 8 therapists at the clinic.

2. Determine the RCI

The RCI specifies the minimum number of points of change that must be observed from one test administration to another for the change to be considered reliable. Recall from Chapter 8 that the formula for the reliable change index is

TABLE 9.2
Data for Clinical Change Analysis Using the OQ-45

Client Number	Intake Score	Last Score
1	64	33
2	61	53
3	57	70
4	41	22
5	64	63
6	64	59
7	65	68
8	71	84
9	75	62
10	76	73
11	77	46
12	79	41
13	82	114
14	83	81
15	87	59
16	87	82
17	90	49
18	93	27
19	94	85
20	95	73
21	99	74
22	106	89
Mean	77.73	63.95
SD	15.83	22.08

$$\text{RCI} = 1.96\sqrt{2S^2(1 - r_{tt})}$$

The RCI establishes a 95 percent confidence interval for interpreting change scores based on the variability of the scores themselves and the reliability of the test.

Since the OQ-45 was specifically developed for use with the clinically significant change model, a recommended RCI of 14 points on the total score is specified in the manual. It can be verified that this value is reasonable if we assume that the reliability of the OQ-45 is $r_{tt} = 0.93$, as indicated previously, and that the standard deviation of scores on the OQ-45 is approximately 20 points, again as indicated in the normative data previously given. Using these parameters, the RCI can be calculated as

$$\text{RCI} = 1.96\sqrt{(2)(20^2)(1 - 0.93)} = 14.67$$

We will use the value of 14 for the RCI recommended in the OQ-45 manual.

3. Establish a Clinically Significant Change Cutoff Score

Again, the authors of the OQ-45 make a specific recommendation that the cutoff for clinically significant change be set at a total score of 63. This is a reasonable cutoff, as illustrated in Figure 9.1. The cutoff of 63 falls just below one standard deviation from the mean of the two clinical samples and just above one standard deviation from the mean of the general community sample. Hence, a cutoff of 63 should optimally differentiate between the clinical (or dysfunctional) population and the general community (or functional) population. Note that the line representing two standard deviations from the respective means extends across the cutoff of 63. This means that classification using this instrument will not be perfect. A few individuals in the dysfunctional population will be mistakenly classified as functional and a few individuals in the functional population will be mistakenly classified as dysfunctional. Lambert and Finch (1999) report that the sensitivity of the instrument (the percent of individuals in the dysfunctional population who were correctly classified as such) is equal to 84 percent when using a cutoff of 63, and that the specificity of the test (the percentage of the individuals in the functional population who were classified as such) is equal to 83 percent. A clinical significance cutoff score of 63 will be used for this analysis.

4. Classify Each Client according to the Established Criteria

Table 9.3 shows the change score (intake score minus final score) for each client. As indicated in column 4, change scores of less than 14 points are deemed not reliable. These individuals are assigned to the no change category. Of the total group of 22 clients, 10 (45 percent) failed to show reliable change. Clients who showed more than 14 points of change and whose final score was 63 or lower are classified as recovered. These individuals met both criteria for clinically significant change. First, the magnitude of the change was reliable. Second, their scores changed from those typical of a dysfunctional population to those typical of a functional population. A total of seven clients (32 percent) of the sample were classified as recovered. A number of clients showed reliable improvement (their scores decreased by 14 points or more), but their final score was still above 63. These individuals were categorized as improved. A total of four clients (18 percent) were classified as improved. Finally, one client was reliably more symptomatic after treatment than before. This individual, representing 5 percent of the group, was categorized as deteriorated.

The analysis reported in Table 9.3 results in an unambiguous taxonomy for the classification of outcomes. A graphic representation of this analysis is provided in Figure 9.2. Each individual client is represented by a point on the scatter plot, with the various classification categories as indicated.

Figure 9.1

Normative data for three samples for the OQ-45 total score. Solid dots show the mean for each group. Boxes around each group's mean represent one standard deviation. Lines extend to two standard deviations. Data are reported in Lambert and Finch (1999).

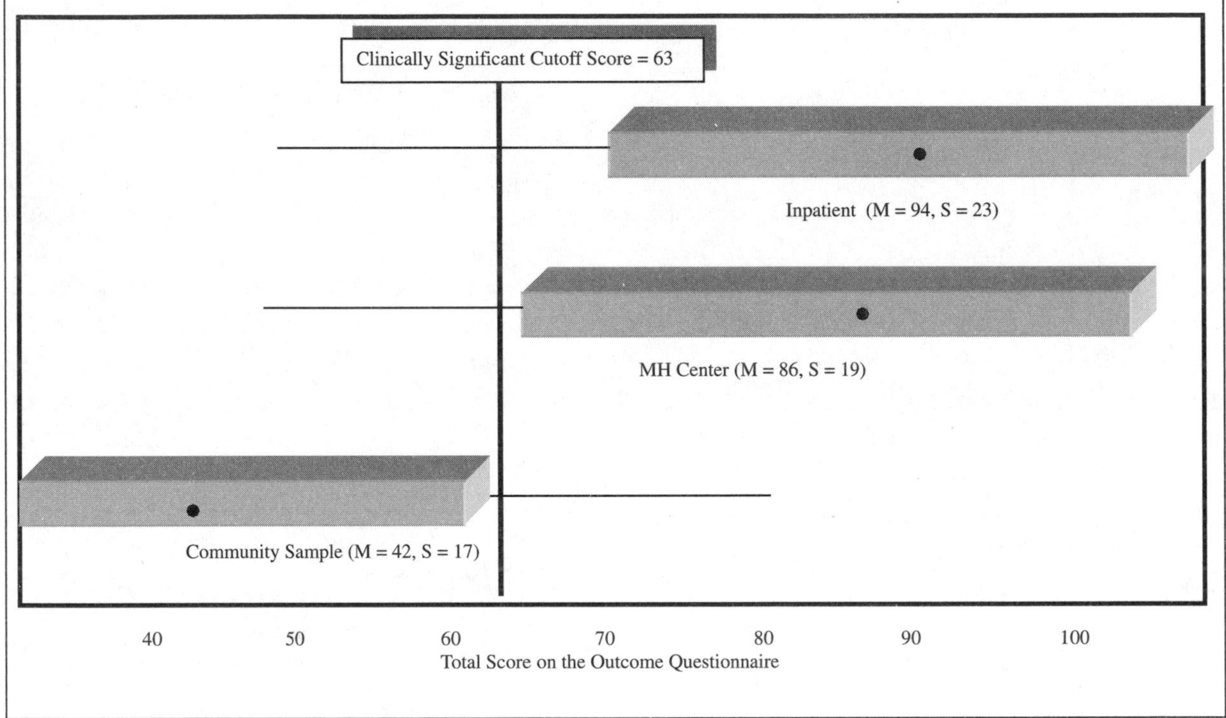

THE SCL-90-R

General Description

The SCL-90-R is a widely used self-report personality inventory that assesses a range of symptoms. As the name implies, it includes 90 items. Each item is rated using the same format: Clients indicate the degree to which they were distressed over the past week (seven days, including today) by each symptom. The rating scale involves indicating the degree of distress as 0 = not at all, 1 = a little bit, 2 = moderately, 3 = quite a bit, and 4 = extremely. An earlier version of the SCL-90 exists, but its use is not recommended (Derogatis, 1994).

The SCL-90-R has been used extensively for research as well as for clinical purposes. It is well suited for assessing client changes over time, since it can be repeatedly administered and it is sensitive to changes in self-perceived symptom distress. A shorter (53-item) version of the instrument called the Brief Symptom Inventory (BSI) also exists. The BSI correlates highly with the SCL-90-R but is not as widely used.

TABLE 9.3
Change Scores and Outcome Classifications for 22 Clients Using the OQ-45 as the Outcome Measure

Client Number	Score	Last Score	Change Score	Outcome
1	64	33	31	Recovered
2	61	53	8	No change
3	57	70	−13	No change
4	41	22	19	Recovered
5	64	63	1	No change
6	64	59	5	No change
7	65	68	−3	No change
8	71	84	−13	No change
9	78	64	14	Improved
10	76	73	3	No change
11	77	46	31	Recovered
12	79	41	38	Recovered
13	82	114	−32	Deteriorated
14	83	81	2	No change
15	87	59	28	Recovered
16	87	82	5	No change
17	90	49	41	Recovered
18	93	27	66	Recovered
19	94	85	9	No change
20	95	73	22	Improved
21	99	74	25	Improved
22	106	89	17	Improved
Mean	77.86	64.05		
SD	15.82	22.08		

Administration and Scoring

The SCL-90-R is almost always self-administered. It usually takes 12 to 15 minutes to complete, although some individuals may require more time. The test assumes a sixth-grade reading level (Derogatis, 1994). In addition to the paper-and-pencil version, the test is also available in an online version and on audiocassette. Scoring may be accomplished by hand using scoring keys, by submitting the answer sheet via surface mail, or by purchasing scoring software.

Taking the average response to the endorsed items in a particular scale generates raw scores on the SCL-90-R. If the client omits an item, it is not included in the scoring. This yields a raw score on the scale of 0 (not at all distressed) to 4 (extremely distressed) used on the answer sheet. A score of 0 indicates that the client did not report distress about any of the items on the scale in question. A score of 1 indicates that the average level of endorsement over the items on the scale is a response of "a little bit." When used for clinical purposes, the raw scores are usually converted to *T* scores. The SCL-90-R utilizes area *T* scores (as opposed to the more traditional linear *T* scores), which serve to normalize the percentages in the resulting *T*-score distribution (Derogatis, 1994). The *T* scores on each of the scales

Figure 9.2

Clinically significant change analysis for the OQ-45 data. As recommended by Lambert and Finch (1999), the RCI was set at 14 points and the cutoff for return to normal functioning was set at 63 points.

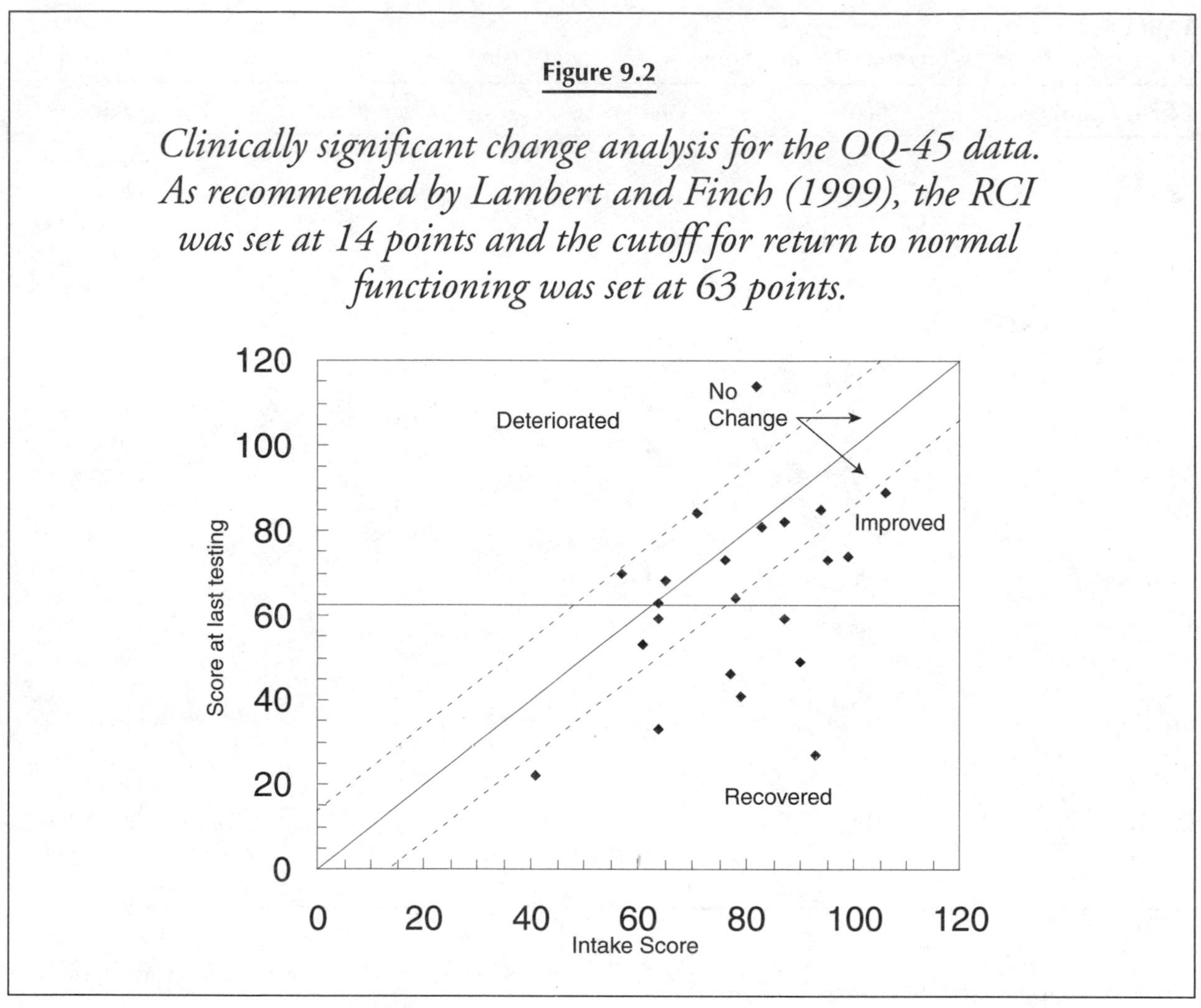

on the SCL-90-R may be reported in a traditional type of profile sheet.

When used for research purposes, SCL-90-R scores are typically reported in terms of raw scores. This format often takes some getting used to, since the scores are on a 0-to-4 scale, resulting in means and standard deviations in the form of decimal numbers. Typical mean scores are often low. For example, in a community sample, the mean overall symptom score is only 0.43, with a standard deviation of 0.17. If it is remembered that on this scale a score of 0 means that the client does not report any distressing symptoms and that a score of 1 indicates that the client experiences the symptoms as distressing "a little bit," the numbers make intuitive sense. It should also be noted that, given this scoring procedure, raw scores on the SCL-90-R tend to show a pronounced positive skew, especially in a clinical population. Again, this makes sense if we remember that the lowest score possible on a scale is 0, indicating no distress. Most individuals, even many psychiatric patients, report minimal distress on most items. However, it is possible that a few clients may report very high levels of distress in many of the items in the scale. This would result in a very high score (the maximum would be 4) for a few patients. The overall pattern of most individuals reporting relatively little symptom distress but a few individuals reporting considerable symptom distress produces a positively skewed distribution of scores. This has some consequences for the interpretation of clinical significance, as described later.

Scales

The SCL-90-R yields nine specific symptom scales and three general indices of distress. Of the general indices, the one most often used for assessing outcome is the Global Severity Index (GSI). The GSI incorporates all 90 items on the test and provides a very reliable measure of overall psychological distress at the time the test is taken. According to the manual (Derogatis, 1994, p. 12), the GSI is the "best single indicator of the current level or depth of the disorder," and "should be used in most instances where a single summary measure is called for." The GSI is in this sense very useful as an overall, general-purpose outcome measure appropriate across a variety of client populations and presenting symptoms.

The SCL-90-R also includes nine subscales that assess specific symptom clusters. These include measures of somatization, obsessive-compulsive behavior, interpersonal sensitivity, depression, anxiety, hostility, phobic anxiety, paranoid ideation, and psychoticism. In addition to their obvious utility for initial assessment and diagnostic purposes, the subscales can also serve as outcome measures to assess improvement in specific symptom dimensions. In these cases, looking at selected subscales and the overall GSI is recommended. If the interest is in only one or two of the subscales, the more efficient approach is to use a measure focused on the symptom cluster to be assessed. For example, if the primary purpose of an intervention subjected to outcome assessment is the treatment of depression, it makes sense to use a measure of depression, such as the Beck Depression Inventory, as the outcome measure instead of the SCL-90-R, which provides a measure of global distress and subscales on dimensions that are not of interest.

Source and Cost

The SCL-90-R must be purchased on a per-use basis. A preview package, which includes a manual and three assessments with profile reports, is currently priced at $33. Answer sheets cost $17 for a package of 25. A complete starter kit, which includes 50 answer sheets and a set of hand-scoring keys, costs $104. Contact the manufacturer for information on prices for scoring services.

Vendor:	National Computer Systems (NCS)
Telephone:	1-800-627-7271
Fax:	1-800-632-9011
Postal address:	P.O. Box 1416, Minneapolis, MN 55440
E-mail:	assessment@ncs.com
Web site:	http://assessments.ncs.com

Normative Data

Normative data will be reported here only for the overall Global Severity Index (GSI) of the SCL-90-R. The reader is referred to the scoring manual (Derogatis, 1994) for normative data on the individual subscales of the SCL-90-R.

Horowitz, Rosenberg, Baer, Ureño, and Villaseñor (1988) report a test-retest reliability coefficient for the GSI of 0.84. Test-retest coefficients for the subscales are reported in Derogatis and Savitz (1999). Edwards, Yarvis, Mueller, Zingale, and Wagman (1978) obtained somewhat higher reliability coefficients in a nonpatient sample in a study. They calculated both internal consistency and test-retest estimates of reliability on the SCL-90. The mean value of coefficient alpha was 0.953, whereas test-retest correlations were estimated to be between 0.93 and 0.94. Although it is difficult to clearly account for the discrepancy in these values, it is safe to assume that the reliability of scores from the SCL-90-R should be high under most circumstances, with coefficients at least in the vicinity of 0.85.

Table 9.4 lists means and standard deviations for several samples with the GSI. These data were drawn from a variety of sources to show the wide range of scores that can be observed on the SCL-90-R. The asymptotic sample was a specially selected group whose members did not report the presence of psychiatric symptoms on a variety of other measures. Both of the nonpatient groups were community samples. A group of psychiatric outpatients provided a clinical sample. The childhood trauma victims were inpatients involved in either an adult sexual trauma recovery program, a dissociative disorders program, or both. Note that there is a considerable gap between the two functional population means and the two clinical or dysfunctional population means. The asymptotic group probably represents the lowest possible mean score on this instrument in a nonclinical population. The inpatient trauma group probably represents the kinds of mean scores to be expected in a highly distressed population. Taken together, these means illustrate the continuum of scores from functional to dysfunctional.

Where to Find Additional Information

The SCL-90-R manual (Derogatis, 1994) provides considerable information about the test. Derogatis and Savitz (1999) wrote a discussion of the use of the SCL-90-R as an outcome measure. Lambert and Lambert (1999) illustrate the use of the SCL-90-R using the clinically significant change approach. An illustration of the use of the GSI scale of the SCL-90-R in a clinically significant change analysis of the outcome of an eye movement desensitization and reprocessing (EMDR) treatment program can be found in Wilson, Becker, and Tinker (1997).

TABLE 9.4
Normative Data for the GSI Measure of the SCL-90-R

Sample	Mean	Standard Deviation	*N*
Asymptotic*	0.19	0.16	82
Nonpatients†	0.31	0.31	974
Nonpatients‡	0.27	0.29	84
Psychiatric Outpatients†	1.26	0.68	1,002
Inpatient Childhood trauma victims§	2.04	0.86	144

*Tingey, Lambert, Burlingame, and Hansen (1996)
†Derogatis (1994)
‡Edwards, Yarvis, Mueller, Zingale, and Wagman (1978)
§Ellason and Ross (1997)

Analysis of Clinically Significant Change Using the SCL-90-R

1. Assemble the Data to Be Analyzed

The use of the SCL-90-R in an analysis of clinically significant change is illustrated using a study published by Wilson, Becker, and Tinker (1997). This study, in turn, was based on an earlier study by Wilson, Becker, and Tinker (1995) that considered the efficacy of eye movement desensitization and reprocessing (EMDR) treatment for trauma-related disorders. The initial study utilized a delayed treatment design and showed significant improvement for those assigned to the immediate treatment group but not for those assigned to the delayed treatment group. The subjects in the Wilson, Becker, and Tinker (1995) study were followed up 15 months later, after all had received treatment, with the follow-up data reported in Wilson, Becker, and Tinker (1997)—the study described here. Results were reported on several outcome measures, including the Impact of Events Scale, the State-Trait Anxiety Inventory, and SCL-90-R. Only the data from the SCL-90-R are presented here.

Data were reported from 64 participants, 32 of whom completely met the diagnostic criteria for Posttraumatic Stress Disorder (PTSD) (full PTSD group) and 34 of whom partially met the diagnostic criteria for PTSD (partial PTSD group). At the time of the pretest—prior to treatment—there was evidence for relatively high rates of psychological distress on the SCL-90-R for both the full PTSD group (mean = 1.34, SD = 0.60) and the partial PTSD group (mean = 0.81, SD = 0.47). Both groups showed a decline in distress immediately following treatment (mean = 0.69 for the full PTSD group; mean = 0.40 for the partial PTSD group). These gains were maintained at the 15-month follow-up assessment (mean = 0.65 for the full PTSD group; mean = 0.35 for the partial PTSD group). Individual scores for all 64 research participants are not reported here.

2. Determine the RCI

Wilson, Becker, and Tinker (1997) calculated the RCI using values of $r_{tt} = 0.953$ for the reliability coefficient and $S = 0.31$ for the standard deviation. Calculating the RCI according to the formula presented in Chapter 8, the resulting index is

$$\text{RCI} = 1.96\sqrt{(2)(0.31^2)(1 - 0.953)} = 0.186$$

The reliability coefficient was obtained from Edwards, Yarvis, Mueller, Zingale, and Wagman (1978) and was based on the value of coefficient alpha in a nonpatient sample. The standard deviation is taken from the normative data for the community sample reported by Derogatis (1994). It might be argued that the value for the reliability coefficient is somewhat high. For example, the test-retest coefficient reported by Horowitz et al. (1988) is lower at $r_{tt} = 0.84$. If this more conservative value for a reliability coefficient is used, the RCI is calculated as

$$\text{RCI} = 1.96\sqrt{(2)(0.31^2)(1 - 0.84)} = 0.34$$

The implications of using a slightly more conservative RCI are considered later.

3. Establish a Clinically Significant Change Cutoff Score

A cutoff score to distinguish functional and dysfunctional populations was derived from the normative data presented in Table 9.4. The distributions of scores for two of these samples are illustrated in Figure 9.3. Setting the cutoff score at a value of 0.62 appears to offer optimal discrimination. Note that this value is exactly one standard deviation above the mean of the community sample (functional population) and also falls about one standard deviation below the mean of the psychiatric outpatient sample (dysfunctional population). It should also be noted that, given the data reported earlier, prior to treatment the participants in the Wilson, Becker, and Tinker (1997) study scored on average in the dysfunctional range, whereas after treatment and at 15-month follow-up the average score had moved across the cutoff of 0.62 and well into the functional range. Wilson, Becker, and Tinker (1997) used a cutoff score of 0.62 to mark clinically significant change on the SCL-90-R.

4. Classify Each Client According to the Established Criteria

Once the parameters for determining the RCI and the cutoff score have been set as just described, each participant in the Wilson, Becker, and Tinker (1997) study can be classified as to outcome. Of the 64 clients participating in the study, 1 (2 percent) was classified as deteriorated, 19 (29 percent) were classified as uncertain change (e.g., change not reliable), 9 (14 percent) were classified as improved but not recovered, and 37 (56 percent) were classified as recovered. These results are illustrated in Figure 9.4, using

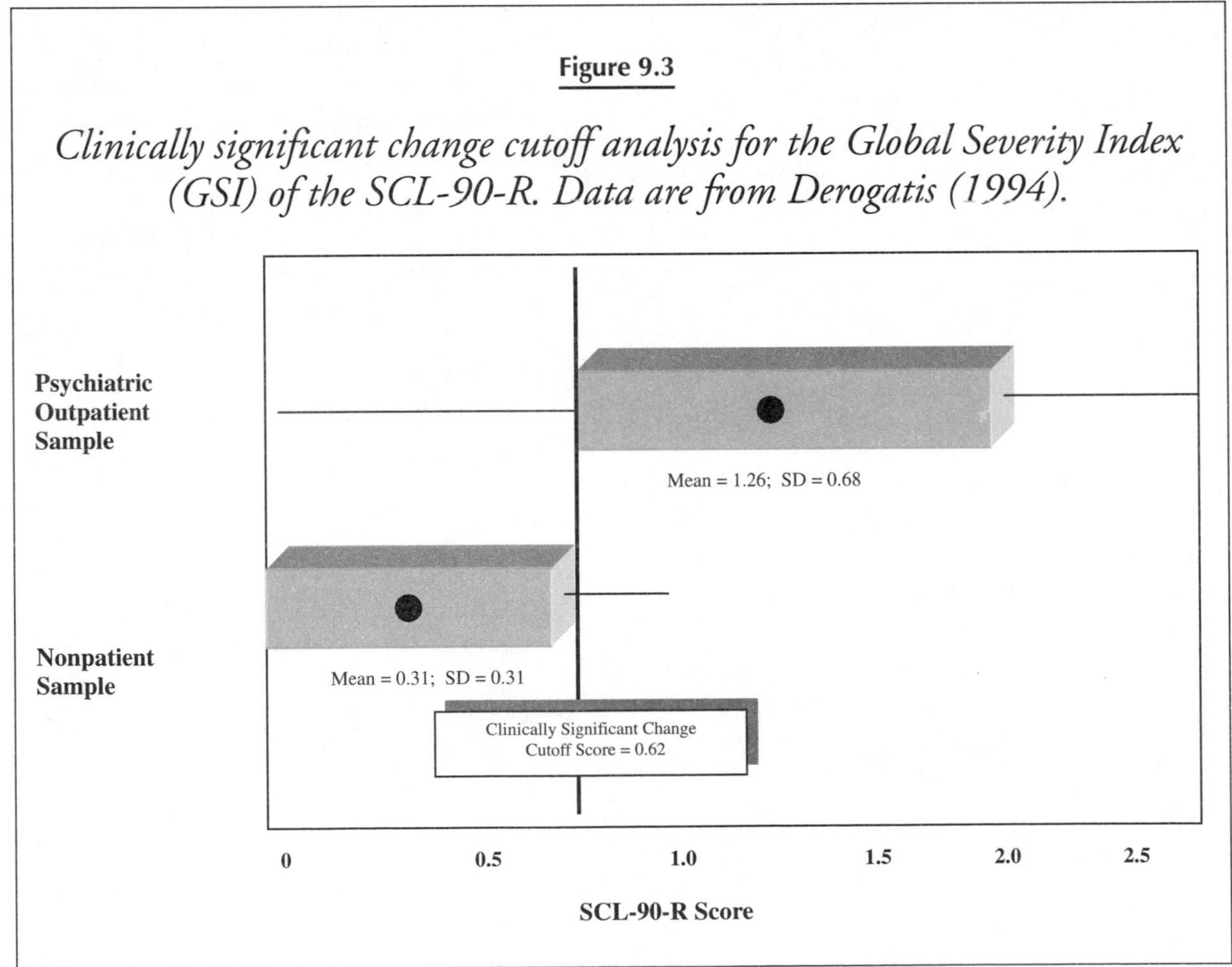

Figure 9.3

Clinically significant change cutoff analysis for the Global Severity Index (GSI) of the SCL-90-R. Data are from Derogatis (1994).

the kind of diagram developed previously. The cutoff for clinically significant change appears as a horizontal line at a value of 0.62. The RCI is represented by the two dashed lines on either side of the diagonal. It should be noted that the band of unreliable change is narrow. This is a consequence of the high value of the reliability coefficient used in the calculation of the RCI. It should also be noted, however, that using a lower value for reliability would only increase the RCI from 0.19 to 0.34. It should be evident in examining Figure 9.4 that this change would only move the dashed line very slightly further away form the diagonal. Just a few additional participants would be classified as no change, as opposed to recovered, improved, or even deteriorated.

THE BDI

General Description

The Beck Depression Inventory (BDI) is a widely used instrument. It is a self-administered inven-

Figure 9.4

Summary of an analysis of clinically significant change using the SCL-90. From S. A. Wilson, L. A. Becker & R. H. Tinker, 1997, "Fifteen-month follow-up of eye movement desensitization and reprocessing (EMDR) treatment for posttraumatic stress disorder and psychological trauma," Journal of Consulting and Clinical Psychology, *65, p. 1053. Copyright 1997 by the American Psychological Association. Reprinted with permission of the author.*

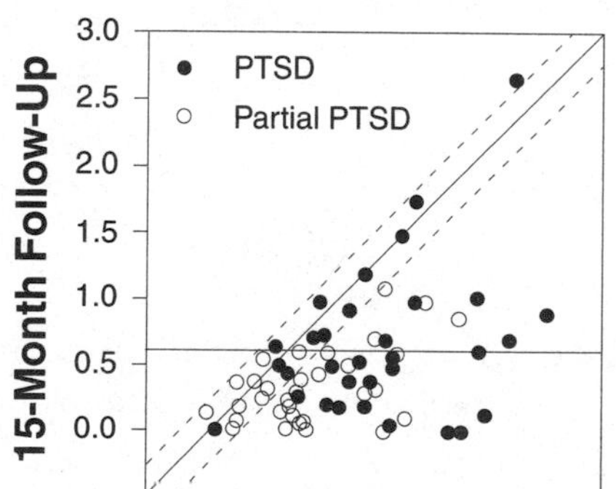

tory consisting of 21 items listing depression-related symptoms. The BDI is highly sensitive to change in self-reported affect, and has been used extensively in outcome studies of the efficacy of various treatments for depression. This property of sensitivity to change, along with its widespread use, makes the BDI an obvious candidate for an outcome measure for depressed clients. The instrument is also often used for assessment purposes. However, Katz, Katz, and Shaw (1999) point out that this can result in misleading interpretation, especially if the instrument is used with a seriously distressed population. In such a population, high BDI scores may reflect a general level of distress and not necessarily clinical depression.

Administration and Scoring

The BDI usually only takes five minutes or so to complete. It can be hand-scored in an equal amount of time. Each symptom is rated on a continuum from 0 (total absence of the symptom) to 3 (severe problems with the symptom). The score is simply the total of the ratings on each of the 21 items. An individual who reported absolutely no symptoms of depression on any item would score 0 on the scale.

Scales

The BDI was designed as a unitary measure of depression, and it contains no subscales. Extensive factor-analytic studies of the BDI suggest the presence of three factors, all of which are highly intercorrelated. These factors include negative attitudes toward self, performance impairment, and somatic disturbance (Beck, Steer, & Garbin, 1988). Since there is likely little clinical utility in subdividing BDI scores into these three dimensions of depression, and since they correlate so highly with each other, almost all outcome studies using the BDI treat it as a single unitary measure.

Source and Cost

The BDI is available from the Psychological Corporation. A complete kit, including the manual and 35 record forms, is available for $61. Additional record forms are priced at $31.50 for a package of 25 or $120 for a package of 100.

Vendor:	The Psychological Corporation
Telephone:	1-800-211-8378
Fax:	1-800-232-1273
Postal address:	555 Academic Court, San Antonio, TX 78204-2498
E-mail:	customer service@harcourt.com
Web site:	www.psychcorp.com

Normative Data

The extensive data on the reliability of the BDI are summarized by Beck, Steer, and Garbin (1988). In 25 studies that reported internal consistency measures of reliability (usually coefficient alpha), the reliability coefficients ranged from 0.76 through 0.95, with a mean value of 0.86. Many studies reported reliabilities greater than 0.90, some using the Spearman-Brown correction. Stability estimates using the test-retest procedure were lower, ranging from 0.60 to 0.83 for nonpsychiatric participants and from 0.48 to 0.86 among psychiatric patients. This discrepancy between internal consistency and test-retest reliability estimates is to be expected, since, as Beck (1967) pointed out, depression is an unstable trait when measured over time. To the extent that the individual's affective state fluctuates from test to retest, changes in scores may be attributed to real changes in the characteristic being measured as opposed to simply being due to measurement error. This issue is discussed in more detail in the next chapter.

There are considerable normative data available on the BDI as well, given its widespread use as both a clinical measure and an outcome measure. In a metanalytic review of this literature, Nietzel, Russell, Kelly, Hemmings, and Gretter (1987) provided the normative data shown in Table 9.5. These data come primarily from functional populations. These included a "nondistressed" group, which served as normal controls in studies that contrasted them with a clinically diagnosed group, a group from the "general population," which consisted mostly of college students, and a "special group," whose participants were undergoing situational or physical stress of some kind. In addition, data from Beck (1967) are reported showing BDI scores for a various categories of depression.

It is evident from Table 9.5 that BDI scores increase in relation to the presence of depression. It can also be noted that, for clinical purposes, the cutoff for a diagnosis of mild depression is usually placed somewhere between a score of 10 and a score of 13.

Where to Find Additional Information

The most complete review of the psychometric properties of the BDI is found in Beck, Steer, and Garbin (1988). Ogles, Lambert, and Masters (1996) provided a thorough discussion and example of using the BDI for the analysis of clinically significant change. A short review of the BDI as an outcome and assessment instrument can be found in Katz, Katz, and Shaw (1999).

Example Analysis of Clinically Significant Change Using the BDI

1. Assemble the Data to Be Analyzed

This example demonstrates an analysis of clinically significant change using a large data set. Assume that the BDI is routinely given at intake and again at the end of treatment at an outpatient unit at a large hospital. The unit specializes in the psychiatric treatment of individuals with chronic medical problems, especially chronic pain, traumatic brain injury, and physical disability. It should be noted that these individuals do not necessarily present with symptoms of depression, though the majority do. In addition, it is likely that the BDI is picking up on overall symptoms of psychological distress in addition to (or

TABLE 9.5
Normative Data for the BDI

Group	Mean	Standard Deviation
Nondistressed	4.6	4.5
General population	7.2	6.5
Situational stress	8.1	5.8
Not depressed	10.9	5.8
Mild depression	18.7	10.2
Moderate depression	25.4	9.6
Severe depression	30.0	10.4

instead of) depression. Given these concerns, it is arguable that the BDI is not necessarily the best outcome measure to use and that a more global measure of symptom distress might be more appropriate. On the other hand, since the instrument is routinely administered and the data are available, there is sufficient reason to conduct an analysis of clinically significant change while keeping in mind the concerns noted. Data from 160 patients are available for this analysis.

2. Determine the RCI

Since there are various sources of normative data that give different values for the mean and standard deviation, and since different studies have yielded different values for the reliability of the BDI, some decisions must be made in order to establish the RCI for this analysis. A very conservative approach to setting this criterion would be to use the lowest estimate of reliability and the highest estimate of the standard deviation. This would result in the widest range for the RCI. The lowest reliability reported by Beck, Steer, and Garbin (1988) was a test-retest coefficient of 0.48. Beck (1997) reported a standard deviation for scores on the BDI equal to 8.10 in a group with minimal depression. Using these parameters, the RCI would be calculated as

$$\text{RCI} = 1.96\sqrt{(2)(8.1^2)(1 - 0.48)} = 16.50$$

This figure requires a very large change in order to be called reliable, and is almost certainly too conservative. As indicated previously, most samples of the BDI have yielded smaller standard deviations (especially in nonclinical populations) than the value used here. In addition, the test-retest reliability coefficient of 0.48 almost certainly reflects changes over time in the actual level of depression as well as measurement error. Consequently, it likely underestimates the reliability of scores on the BDI.

On the other hand, taking a very liberal approach to the estimation of the RCI, we could use the standard deviation of 4.46 reported by Nietzel, et al. (1987) in a nondistressed group of individuals. In an estimate of the internal consistency of the BDI, Beck, Rial, and Rickels (1974) reported a split-half reliability of 0.93 after using the Spearman-Brown correction. Using these parameters to calculate the RCI results in the following value

$$\text{RCI} = 1.96\sqrt{(2)(4.46^2)(1 - 0.93)} = 3.27$$

This value for an RCI is likely too narrow, and would likely result in changes on the BDI due to measurement error being classified as reliable.

Calculating an RCI requires making some assumptions about the variability and the reliability of scores on the BDI. Although the standard deviations of scores in various nonclinical populations (see the normative data listed previously) seem to run between 5 and 6 points, scores in clinical populations are a little more variable. Beck (1967) reported a standard deviation of 8.1 in individuals with minimal depression. Further, in the present sample the standard deviation of pretest scores on the BDI was equal to 9.51, and that of the posttest scores was equal to 8.50. Given the wide range of depression scores among the patients in the present example, using a larger (more conservative) estimate of the standard deviation of the scores on the BDI seems appropriate. We will use the value of 8.50, which is the standard deviation of the posttest scores in the present example. To obtain an estimate of reliability, Beck et al. (1988) reported that estimates of internal consistency reliability range from 0.73 to 0.95, whereas test-retest reliability estimates range from 0.48 to 0.86. For reasons that are described in detail in Chapter 11, test-retest procedures are likely to underestimate the reliability of measures of personality traits that may change over time. Consequently, for this example we will use an estimate of reliability of 0.84. This value is at the upper end of the test-retest estimates and midway between the various internal consistency estimates. Using these parameters, the RCI for this example can be estimated as

$$\text{RCI} = 1.96\sqrt{(2)(8.50^2)(1-0.84)} = 9.42$$

Based on this calculation we will set the RCI at 9 points for this example. It should be noted that this value is identical to that derived by Ogles et al. (1996) based on a slightly different set of assumptions. It should also be pointed out that this RCI value of 9 points is roughly halfway between the extreme high and low values of 16.5 and 3.27 calculated previously.

3. Establish a Clinically Significant Change Cutoff Score

Establishing a cutoff for indicating return to normal functioning using the BDI is more straightforward. Using Cutoff a as suggested by Jacobson and Truax (1991), the cutoff should be set at two standard deviations above the mean of the functional population. The best estimate of parameters of the functional population comes from the values reported by Nietzel et al. (1987) for scores in the nondistressed group consisting of individuals selected as normal controls in clinical outcome studies. Given a mean of 4.54 and a standard deviation of 4.46 for this group, a cutoff score of two standard deviations above the mean would be set at 13.46 points. This value is almost identical to the cutoff score of 13 points that is recommended if the BDI is used for general screening for depression (Bosco, Krebaum, & Rush, 1997). A clinically significant change cutoff score of 13 points on the BDI will be used for this example.

4. Classify Each Client according to the Established Criteria

The results of this analysis of clinically significant change using the BDI are shown in Table 9.6. Of the 160 patients in the sample, 18 (11 percent) showed deterioration over the course of their treatment at the hospital. A total of 83 patients (52 percent) failed to show a reliable change. The remaining patients improved significantly. Of these, 5 (3 percent) showed reliable improvement but failed to meet the cutoff for return to normal functioning. Fifty-four patients (34 percent of the total) were classified as recovered, showing both a change greater than 9 points and a posttest score below 13 points on the BDI. While at first glance these results may seem discouraging, given the nature of the treatment population in this example, they are not surprising.

To further understand this example, a graphic presentation of the outcome is shown in Figure 9.5. The boundaries for reliable change are represented as two dashed lines parallel to the diagonal (9 points away in this case) and the clinically significant change cutoff is represented by a horizontal line across the graph (at a score of 143 in this example). The dots on the graph represent individual patients. Note that a sunflower plot is used, where each additional marker line ("petal") at a given data point represents an additional patient with that particular pre- and posttest score. Given the relatively large sample in this example, it is not surprising that different patients might score identically on pre- and posttreatment administrations of the BDI.

Several features of this example are worthy of additional discussion. First, a relatively large pro-

TABLE 9.6
Classification of Outcome Using the BDI

Pre-treatment Score	Post-treatment Score	Change	Outcome	Pre-treatment Score	Post-treatment Score	Change	Outcome
9	1	8	No change	15	26	−11	Deteriorated
14	1	13	Recovered	17	4	13	Recovered
26	23	3	No change	26	24	2	No change
13	17	−4	No change	2	10	−8	No change
32	15	17	Improved	28	8	20	Recovered
20	8	12	Recovered	22	20	2	No change
33	27	6	No change	26	31	−5	No change
14	3	11	Recovered	17	24	−7	No change
10	37	−27	Deteriorated	9	7	2	No change
16	8	8	No change	27	6	21	Recovered
10	1	9	No change	2	35	−33	Deteriorated
26	27	−1	No change	1	12	−11	Deteriorated
23	9	14	Recovered	4	7	−3	No change
18	14	4	No change	15	11	4	No change
7	17	−10	Deteriorated	10	8	2	No change
24	4	20	Recovered	20	15	5	No change
27	9	18	Recovered	15	0	15	Recovered
16	8	8	No change	8	17	−9	No change
18	20	−2	No change	18	0	18	Recovered
6	9	−3	No change	18	6	12	Recovered
18	6	12	Recovered	17	5	12	Recovered
13	11	2	No change	24	16	8	No change
26	15	11	Improved	22	28	−6	No change
12	5	7	No change	13	14	−1	No change
20	3	17	Recovered	17	6	11	Recovered
22	13	9	No change	25	19	6	No change
6	5	1	No change	9	11	−2	No change
23	16	7	No change	35	13	22	Recovered
33	0	33	Recovered	26	2	24	Recovered
1	8	−7	No change	18	22	−4	No change
10	12	−2	No change	39	13	26	Recovered
25	8	17	Recovered	5	6	−1	No change
8	9	−1	No change	8	35	−27	Deteriorated
8	18	−10	Deteriorated	2	4	−2	No change
15	7	8	No change	6	18	−12	Deteriorated
20	11	9	No change	16	1	15	Recovered
7	7	0	No change	18	4	14	Recovered
13	14	−1	No change	6	15	−9	No change
17	5	12	Recovered	22	29	−7	No change
13	1	12	Recovered	17	23	−6	No change
28	21	7	No change	11	8	3	No change

TABLE 9.6
(Continued)

Pre-treatment Score	Post-treatment Score	Change	Outcome
42	17	25	Improved
5	25	−20	Deteriorated
16	1	15	Recovered
43	4	39	Recovered
14	4	10	Recovered
21	8	13	Recovered
33	20	13	Improved
34	11	23	Recovered
26	3	23	Recovered
17	2	15	Recovered
6	3	3	No change
15	5	10	Recovered
12	4	8	No change
11	16	−5	No change
48	8	40	Recovered
4	3	1	No change
2	15	−13	Deteriorated
31	12	19	Recovered
10	27	−17	Deteriorated
34	0	34	Recovered
22	11	11	Recovered
9	14	−5	No change
20	15	5	No change
18	6	12	Recovered
5	15	−10	Deteriorated
26	7	19	Recovered
12	15	−3	No change
3	5	−2	No change
1	16	−15	Deteriorated
13	19	−6	No change
14	3	11	Recovered
14	0	14	Recovered
21	5	16	Recovered
29	5	24	Recovered
4	2	2	No change
13	5	8	No change
11	26	−15	Deteriorated
16	11	5	No change
1	12	−11	Deteriorated
26	20	6	No change
11	21	−10	Deteriorated

Pre-treatment Score	Post-treatment Score	Change	Outcome
17	9	8	No change
4	21	−17	Deteriorated
5	7	−2	No change
10	2	8	No change
9	3	6	No change
10	5	5	No change
7	11	−4	No change
36	12	24	Recovered
30	6	24	Recovered
23	14	9	No change
18	4	14	Recovered
12	5	7	No change
14	4	10	Recovered
13	10	3	No change
21	21	0	No change
13	11	2	No change
31	47	−16	Deteriorated
11	13	−2	No change
10	19	−9	No change
17	13	4	No change
25	7	18	Recovered
6	13	−7	No change
9	3	6	No change
20	9	11	Recovered
21	9	12	Recovered
1	10	−9	No change
20	21	−1	No change
8	12	−4	No change
15	2	13	Recovered
1	5	−4	No change
17	0	17	Recovered
12	4	8	No change
17	7	10	Recovered
25	14	11	Improved
13	13	0	No change
10	9	1	No change
29	5	24	Recovered

The RCI was set at 9 points and the clinically significant change was set at 13 points.

Figure 9.5

Clinically significant change plot of the BDI data described in the text. This is a sunflower plot, where additional lines on a data point indicate multiple cases at that coordinate.

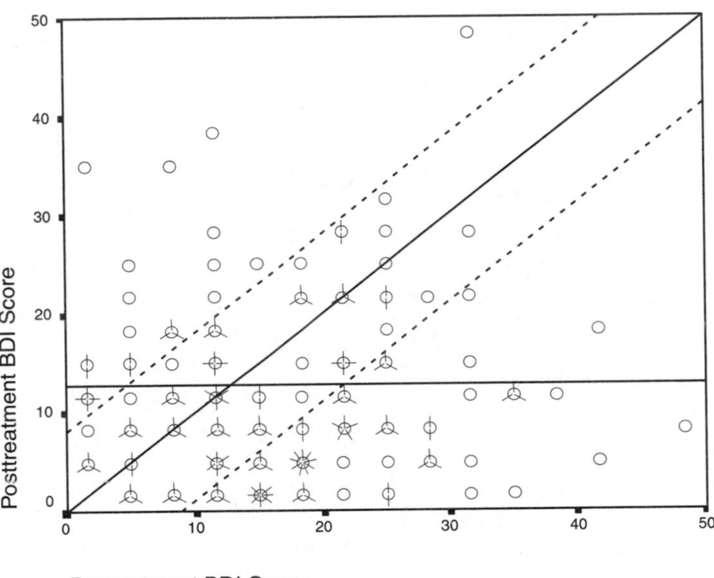

portion of patients started treatment with BDI scores in the functional range. In fact, more than one-third (36 percent) of the sample had pretreatment scores lower than 13. This is not surprising if we recall that the patients were not necessarily presenting for the treatment of depression per se. This does mean that a large number of the patients who did not show reliable change in BDI scores over the course of treatment did not start out with high depression scores in the first place. It also does not imply that these individuals did not benefit from treatment, since their treatment goals could well have been focused on areas other than relieving psychological distress. Second, there is a wide range of BDI scores represented in this sample. Prior to treatment almost 30 percent of the sample scored over 21 on the BDI, and there were a number of scores of 30 and higher. Scores in this range are generally indicative of severe depression. It is encouraging to observe that the majority of patients who began treatment reporting relatively high levels of distress on the BDI showed considerable improvement over the course of treatment. In fact, most were classified as recovered at the end of treatment. Finally, it must also be noted that a substantial minority of the patients (slightly over 10 percent) showed deterioration over the course of treatment, often starting out with BDI scores in the functional range and finishing with scores indicative of considerable distress. It is difficult to account for this result without more specific knowledge about the particular cases involved. Given the nature of the treatment population, it is possible that some of these individuals experienced worsening of their physical condition over the course of treatment due to chronic illness. It would not be surprising if some of these individuals concurrently experienced greater psychological distress. A case-by-case review of these patients could verify the cause of the higher BDI scores. In this sense, an analysis of clinically significant change can provide information about what is not working in treatment as well as what is.

The BASIS-32

General Description

The BASIS-32 was designed as a brief but comprehensive measure of mental health status. It was originally intended as an outcome measure, not as an instrument for assessment and diagnosis. The measure was developed for an acutely ill psychiatric inpatient population. As such, it includes measures of more severe and problematic areas such as substance abuse and psychotic symptoms that are not included on most self-report outcome measures. It includes self-rated measures of both symptoms and behavioral functioning. The instrument is not keyed to specific diagnoses, and hence is suitable for a wide range of client populations.

Administration and Scoring

The BASIS-32 can typically be completed in about 10 minutes. Clients usually fill out the instrument by themselves. Care has been taken to make the questions and format easy to understand. The instrument may also be administered in a structured interview format, either face to face or over the telephone. The instrument includes 32 items. For each item the client is asked to rate the degree of difficulty experienced during a one-week period. The rating scale is straightforward: 1 = no difficulty, 2 = a little difficulty, 3 = moderate difficulty, 4 = quite a bit of difficulty, and 5 = extreme difficulty. Scores are reported as the average rating on this 0- to 4-point scale, and hence are easily interpretable.

Scales

The BASIS-32 generates scores on five subscales. These include: (1) relation to self and others (seven items assessing such things as difficulty within and outside of the family, self-confidence, emotional control, and realistic goal setting), (2) daily living and role functioning (six items assessing areas such as life satisfaction, cognitive functioning, independence, and management of day-to-day living tasks), (3) depression and anxiety (seven items assessing self-rated symptoms in areas such as depression, anxiety, suicidality, and life stress), (4) impulsive and addictive behavior (six items assessing problematic behavior in such areas as chemical and drug use, compulsive behavior, and violent or illegal behavior), and (5) psychosis (four items assessing difficulties in areas such as hallucinations, bizarre behavior, sexual preoccupation, or experiencing unreal thoughts). Factor analyses have consistently provided good support for the underlying factor structure that corresponds to the subscales. The subscales are intercorrelated. The exploratory factor analyses were conducted using an oblique rotation, since the instrument's developers assumed the subscales were intercorrelated because scores on the various scales are not independent (e.g., that patients experiencing difficulty in one area may likely report difficulties in other areas as well; Eisen & Culhane, 1999).

Source and Cost

The BASIS-32 is available through McLean Hospital. Its use requires the purchase of a site license, which carries an annual fee of $100 per site. Arrangements can be made to reproduce the questionnaire for research purposes. Contact the vendor for more information.

Vendor: McLean Hospital
Telephone: 1-617-855-2424
Fax: 1-617-855-2948
Postal address: Department of Mental Health Services Research
McLean Hospital
115 Mill Street
Belmont, MA 02478
Web site: www.basis32.org

Normative Data

The BASIS-32 demonstrates good reliability, especially for the overall or total score. Internal consistency (coefficient alpha) for the entire scale is 0.89, with an average test-retest reliability over all scales reported at 0.85. Reliabilities for individual subscales are necessarily lower, as indicated in Table 9.7. It is notable that on this measure the test-retest and internal consistency indicators of reliability are very similar. This is not the usual pattern observed with measures that are sensitive to change.

The BASIS-32 has been administered to a variety of different clinical samples. Since it was designed to assess outcome in an inpatient population, most of the normative data are from psychiatric inpatients or from outpatients receiving treatment in a hospital setting. Data from a number of studies showing means and standard deviations for the BASIS-32 subscales are reported in Table 9.8. Means are reported for scores on the BASIS-32 upon admission. Mean scores for the measure at discharge, at follow-up, or both are also available in the sources cited. As might be expected, scores for the outpatient sample appear to be slightly lower than mean scores for the inpatient samples. At present, there do not seem to be normative data on the BASIS-32 from a community sample or other functional population.

TABLE 9.7
Reliability Data for the BASIS-32

	Reliability Indicator	
Scale	**Test-Retest**	**Internal Consistency**
Relation to self and others	0.80	0.76
Daily living skills and role functioning	0.81	0.80
Depression and anxiety	0.78	0.74
Impulsive and addictive behavior	0.65	0.71
Psychosis	0.76	0.63
All items	0.89	0.85

Source: Eisen, Dill, and Grob (1994)

TABLE 9.8
Means and Standard Deviations on the BASIS-32 at Admission for Four Clinical Samples

	Inpatients* (N = 247)		Inpatients† (N = 949)		Inpatients‡ (N = 258)		Outpatients§ (N = 223)	
Subscale	**Mean**	**SD**	**Mean**	**SD**	**Mean**	**SD**	**Mean**	**SD**
Relation with self and others	1.47	0.93	2.16	1.03	2.41	0.81	2.02	0.98
Daily living and role functioning	1.77	1.05	2.24	1.04	2.44	0.83	2.01	1.01
Depression and anxiety	1.93	1.05	2.40	1.04	2.75	0.85	2.05	1.03
Impulsive and addictive behaviors	0.86	0.86	1.13	0.85	1.57	0.91	0.90	0.74
Psychosis	0.77	0.91	0.86	0.88	1.29	0.96	0.73	0.79
All subscales	1.34	0.68	1.81	0.80	2.31	0.67	1.58	0.78

*Eisen et al. (1994)
†Eisen and Dickey (1996)
‡Russo et al. (1997)
§Eisen, Wilcox, Schafer, Culhane, and Leff (1997), reported in Eisen and Culhane (1999)

Where to Find Additional Information

A thorough review of the initial stages of development of the BASIS-32 can be found in Eisen et al. (1994). A more recent summary of the psychometric properties of the instrument, along with several case examples illustrating its use, is provided in Eisen and Culhane (1999).

Analysis of Clinically Significant Change Using the BASIS-32

1. Assemble the Data to Be Analyzed

To illustrate the analysis of clinically significant change using the BASIS-32, data from only a single hypothetical client will be considered. Unlike the previous examples in this section, where pre- and posttreatment scores from small or large groups of individuals are analyzed, the following example shows how these procedures can also be applied to an individual case. A second difference in this example is that we will consider scores on each of the subscales as well as looking at the overall score.

To make the case more concrete, assume that a client—a female in her midthirties—presents for treatment in an agitated and anxious state. The individual reports severe disturbance in family relationships and considerable psychological distress primarily in the form of anxiety and depression. She also admits to occasional excessive alcohol use. The client reports a history of prior treatment for anxiety and depression, including one period that required hospitalization. At the time she begins psychotherapy, the client starts taking prescribed medication for treatment of her anxiety and depression. The client is seen for 20 sessions, and treatment goals focus on stabilizing and improving family relationships and on reducing symptoms of anxiety and depression. The client complies well with treatment recommendations and remains on the medication as prescribed. Assume that the BASIS-32 is administered prior to the first session and prior to the last session of therapy. Table 9.9 indicates the client's scores at the beginning and end of treatment.

TABLE 9.9
Pre- and Posttreatment Scores on the Subscales of the BASIS-32 for an Individual Client

Scale	Pretreatment Score	Score at Termination
Relation to self and others	2.79	1.29
Daily living skills and role functioning	1.14	0.85
Depression and anxiety	3.13	0.75
Impulsive and addictive behavior	2.26	1.50
Psychosis	0.50	0.00
All items	2.10	0.98

2. Determine the RCI

Since a pre- and posttreatment comparison on each of the subscales of the BASIS-32 is desired, a reliable change index must be calculated separately for each subscale. To accomplish this, estimates of both the reliability of each subscale and the standard deviation of each subscale must be available. This information is provided in Tables 9.7 and 9.8. It is helpful that reliability estimates on this instrument are so similar using test-retest and internal consistency measures. Since the coefficients are within a few points of each other, we will use the average of the two values as the reliability estimate for this analysis. These average values of the reliability coefficient are listed in the first column of Table 9.10. As indicated in Table 9.8, estimates of the variability of the scales on the BASIS-32 are similar across the normative samples listed, but vary somewhat. Since the samples do vary in size, it is not appropriate to simply average the values of the standard deviation across the samples. One strategy would be to use the values from the largest sample. Another strategy, which we used in this example, would be to calculate a pooled standard deviation weighted by the sample size. This can be accomplished by multiplying each standard deviation by the size of the sample, and then dividing by the total number of subjects across all four samples (total $N = 1{,}677$ in this case). The pooled standard deviations are listed in the second column of Table 9.10. Note that the values are almost identical to the values for the sample with the largest number of subjects.

TABLE 9.10
Calculation of a Reliable Change Index for Each of the Subscales on the BASIS-32

Scale	Reliability	Standard Deviation	RCI
Relation to self and others	0.78	0.97	1.26
Daily living skills and role functioning	0.80	1.00	1.24
Depression and anxiety	0.76	1.01	1.37
Impulsive and addictive behavior	0.68	0.85	1.33
Psychosis	0.69	0.84	1.30
All items	0.89	0.76	0.70

Values for the reliability coefficient and the standard deviation are derived from Tables 9.7 and 9.8, as explained in the text. The RCI was calculated using the formula previously derived.

There are several noteworthy patterns in the RCI data presented in the last column of Table 9.10. First, despite some differences in reliability coefficients and standard deviations, the RCIs for each of the subscales are very similar. A case could be made for setting a single RCI between 1.25 and 1.30 and using the same value for each subscale. Second, the RCI for the subscales is relatively large. Clients must show a change score of over 1 standard deviation in order for change to be classified as reliable. This is primarily because the reliability coefficients for the subscales are relatively low, a reflection of the small number of items comprising each subscale. Reliability estimates, especially those based on internal consistency, do vary as a function of the number of items on a test. The easiest way to improve the reliability of an instrument is to make the instrument longer. Finally, the RCI for the overall score (all items) is considerably smaller than that for the subscales. Again, this is a reflection of the enhanced reliability of the entire 32-item test as compared to the reliability of the individual subscales. This implies that we can be less confident that a change on the subscales is reliable than we can if a similar change is observed on the overall score. This is not a problem with the instrument; rather, it is a natural consequence of the fact that subscales are necessarily composed of relatively few items and hence have lower reliability coefficients.

3. Establish a Clinically Significant Change Cutoff Score

Setting a cutoff score to mark return to normal functioning is problematic for the BASIS-32. This is primarily because normative data for a functional population are not currently available. Means and standard deviations are available, however, for the dysfunctional population (e.g., psychiatric patients at intake). Using these data, a criterion could be set at one or two standard deviations below the mean at admission using the data in Table 9.8. If a cutoff of one standard deviation below the mean were established, scores on the relation to self and others, daily living, and depression and anxiety subscales would have to fall below a value of approximately 1.00 to be classified as clinically significant. On the impulsive and addictive behavior and psychosis subscales, the score would have to be very close to 0 to be classified as clinically significant. If the more stringent criterion of two standard deviations below the mean were used (as suggested by Jacobson & Truax, 1991), scores would effectively need to drop to 0 on all of the subscales.

There is a rational basis for assigning a cutoff in the area of 1.00 in the first three subscales and a cutoff of 0 for the last two, keeping in mind that a score of 0 means the area was rated as no difficulty, a score of 1.0 indicates an average rating of a little difficulty, a score of 2.0 indicates an average rating of moderate difficulty, and a score of 3.0 indicates an average rating of quite a bit of difficulty. If normative data for a community sample or other functional population were available, it is likely that even among a nonpsychiatric population individuals would report a little difficulty on some items relating to interpersonal relations, meeting day-to-day role expectations, and psychological distress. In other words, mean scores for the functional population on these subscales could be expected to be greater than 0 but less than 1. For the remaining subscales—addictive/impulsive behavior and psychotic symptoms—it is much more likely that individuals in the functional population would not report any difficulty. In other words, an individual from the functional population would likely score close to 0 on these scales. However, in the absence of such normative data, the precise locations of the mean and standard deviation of the functional population are impossible to determine. Given this, the clinician interested in conducting a clinically significant change analysis using the BASIS-32 has two alternatives. The first is to set a cutoff based on distance below the mean of the dysfunctional population—most likely one standard deviation below the mean. The second alternative is to omit making a judgment concerning return to normal functioning. Clients can still be classified as deteriorated, no change, or improved based on the RCI calculated earlier.

There is a further argument for adopting the second alternative (omitting a classification of return to normal functioning) if we remember that the BASIS-32 is typically utilized with an inpatient psychiatric population often diagnosed with chronic mental illness, and thus the likelihood of a given client from an inpatient psychiatric population shifting from the dysfunctional to the functional population may be low. In fact, the treatment goals for this population are often met if improvement can be shown. In some cases, maintaining a given level of functioning (as opposed to deterioration) may be considered successful. Scoring in the range of the functional population may not be possible for such clients. Even if such a score can be demonstrated, it is also questionable whether such gains can be maintained indefinitely.

4. Classify Each Client according to the Established Criteria

Since only one client is described in this example, this discussion will focus on the improvement or lack thereof observed on the various subscales of the BASIS-32. A summary of the outcome for the client previously discussed is provided in Table 9.11. Overall, at the time of initial assessment, the client was reporting a score of 2.07 indicative of a moderate level of difficulty. Problems were especially noteworthy in the areas of interpersonal and intrapersonal relationships, depression and anxiety, and impulsive/addictive disorders. At intake, the client reported "a little" difficulty with daily living and role functioning and did not report psychotic symptoms.

Assuming that the treatment goals for this client did not presume a return to normal functioning, a cutoff score for clinically significant change was not established. However, the client's overall level of functioning based on the self-report recorded by the BASIS-32 will be considered. Change scores from before to after treatment are of interest and are reported in Table 9.11. In addition, scores on each subscale are classified as improved or no change depending on whether the difference score exceeds the reliable change index established for each subscale in Table 9.10.

TABLE 9.11
Pre- and Posttreatment Scores on the Subscales of the BASIS-32 for an Individual Client

Scale	Pre	Post	Difference	Outcome
Relation to self and others	2.79	1.29	1.50	Improved
Daily living skills and role functioning	1.14	0.85	0.29	No change
Depression and anxiety	3.13	0.75	2.38	Improved
Impulsive and addictive behavior	2.81	2.01	0.80	No change
Psychosis	0.50	0.00	0.50	No change
All items	2.10	0.98	1.12	Improved

According to Table 9.11, the client improved after treatment. The client was rated as reliably improved in relation to self and others and in depression and anxiety. In other words, reliable improvement was noted over the course of treatment in the individual's interpersonal and intrapersonal functioning, and in self-reported symptoms of psychological distress. It should be noted that these areas were the primary focus of the treatment. There was little change in the area of daily living skills and role functioning. However, this area was reported to be of only minimal concern before treatment started. The area of impulsive and addictive behavior was a concern before treatment. Even though the client exhibited some self-reported improvement in this area, it was not reliable. Further, the overall score remains in the moderate difficulty range. Focus on issues of chemical use most likely remains as a primary area of concern. The last subscale, psychosis, was not a concern either before or after treatment. Over all of the items, the client showed reliable improvement on the BASIS-32, and her scores dropped from an average of moderate difficulty to an average of a little difficulty.

SUMMARY

This chapter provides an in-depth review of the utilization of four common outcome measures for the analysis of clinically significant change. Even if the clinician does not intend to use one of these specific measures, these detailed examples should provide useful models for the application of these procedures to other outcome measures as well. It is hoped that the parallel presentation of the calculations and layout illustrating each of the four measures emphasizes the underlying process behind the clinically significant change approach. While each measure requires its own calculations, the underlying procedural assumptions are the same regardless of the specific instrument(s) used to assess outcome.

The next chapter extends application of the model to other measures. This discussion will be more general, and detailed examples using suggested measures will not be provided. The reader is encouraged to return to this chapter as needed to review the details of the analytic procedures.

10

SELECTING STANDARDIZED OUTCOME MEASURES

The previous chapter provides a thorough review of several widely applicable standardized outcome measures. The measures presented assess fairly global traits. As such, these measures are appropriate for a broad array of symptom change in a wide range of settings. This does not imply that the few measures reviewed in depth will meet the needs of every clinician or be suitable in every setting. Often there is a need for a more specific outcome measure that directly assesses the population served at a particular site or is tailored to the treatment goals at a particular site. Designing a system of outcome evaluation for a setting that treats chemical dependency, eating disorders, sex offenders, or any other specialized population may require an outcome measure specific to that population. Although a detailed review of a large number of such specific measures is beyond the scope of this book, a listing of useful sources where such measures can be found is provided in the next section.

Literally hundreds of scales and tests have been developed for specific disorders, treatment populations, or other types of treatment programs. Some of these are commercially available, although many more are in the public domain or may be used with the permission of the author. At least rudimentary data on reliability and validity are available for most of these measures. It is likely that someone, somewhere, has developed a suitable outcome measure for just about every imaginable situation. The problem is to find just the right instrument and obtain it.

What Makes a Useful Outcome Measure?

The selection of one or more outcome measures is perhaps the key decision in the development of any program of outcome evaluation. Too often outcome assessment is made difficult or impossible by selecting measures that are inappropriate, time-consuming, expensive, or generally lacking in user-friendliness. There is no single set of rules that can be followed to guarantee a good set of outcome measures. Rather, each outcome evaluation must be considered in its own context. Compromises and trade-offs are always part of the process of designing the outcome investigation. What follows are some general suggestions and hints for selecting outcome measures. No single measure or set of measures will meet all of the following criteria; however, these criteria do provide general practical suggestions for selecting outcome measures. Many of these suggestions are consistent with the guidelines developed by a panel of experts sponsored by the National Institute of Mental Health (Ciarlo, Brown, Edwards, Kiresuk, & Newman, 1986; Newman, Ciarlo, & Carpenter, 1999).

The suggestions that follow presuppose a general approach to normative outcome assessment as outlined in the previous chapter. In other words, the plan for assessing outcome will involve the administration of pre- and posttreatment measures, and comparisons with normative data on the measures will be made to assess the degree of improvement of each client. The goal of the assessment is to determine whether a client has shown clinically significant change over the course of treatment.

1. Keep the Instruments Short and the Procedure Simple

People don't like to fill out forms. It is usually easiest to get data from clients at intake; the outcome measure can be slipped in with the other paperwork and diagnostic testing that is being conducted. The follow-up data are harder to come by. Most outcome studies include plenty of pretreatment scores. Posttreatment scores are less common, and long-term follow-up measures are rarer still. The easiest way to encourage compliance with an outcome assessment program is to make it easy for the client to do the paperwork. This starts with keeping the forms short. The more times you ask clients to rate themselves, the shorter the form should be. Try to limit questionnaires to one page, if possible.

2. Use Instruments That Are Easy to Administer and Score

Ease and efficiency apply to those administering and scoring the instruments as well as those filling them out. A well-designed outcome evaluation program should become an integral part of your clinical practice. That means that the tasks of administering, collecting, scoring, and entering data will be repeated over and over again. The key to ease of use is simplicity and routinization.

3. Measure the Specific Outcome(s) at Which Your Intervention Is Aimed

We tend to select outcome measures that are at some distance from the focus of the intervention. Resist selecting an outcome measure only because it is readily available or easy to administer. For example, assume that in a group treatment program for female victims of sexual abuse the Beck Depression Inventory (BDI) is routinely given when women start the group. Assume that the focus of the group is to help women change their life circumstances and to improve the quality of their relationships, not to provide therapy for depression and anxiety. Nonetheless, the therapist may be tempted to use the Beck Depression Inventory as the outcome measure because it is already administered at the beginning of treatment. Also, it could be argued that women who successfully complete the group should be less depressed. However, using the BDI as the sole outcome measure is not a good idea. For one thing, the group may be judged successful in achieving its aims even if there is not a change in depression symptoms. At the same time, demonstrating a reduction in depression does not necessarily mean that the group is meeting its primary goal—to help women change their life circumstances and improve relationships. Consequently, choosing one measure that is more closely directed at rating changes in life circumstances and another that considers quality of relationships would be better. Note that this does not mean that it might not also be a good idea to include the BDI as well, but that the BDI should not be the sole outcome measure.

Outcome measures may also be distant from the intervention being assessed in terms of time. Generally, the most success will be shown with measures administered at the end of treatment or at short-term follow-up. However, it might be argued that the success of a chemical dependency treatment program is best assessed in terms of long-term abstinence from chemical use in the months or years after program completion. Although this is a worthy goal, there are several problems with using long-term abstinence as the primary outcome measure. First, it takes a long time to collect the data, since the clinician must wait to see how program completers fare over a period of months or even years. Second, it is difficult to track individuals over time and to obtain their cooperation in gathering long-term outcome data. The time and effort spent in such tracking often has a poor payoff in terms of actual data collected. Third, relapse rates are extremely high in many such programs. Setting long-term abstinence as the only treatment goal makes it very likely that many treatment programs will not appear to be successful in the long run. Measures more immediate to the intervention might include a client's understanding of the educational goals of the treatment program or self-rated strategies for dealing with problematic situations that in the past have led to chemical use. The point is to look for immediate, measurable changes that should have occurred as a result of the intervention. This is not to say that long-term behavioral data on abstinence, job performance, or interpersonal relationships are not useful or desirable. If the time and resources are there to obtain such data, by all means collect them. However, difficulty in obtaining such data in no way precludes assessing the outcome of the intervention, and there is much to be said for using measures that are specific to the purpose of the intervention.

4. Use Measures That Provide Clinically Useful Information

Whenever possible, use instruments that can do double duty at intake for diagnosis and initial assessment of the client as well as provide a baseline for tracking outcome. Similarly, ongoing assessment of outcome helps the therapist monitor clinical progress as well as providing information to outside parties regarding treatment effectiveness. Although not all outcome measures are necessarily clinically useful in this way, using such measures when appropriate has obvious advantages.

5. Use Measures That Are Sensitive to Change

The reason for conducting an outcome evaluation is to show that your interventions result in measurable change in the clientele you serve. The entire purpose of the outcome assessment is defeated if the measures selected are insensitive to change. This is one of the reasons why some commonly used assessment instruments like the Minnesota Multiphasic Personality Inventory-2 (MMPI-2) are not generally useful as outcome measures. Many of the scales on the MMPI-2 assess characterological traits that remain relatively invariant over time. Although this characteristic may be useful in a diagnostic instrument, it is undesirable in an outcome instrument. Rather, a desirable outcome instrument will show change over the course of treatment. This is one reason many outcome measures focus on immediate symptoms. Even over a short number of sessions it would be reasonable to expect to see reduction in symptoms like anxiety and depression. Major personality restructuring might be expected to take longer.

This is not to say that an instrument like the MMPI-2 or the Millon Clinical Multiaxial Inventory (MCMI) might not be considered as an outcome measure for a long-term treatment program whose goal is characterological change. However, even in this case the length and cost of these instruments argue against their use as outcome measures. Behavioral measures may be subject to the same concern.

6. Look for Measures for Which Normative Data Are Available

The procedure for assessing clinically significant change described in the previous chapter requires some normative information about the measure. Ideally, data should be available about the reliability of the instrument, the mean and standard deviation of scores on the instrument for a functional population (i.e., individuals who do not have the disorder being treated), and the mean and standard deviation of scores on the instrument for a dysfunctional population (i.e., individuals who have the disorder being treated). Without this information it is difficult to utilize the procedures for assessing clinically significant change suggested by Jacobson and Truax (1991).

It should be noted that the procedures may sometimes be applied in cases where only some normative data are available. If information on the reliability of the test cannot be obtained, judgments of clinically significant change can be made without making an allowance for measurement error. If this is the case, small changes in scores over treatment should be interpreted with extreme caution. Similarly, data may be available only for the dysfunctional population. If it is reasonable to assume that individuals who no longer score in the dysfunctional range on the instrument are in fact recovered, decisions regarding clinically significant change may be made using the available cutoff information. It is also possible to interpret pre- and posttreatment changes simply in terms of whether the client improved.

Even if published norms are not available for an instrument, clinicians should not be discouraged from developing their own norms. Once intake data are collected on a reasonably large number of clients, estimates of the mean and standard deviation of the dysfunctional population can be made. It is also not difficult to estimate the internal consistency reliability coefficient of a measure from a sample of scores. If a program of outcome assessment is consistently implemented over time, the resulting database may well be the preferred source for normative data. It is especially appropriate to obtain means and standard deviations for the specific range of dysfunction seen in a specific practice.

7. Keep Costs Down

Therapists have choices regarding cost when selecting outcome measures, As with the purchase of any other product, it is not necessarily true that more expensive means better quality. The most expensive outcome evaluation systems tend to be complete "turnkey" systems supplied by companies that specialize in developing large data-based systems. Although a number of these are available, they tend to be used by larger hospitals, clinics, and managed care organizations. Smaller settings (and many large ones) may rely on a collection of individual instruments tailored to the interventions being offered. Here the issue of cost usually revolves around the issue of one-time versus unlimited use and copyright issues. The most expensive instruments tend to be those marketed on a fee-for-use basis, where the instrument must be purchased individually for each administration. Many standard psychological tests fall into this category. Sometimes the purchase price includes computer scoring as well as the test itself. Another option involves instruments where a site license for unlimited use may be purchased. These tend to be cheaper on a per-use basis if there is sufficient volume. Least expensive, of course, are instruments that are in the public domain. There are many such measures, often developed for research purposes, that can be used at no cost. Often the only requirement is to request permission of the author. In the following chapters, we will focus on low-cost or public domain instruments whenever possible.

8. Use a Personal Touch to Gather Data While the Client Is Present

It is always difficult to collect outcome data. The difficulty seems to increase as a function of the physical and temporal distance of the client from the therapist's office and from the therapist him- or herself. The best return rate is obtained when the therapist hands the client the forms to fill out at the end of the designated session and says, "I would really appreciate it if you could take a few minutes to fill these out right away." The compliance rate is lower if the office manager or receptionist gives the client the forms and asks the client to fill them out right away. Sending the forms home with the client greatly reduces the response rate. Mailing out forms at some later date after treatment isn't much better. Calling up clients and asking or reminding them to fill out and send in the forms may help, but is both time-consuming for the office and intrusive for the client. The best solution is for the therapist to ask clients for the data before they leave the appointment.

9. Think of Outcome Evaluation as an Ongoing Program Rather Than a One-Time Project

In traditional research, a study is designed, data are collected and analyzed, and the study is written up. Then, that study is over and it is time for another one. Some outcome assessments may work that way too (e.g., an outcome study conducted for purposes of meeting a requirement for an accreditation self-study). Even in this case, the project would be easier if the outcome data were gathered routinely. For most purposes, it is desirable to implement a program of outcome evaluation that becomes an integral part of the treatment program in a particular setting.

SOURCES FOR INFORMATION ABOUT STANDARDIZED MEASURES

The most familiar source for information on standardized psychological tests is the *Mental Measurements Yearbook* series developed by the late Oscar Buros and published by the University of Nebraska Press. The series is currently in its 13th volume. The hardcover version is probably best accessed at a library. The Buros Institute Web site can be accessed at www.unl.edu/buros. An updated version of the most recent editions of the yearbook is also available on CD-ROM and over the Internet from SilverPlatter Information Services (go to the silverplatter Web site or call 1-800-343-0064).

A recently published book titled *The Use of Psychological Testing for Treatment Planning and Outcomes Assessment* (2nd edition), edited by

Maruish (1999b), includes a thorough discussion of methodological issues involved in the implementation of outcome research, as well as a detailed review of over 40 specific outcome measures. This book is particularly useful because its emphasis is on the use of measures for outcome assessment in addition to initial assessment.

Fischer and Corcoran's (1994a, 1994b) two-volume *Measures for Clinical Practice* lists a wide variety of measures aimed at specific treatment populations or presenting symptoms. These books provide an extensive listing of outcome measures for children and families (volume 1) and for adults (volume 2). Descriptions include a summary of data on reliability and validity, information about how to obtain the instrument, references for research conducted using the instrument, and often a complete version of the instrument itself. Many of the instruments listed are in the public domain, or can be used if permission of the author is obtained.

For outcome measures in medical or health-related settings, a paperback book by Bowling (1997) titled *Measuring Health: A Review of Quality of Life Measurement Scales* is very useful. This book provides critical reviews of over 50 measures, including measures of functional ability, health status, social support, and life satisfaction.

Another useful resource is a CD-ROM titled *Health and Psychosocial Instruments* (HAPI), which indexes a large number of scales and instruments. Copies of instruments are often available on the disk. Again, many of the instruments are in the public domain. The database is updated quarterly, and a subscription costs $295 a year (at the time this book was published). HAPI is distributed by BMDS, P.O. Box 110287, Pittsburgh, Pennsylvania 15232. The HAPI database is also available at many academic libraries.

A less useful resource is Goldman and Mitchell's (1996) seven-volume *Directory of Unpublished Experimental Mental Measures.* This series includes brief references to a wide variety of measures described in psychology journals over the years; however, most of the measures are not clinically focused.

Finally, several books on outcome assessment list various measures and provide suggestions and examples for implementing an outcome assessment program. The first, *Assessing Outcome in Clinical Practice,* by Ogles, Lambert, and Masters (1996), lists commonly used measures for assessing outcome in clinical practice and provides detailed strategies for implementation. The general approach to outcome assessment these authors focus on is the clinically significant change approach, compatible with the approach outlined in this book. *The Measurement and Management of Clinical Outcomes in Mental Health,* by Lyons, Howard, O'Mahoney, and Lish (1997), provides a summary of methodologies and measures for outcome assessment, quality assurance, customer satisfaction, and outcome management focused especially on managed care settings. *Outcomes and Incomes,* a short book by Clement (1999), lists a number of outcome measures in the context of a unique system of data analysis. Finally, Strupp, Horowitz, and Lambert (1997) have edited a book that reviews key issues in the selection of outcome measures specifically for mood, anxiety, and personality disorders.

Additional Outcome Measures for Various Settings and Populations

It is not possible to provide a detailed review in this text of more than a handful of the hundreds of potential outcome measures that are available, but the detailed review of the four different measures provided in Chapter 9 can be used as a model that can be applied to other measures. Clinicians who work with children, who specialize in family and couples counseling, or who treat individuals with addictions may prefer to use a measure other than the ones described in Chapter 9.

A few additional suggestions for outcome measures are provided in the following section. The list is by no means exhaustive, and many other suitable measures are not listed either because of space limitations or because the author is not aware of them. In addition, no claim is made that the instruments listed here are the best instruments, or that they are to be preferred over other instruments. No instrument is perfect, and none will meet all of the suggested criteria listed earlier. The instruments presented are roughly organized into functional categories.

Measures for Use with Children and Adolescents

The Child Behavior Checklist (CBCL)

This is a widely employed instrument used to assess children and adolescents. It is sometimes referred to simply as the Achenbach after its author. It includes scales that measure internalizing problems (withdrawal, somatic complaints, and anxiety/depression), externalizing problems (delinquent behavior and aggressive behavior), and social, thought, and attention problems. The CBCL may be filled out by parents, teachers, or others who observe the child. It is also available in a self-report form for older children. Normative data are provided in the manual (Achenbach & Edelbrock, 1983). Detailed information on the use of the CBCL for outcome assessment may be found in Achenbach (1999). The CBCL may be obtained from University Associates in Psychiatry.

Address:	1 South Prospect Street, Burlington, Vermont 05401
Phone:	802-656-8313
E-mai:l	checklist@uvm.edu
Web site:	www.uvm.edu/~cbcl

The Youth Outcome Questionnaire (Y-OQ)

The Y-OQ was developed as a counterpart to the OQ-45 (described in Chapter 9). It is a parent-report measure designed specifically to track treatment progress in children and adolescents. Most parents can complete the instrument in five to seven minutes. In addition to an overall score, the Y-OQ yields subscales in six domains of functioning, including intrapersonal distress, somatic concerns, interpersonal relations, social problems, behavioral dysfunction, and critical items. The critical items subscale targets serious concerns that may require immediate intervention (e.g., suicidality, psychotic ideation, eating disorders). For a thorough review of the Y-OQ, see Wells, Burlingame, and Lambert (1999). The instrument is available from American Professional Credentialing Services.

Address:	P.O. Box 477, Wharton, New Jersey 07885-0477
Phone:	1-888-MH-SCORE
Fax:	1-973-366-8665
E-mail:	apcs@erols.com
Web site:	www.oqfamily.com

The Children's Depression Inventory (CDI)

The CDI is a self-report measure of depressive symptoms in youth ages 7 to 17 years. It can be administered in 15 minutes or less, and, as its name implies, is similar in focus to the Beck Depression Inventory. Normative data are available in the test manual (Kovacs, 1992). A recent review of the instrument may be found in Sitarenios and Kovacs (1999). The instrument is available from Multi Health Systems.

Address:	MHS Inc., 908 Niagara Falls Boulevard, North Tonawanda, New York 14120-2060
Phone:	800-456-3003
E-mail:	customerservice@mhs.com
Web site:	www.mhs.com

Global Measures of Outcome

The Symptom Assessment-45 (SA-45)

This instrument uses a subset of the items from the SCL-90-R to assess symptomology across nine psychiatric domains. Like the SCL-90-R, it also includes a global index of overall psychological distress. It is available in a paper-and-pencil version and in a Windows-based computerized version. Normative data are provided in the manual (Strategic Advantage, 1997). A recent review of the instrument, including suggested criteria for an analysis of clinically significant change, can be found in Maruish (1999a). The instrument is available from Multi Health Systems.

Address:	MHS Inc., 908 Niagara Falls Boulevard, North Tonawanda, New York, 14120-2060
Phone:	800-456-3003
E-mail:	customerservice@mhs.com
Web site:	www.mhs.com

Measures for Specific Diagnostic Categories

The State-Trait Anxiety Inventory (STAI)

The STAI is arguably the most widely used measure in research on anxiety in both clinical and nonclinical settings. Originally developed by Spielberger, Gorusch, and Lushene (1970), the instrument was extensively revised some years later (Spielberger, 1983). A unique feature of the inventory is the separate measurement of anxiety as an immediate emotional state and as a more enduring personality trait. The instrument consists of 40 items (20 assessing state anxiety and 20 assessing trait anxiety) self-rated on a 4-point scale. Scores on the trait component of the STAI should show change over treatment for individuals with panic disorder, generalized anxiety disorder, and phobia. The state component of the STAI is useful in evaluating progress in working with anxiety responses to specific stimuli or situations (e.g., test anxiety). The STAI has been translated into more than 30 languages, and extensive norms are available. A recent review of the STAI can be found in Spielberger, Sydeman, Owen, and Marsh (1999). The STAI is available from the Mind Garden, Inc.

Address:	1690 Woodside Road, Suite 202, Redwood City, California 94061
Phone:	650-261-3500
Web site:	www.mindgarden.com

Measures for Marriage and Relationship Issues

The Dyadic Adjustment Scale (DAS)

The DAS is a self-report measure of relationship satisfaction for married or cohabiting couples. The instrument consists of 32 items rated on a Likert-type scale, and provides an overall measure of relationship satisfaction as well as scores on four subscales (satisfaction, cohesion, consensus, and affectional expression). The DAS has been widely used in marriage research, and appears to be sensitive to changes in relationship quality over the course of marital therapy. Normative data are provided in the article by Spanier (1976) that first described the DAS. The instrument is available from Multi Health Systems.

Address:	MHS Inc., 908 Niagara Falls Boulevard, North Tonawanda, New York 14120-2060
Phone:	800-456-3003
E-mail:	customerservice@mhs.com
Web site:	www.mhs.com

The Marital Satisfaction Inventory-Revised (MSI-R)

Consisting of 150 true/false items, the MSI-R has been used for both treatment planning and outcome assessment in working with couples in distressed relationships. The instrument takes about 25 minutes to complete, and includes two validity scales, a measure of global distress, and 10 subscales that assess specific aspects of marital satisfaction (including such areas as problem solving, aggression, finances, sex, childrearing, and communication). A Spanish translation is available. Normative data are provided in the scoring manual (Snyder, 1997). A recent article describing the MSI-R was written by Snyder and Aikman (1999). The instrument is available through Western Psychological Services.

Address:	12031 Wilshire Boulevard, Los Angeles, California 90025-1251
Phone:	1-800-648-8857
Web site:	www.wspublish.com

Measures of Quality of Life and Health Issues

The SF-36 Health Survey (SF-36)

The SF-36 is a short (36 items) instrument designed as a generic measure of health status. The instrument yields two summary measures—Physical Health Status and Mental Health Status—with four subscales embedded within each. The SF-36 has been widely used as an outcome measure when health assessment is required. It has been translated into a number of languages, and normative data have been collected in over 40 countries. Information about the SF-36, including a summary article and extensive bibliography, can be found at its Web site at www.sf-36.com. Detailed information about the SF-36, including normative data, can be found in the user's manuals (Ware, Kosinski, & Keller, 1994; Ware, Snow, Kosinski, & Gandek, 1993). A recent review of the SF-36 was written by its author, John Ware (1999). The instrument itself is distributed by the Medical Outcomes Trust.

Address:	PMB #503, 198 Tremont Street, Boston, Massachusetts 02116-4705
Phone:	617-426-4046
Web site:	www.outcomes-trust.org

The Quality of Life Inventory (QOLI)

Designed as an overall measure of positive mental health, the QOLI assesses life satisfaction across 16 domains, which include such areas as health, work, play, money, relationships, learning, community, and home. The measure is based on empirical study of the kinds of qualities people seek to include in their lives. Respondents rate both the importance of each domain and their satisfaction with each domain, yielding an overall score that is weighted in terms of its importance to the individual. Comprising only 16 items, the QOLI can be completed in approximately 5 minutes. Michael Frisch developed the QOLI, and information and normative data may be found in Frisch (1992, 1999) and Frisch, Cornell, Villaneuva, and Retzlaff (1992). Information about the use and interpretation of the QOLI can also be found in the treatment manual (Frisch, 1994a, 1994b). The QOLI is available from National Computer Systems (NCS).

Address:	P.O. Box 1416, Minneapolis, Minnesota 55440
Phone:	1-800-627-7271
Web site:	http://assessments.ncs.com

DEVELOPING YOUR OWN NORMATIVE OUTCOME MEASURES

Developing and norming an assessment instrument may seem like a daunting task; however, if no appropriate instruments are available, you might consider developing a short instrument to assess outcome. Such an instrument might be an extension of some of the kinds of rating scales described in Part II of this text. For these purposes, however, the instrument cannot be individually scaled for each client. To be adequately normed, the items on the instrument must be refined and the instrument must be administered repeatedly. The process of writing items for a test need not be overwhelming if a straightforward rating scale is used. Keep in mind the psychometric properties of a good rating scale, outlined in Chapter 4. Another possibility would be to find an existing instrument that would meet your needs with some modification. Once the instrument is modified, existing norms may no longer apply, but the instrument might provide a model for a more appropriate scale. Of course, you must be aware of copyright restrictions if you use items verbatim from a protected measure.

Another situation may arise if a useful instrument is found, but normative data are not available for it. In this case, you are saved from developing an instrument, but you must still collect normative data to conduct an outcome analysis.

To conduct a reliable change analysis, information about the reliability of scores on the instrument must be obtained. This is most easily accomplished using a measure of internal consistency, like Chronbach's coefficient alpha. Once sufficient scores on the instrument are collected (a sample of 40 to 50 individuals may be adequate, although somewhat larger samples are desirable), the alpha statistic may be easily calculated using a standard statistical software package like SPSS. The process for collecting normative data to calculate a clinically significant change cutoff score is similarly straightforward. Once the population is identified and the sample data are collected, it is necessary to calculate means and standard deviations of the relevant groups. If an instrument is routinely administered in clinical practice, obtaining a clinical sample will occur as a matter of course. The mean and standard deviation for all clients at intake, or for all clients with certain diagnoses at intake, should provide normative data for the dysfunctional population. Obtaining a community sample for parameter estimates for the functional population may be more difficult. Unless you are willing to provide compensation, it may be difficult to assemble a large enough representative sample of nondistressed individuals for normative purposes. This can present some interpretation difficulties in assessing clinically significant change. As discussed in Chapter 11, these difficulties may or may not be insurmountable.

In general, the construction and norming of a new or modified instrument should be approached cautiously. Unless experienced in psychometric methods, the clinician is advised to seek consultation from an individual with appropriate methodological expertise if he or she intends to develop an outcome measure.

SUMMARY

This chapter provides details on the process of selecting an outcome measure (or measures) for specific settings. Ten general criteria are suggested on which to evaluate the utility of a specific scale for the purpose of outcome assessment. These criteria focus on the pragmatic demands and constraints of the applied clinical setting. It is emphasized that decisions regarding the selection of outcome measure(s) should be made with regard to clinical needs and requirements rather than abstract psychometric principles or research findings. A nonexhaustive listing of several additional outcome measures is also included, as well as resources for locating additional measures.

Time given to searching for an outcome measure particularly appropriate to a specific setting is time well spent. It should also be noted that the field of outcome assessment is growing rapidly. The clinician should be alert for new measures and for additional normative data on existing measures.

Again it should be emphasized that the authors are not endorsing any of the outcome measures listed in the book. Nor should lack of mention of a potential outcome measure in any way be considered a criticism of that measure. The specific measures listed in Chapters 9 and 10 were chosen primarily because of their widespread use, general availability, and utility in a wide variety of clinical settings. Their inclusion in this book should in no way be construed to imply that these are the best measures or the recommended measures for any particular application.

The next chapter continues the detailed review of clinically significant change analysis, this time focusing on data analysis.

11

COLLECTING AND ANALYZING NORMATIVE OUTCOME DATA

Following an outcome analysis is easy when the examples appear neatly laid out in a text. The data are already collected, analytic decisions have been made, and conclusions have been drawn. The actual practice of developing an outcome assessment system can be much more difficult. Questions about procedure, analysis, and interpretation arise at every step of the process. No text can answer all of these questions ahead of time; however, the authors have anticipated as many as possible to help guide clinicians through the process of setting up an outcome evaluation system using normative measures. Do not expect a cookbook approach. Every clinical setting is unique, and no universal instrument or set of procedures for outcome assessment will apply to all settings, any more than a single approach to therapy can be universally applicable. This chapter provides sufficient information for the clinician to make reasonably informed decisions at the various choice points of conducting an outcome assessment using normative measures. Some of the information in this chapter is necessarily technical. However, the authors have kept the details of these procedures as accessible and user-friendly as possible.

First, we describe various aspects of planning and implementing a procedure for collecting normative outcome data. Then we focus on analyzing normative outcome data, considering details of the decisions that must be made in order to establish the reliable change index (RCI) and cutoff scores so that an analysis of clinically significant change can be conducted. Finally, we discuss issues surrounding the analysis and interpretation of data obtained via an analysis of clinically significant change.

Overall Strategies for Outcome Assessment Using Normative Measures

The term *design* can be an intimidating one when used in the context of conducting outcome assessment or outcome research. This is especially true if the connotation is that of research design. Clinicians may have memories of graduate courses in research design in which complex methodologies required control groups, randomization, double-blind observation, and the like. Although these methods are well suited, or even necessary, for conducting experimental research under highly controlled laboratory-like conditions, the procedures seem far removed from the world of clinical practice. Principles of experimental research design are not relevant to the kinds of outcome assessment discussed in this book. The authors do not assume that the clinician will establish a randomly assigned control or comparison group, that ratings need be done in a blind fashion, or that treatments need to be administered for a specified duration in a consistent manner. These requirements are characteristic of efficacy research, as discussed in Chapter 1. The procedures described in this text are designed to provide evidence for the effectiveness, not the efficacy, of treatment (Seligman, 1996; Wells, 1999). The kinds of normative assessment procedures described in this book have also been referred to as *practice research* or *quality of care research* (Brooks & Lohr, 1985; Holloway & Ringel, 1998). It is not the purpose of this kind of assessment to demonstrate that clients who receive treatment are better off than clients who do not receive treatment. Rather, the clinician is attempting to document the kinds of changes and the amount of change that have been observed in the client over the course of treatment.

Given that the purpose of normative outcome assessment is to document client change, the focus is on data collection in real clinical settings, in which the assessment procedures are designed to fit the setting, not the other way around. Clinicians attempting to implement programs of outcome assessment in their practices need not be concerned about traditional research design issues like randomization and standardization of procedures. The primary goal of outcome assessment is to provide reasonably reliable and valid indicators of individual client progress. A secondary goal may be to provide an overall assessment of the treatment effectiveness of a specific practice or clinic. The clinician is not attempting to demonstrate the efficacy of treatment, nor will the data collected generalize beyond the specific practice and clients assessed.

If these principles are kept in mind, many of the design questions that arise when implementing a program of normative outcome assessment can be answered. Here are some common kinds of issues that arise in the course of conducting outcome assessments, along with possible answers:

I forgot to give the client the instrument at the first session. Is it okay to have him or her fill it out at the second session? Why not? Make a note of the timing of the "pretest" when the scores are recorded.

A particular client has very poor reading skills. Is it okay for me to read the questions to him or her so that I am sure he or she understands them? Certainly, if you feel that the instrument as read is a valid indicator of the client's psychological state.

My client inadvertently took the outcome measure home after the last session. The client later called to ask if it was okay to mail it in. Is it? None of the other clients are mailing in their surveys. Of course, as long as you feel that the client was reasonably honest and accurate when filling out the instrument.

My clients receive very different numbers of sessions. Some only come once or twice; some are in therapy for several months or longer. Can I compare outcomes for all of these individuals in a single analysis? The answer here must be a qualified yes. If the short- and long-term clients represent different kinds of clinical populations, it may be problematic to mix them together in overall analysis. The best course of action may be to keep track of outcomes separately. This can easily be accomplished on a graph of clinically significant change by using different symbols to represent long- and short-term clients.

I use different treatment approaches with different clients. Do I have to keep track of which treatment approach was used and compare them in my outcome analysis? Such a comparison would be difficult to make in most settings. Given sufficient data collected over time, an analysis of this kind might be attempted. However, the purpose of the outcome analysis is to evaluate the effectiveness of your treatment program, not to determine which treatments work the best. The short answer is no.

I see a number of different types of clients. Do I have to keep track of different client populations or diagnoses when conducting a normative outcome analysis? On a case-by-case basis, information about diagnoses and presenting problems is already recorded, and must be considered in evaluating the outcome for the individual client. Given sufficient data collected over time, comparisons might be made between outcomes for different treatment populations. However, this is certainly not the primary focus of the normative outcome assessment. Of more concern in this case is the selection of outcome measures. It is possible that different measures would need to be used depending on the type of client being treated and the treatment goals for that client.

When and How Often to Assess

The critical element in the design of an outcome assessment is to obtain two data points from the client. It is not possible to observe change over time in client functioning unless measures are taken at least twice. Ideally, this means that the outcome instrument is administered prior to treatment and at the end of treatment. As discussed in the previous section, small variations on this are not of major concern. There is no cause for concern if the assessment is given on the second session instead of the first, or if what was thought to be the final session turns out to be followed by several ad hoc appointments. It must be stressed, however, that at a minimum the clinician who intends to track outcome using normative measures must design the program of outcome assessment to obtain two measures (pre and post) from each client.

It is possible to collect normative outcome data more often. Earlier in this book a strong case was made for collecting at least some individual outcome data from clients at each session. Collecting normative outcome data this frequently is typically not as useful, for several reasons. First, if the outcome measure takes more than even a few minutes to fill out, clients will likely resist completing the instrument each session. Second, session-to-session changes may not be reliable when normative measures are used. Finally, if the normative measure must be purchased on a per-use basis, frequent administration can be costly. These caveats notwithstanding, there are situations where more frequent administration of normative outcome measures may make sense. Some measures are very short and can be administered each session if desired. The Beck Depression Inventory (BDI), the Outcome Questionnaire-45 (OQ-45), and the Behavior and Symptom Identification Scale-32 (BASIS-32) fall into this category. For example, Kadera, Lambert, and Andrews (1996) illustrated the use of the OQ-45 on a session-by-session basis. The progress of each client is plotted separately, showing change over time. The pattern for most clients is quite consistent. The pattern of improvement is variable, of course, with some clients showing rapid improvement, some slow but steady improvement, and others little change or variable scores with no particular pattern. The regular administration of normative measures can provide a useful adjunct to the kinds of individual evaluation procedures outlined in Part II of this book. An added advantage of multiple testing is the increased likelihood that a measure will in fact be obtained close to the end of treatment. As discussed in the next section, this often determines whether any outcome data are available at all.

Another situation where more frequent administration of outcome measures is in order is when treatment extends over time. If the client is being treated in fewer than 10 to 12 sessions, a pre- and posttreatment assessment of outcome is likely sufficient. What if the treatment program lasts for 20 sessions or more, however? In this case, assessing outcome at midtreatment can provide useful information about client progress. If normative outcome measures are adminstered regularly—say, every 10 to 12 sessions—separate analyses of clinically significant change can be made from the baseline measurement to each of the midtreatment measurement points. It would even be theoretically possible to assess for clinically significant change (or at least for reliable improvement) from one midtreatment measurement point to another. The usefulness of implementing midtreatment evaluations depends on the requirements of the particular setting, as well as the length of treatment.

A final option for normative outcome assessment involves the collection of follow-up data. Here, the client is contacted at some point after the termination of treatment and asked to fill out the normative assessment instrument again. Typical follow-up assessment periods range between one and six months posttreatment. Practical considerations of cost and client availability usually constrain the collection of follow-up outcome data. However, if the goal of the treatment program is long-term change, reviewing how clients are doing some time after treatment is completed can provide useful information.

IMPLEMENTATION ISSUES

Assume that after careful consideration the clinician has identified an instrument for normative outcome assessment, obtained permission to use the instrument, and obtained a copy of the instrument. The clinician has decided when to administer the instrument and has assembled normative data for the analysis. The difficult part of conducting an outcome assessment can now begin.

Depending on the setting, there is likely to be some resistance to implementing an outcome assessment program. If the therapist is in private practice, the source of the resistance and the solution to it are straightforward. However, in larger practices, clinics, agencies, or institutional settings where the treatment staff are employees, at least some of the staff can be expected to actively or passively resist the implementation. Lyons, Howard, O'Mahoney, and Lish (1997) note that resistance may be indirect. Concerns may be voiced about "confidentiality, dehumanization of the therapeutic process, reductionism that fails to capture human experience, and interference with the transference relationship" (p. 136).

Often, the end result of such staff or provider resistance is that outcome data are not collected. If we also consider evaluations that are not distributed to clients through oversight or hurried schedules, it is clear that obtaining outcome data is easier to plan than to implement.

A common pattern of missing data in outcome assessment involves the end-of-treatment measure. For example, in an outcome assessment program conducted at a small clinic, Hyink-

Huttemier (2000) reported that over the course of the project, 88 clients consented to participate and filled out the assessment instrument at intake. However, only 35 forms were completed at 5 sessions, 15 forms at 10 sessions, and 5 forms at 15 sessions. In other words, less than half of the clients who filled out the pretreatment instrument completed a second instrument.

One problem is remembering to distribute the instrument. Implementing the kind of regularly scheduled program of outcome assessment recommended in this book can help greatly with this problem. A more difficult issue is that often clinicians do not know ahead of time exactly which session will be the last. Perhaps the client is left with the instruction to "call if you have more issues to work out," or the client misses several appointments and then drops out of therapy, or the client is feeling better as the final sessions approach, and calls in to cancel the last session or two. The tendency for clients not to return is perhaps the most compelling reason to administer the outcome assessment instruments periodically during the course of treatment, thus maximizing the chances of obtaining usable data with which to evaluate client progress. A similar strategy would be to administer the outcome assessment close to the end of treatment, but not to wait for the last session. There is evidence that assessments made late in treatment are good approximations of scores obtained at the end of treatment. Speer (1994) calculated that the use of such measures obtained late in the course of treatment may underestimate final improvement rates by only about 2 percent. It appears that a measure collected close to the end of treatment will yield results very similar to those collected at the end of treatment.

Any program of outcome evaluation will only be successful if the individuals responsible for data collection support the program and see its value. Achieving this degree of support has been called *buy-in* in some settings (Cohen, 1998). Data will be collected haphazardly, or not at all, if those responsible do not understand the value of the outcome assessment program, are not given credit for the time it takes to collect the data, or feel threatened by the assessment program.

Another challenge to successful implementation of an outcome assessment program is to develop a regular process by which the data are routinely collected. Lyons et al. (1997) referred to difficulties in this area as "operational friction." It is critical to clearly specify the procedures to be followed in collecting the data. Who will distribute the instrument to the client? Will the instrument be given to the client at the end or the beginning of the visit? These and other procedural issues need to be carefully worked out. Although each setting is unique, two recommendations can be made for enhancing implementation procedures. First, most often the best time for the client to fill out the instrument is at the beginning of the session or visit. Most clients wait at least a few minutes before beginning a session; this is an ideal time to complete paperwork. At the end of the session the client is usually anxious to leave for his or her next appointment. The second recommendation is that the therapist hand out the instrument. Although it is also reasonable for a receptionist or office manager to hand out the forms, we noted earlier that clients give more weight to the task if the therapist requests the information. However it is done, it is critical to have someone actually hand the forms to the client. Leaving them in a folder in the waiting room with the instructions to "Fill one out when you come in" is a guarantee of a minimal response rate. Mailing forms out is not recommended either. The response rate is lower and the cost is higher than when the instrument is personally handed to the client.

Client compliance may also be an issue in obtaining outcome data. The longer the instrument and the more often it is administered, the greater the likelihood the client will resist completing it. Obtaining data can be even more difficult when working with children, when a parent or other collateral must fill out the evaluation form. However, if the procedure for filling out the instruments is clearly explained, if the instruments are handed out in a manner that facilitates immediate completion, and if the importance of the data collection is emphasized, most clients will comply with the request to fill out the instrument. In other words, if the therapist has bought in to the outcome assessment plan, if the instrument is user-friendly, and if there is a smooth flow of operations for actual data collection, clients will respond with a very high compliance rate.

DETERMINING THE RCI: SELECTING THE RELIABILITY COEFFICIENT

Outcome assessment is about detecting change. Has the client changed for the better, changed for the worse, or stayed about the same? The reliable change index is concerned with the last of these, denoting whether there is evidence of change over the course of treatment. If our measurements were perfect, such that a score on a psychological test was an exact and precise indicator of the internal state of the individual, we would not have to worry about whether or not change was reliable. If our instruments were not subject to any error of measurement, all change recorded by the instruments would be real or reliable change. Unfortunately, measurement in psychology (or in any field, for that matter) is never exact. A score on an instrument is always subject to a certain amount of measurement error. *Error* in this case doesn't mean a mistake; rather, it refers to the degree of imprecision inherent in the measurement process itself. A basic understanding of the nature of measurement precision, or reliability, is critical to understanding the concept of reliable change in outcome assessment.

The degree of precision to be expected when using a measurement instrument is quantified in the instrument's reliability coefficient. In essence, the reliability coefficient tells us how the test correlates with itself. If the test correlates perfectly, such that identical scores are obtained each time the test is administered to the same person, it can be said that the test is perfectly reliable. That is, it gives the same result every time. A test like this would have a reliability coefficient equal to 1.00. In practice, test reliabilities tend to be high, but never perfect. Reliability coefficients in the 0.90 range are considered very strong; that is, the test gives almost the same result every time it is administered. Reliability coefficients in the 0.80 range are considered adequate; that is, the test gives reasonably consistent results each time it is adminstered, although there is some random variation in the test scores. Reliability coefficients in the 0.70 range are generally considered marginal. Much of the variability in the test scores is attributable to random measurement error. A reliability coefficient of 0.70 in fact implies that 30 percent (1 minus 0.70 or 70 percent equals 0.30 or 30 percent) of the variability in the scores is due not to differences in the trait being measured but to chance factors. It should also be noted that longer tests tend to be more reliable. This is why the subscales on a test usually have lower reliability coefficients than the overall total score; there are more items going into the total score than into the individual subscales.

These points are essential to understanding the concept of the reliable change index (RCI) because a value for the reliability of scores from the outcome instrument must be used in its calculation. If a high value is used for the reliability coefficient, the resulting band for unreliable change will be relatively narrow. This is desirable, since it means that a higher percentage of observed changes in client functioning can be classified as reliable. On the other hand, if the reliability coefficient is low, the RCI band will be wider. This is less desirable since the client will have to show a fairly large change in test scores before the change can be deemed reliable.

Estimates of the reliability of scores from a test are usually calculated in one of two ways. The first, test-retest reliability, simply involves administering the test twice to the same individuals and calculating the correlation coefficient between the two sets of scores. If individuals score about the same both times they take the test, the correlation is high and the reliability is strong. If there is more variability in the scores from the two administrations, the reliability coefficient is correspondingly lower. Test-retest reliability is not difficult to calculate, but it does require having a group of individuals sit for the same test twice. The second estimate, internal consistency reliability, involves correlating the test with itself based on a single administration. The older procedure for doing this was called split-half reliability because the test items were randomly divided into two equal halves and the correlation between the two halves was calculated. If the two halves yielded about the same score for a particular individual, the reliability coefficient would be high. If, on the other hand, each half yielded different scores, the reliability coefficient would be correspondingly lower. There are some problems with the split-half procedure, stemming from the fact that the random allocation of items into the two halves can affect the reliability coefficient. Consequently, current practice is to calculate a statistic called coefficient alpha as a measure of internal consistency reliability (Pedhazar & Schmelkin, 1991). Alpha represents the average of all possible split-half combinations. Coefficient alpha is easy to calculate because it only requires administering the test once to a reasonably representative sample. A third procedure for assessing reliability—developing an alternate form of a test—is more expensive and time-consuming. Few, if any, outcome measures exist in alternate forms.

When reliability data for an instrument used for outcome assessment are reported, coefficients for both test-retest reliability and coefficient alpha are often given. These two coefficients may have different values, requiring therapists to decide which value to use in calculating the reliable change index. An important point to consider in making this decision is that most outcome measures are sensitive to change. That is, they are designed to reflect day-to-day changes in client mood, functioning, anxiety level, or behavior. Since the goal of intervention is to produce change, using measures that are sensitive to change makes sense. However, this characteristic of outcome measures makes the determination of test-retest reliability somewhat problematic. A test-retest reliability coefficient only makes sense if the individual is in the same psychological state both times the test is administered. If the level of psychological distress is the same at test and retest, then any differences in test scores must be due to the measurement error of the test itself. The problem is that the individual is probably not in exactly the same psychological state at the retest period as at the first administration of the instrument. Consequently, at least some of the variability in the scores from test to retest is due to real changes in the client. This is not measurement error; the client has really changed, and the test is accurately reflecting that change. The end result is that test-retest reliability coefficients for unstable internal states (like depression and anxiety) tend to be low—at least lower than internal consistency estimates. This is especially problematic for outcome assessment measures, since most are in fact measures of internal states that are subject to change and can fluctuate from day to day in response to both internal and external events.

These issues can be illustrated by a review of the extensive reliability data on the Beck Depression Inventory (BDI). As described in Chapter 9, estimates for the test-retest reliability of the BDI range from 0.48 to 0.86 (Beck, Steer, & Garbin, 1988). As might be expected, estimates taken over shorter time intervals tend to be somewhat higher than estimates taken over longer intervals. In fact, there is a correlation of −0.30 between the reliability estimate and the number of days in the test-retest interval. As the interval becomes longer, reliability estimates become lower. In addition, test-retest estimates for normal populations tend to be somewhat higher than test-retest reliability estimates for clinical populations. This makes sense if we assume that there is more day-to-day fluctuation in depression levels in a clinical population than in a nonclinical one. Estimates of internal consistency using coefficient alpha, on the other hand, tend to be much higher, with an average value of 0.86 and many coefficients in the 0.90 range (Beck, 1988).

At last we are at a point where the question of which reliability coefficient to use can be answered with some basis. Test-retest estimates of reliability, especially those taken over a longer period of time, probably underestimate the reliability of scores obtained using common clinical outcome measures. On the assumption that individuals can and do consistently rate how they feel at a particular point in time, internal consistency estimates of reliability may be a more accurate reflection of the reliability of outcome scores. We should be cautious, however, of extremely high values of coefficient alpha, especially for longer tests. In the case of the BDI, note that the average coefficient alpha over several studies is equal to 0.86. Similarly, the high end of test-retest estimates is equal to 0.84. Using a value for reliability in the mid 0.80s would seem reasonably conservative in calculating a RCI for the BDI.

There is one more important general point to make about reliability. Reliability is often referred to as a property of a test instrument itself. How often have you heard someone say that Test ABC is a very reliable measure, whereas Test XYZ is not very reliable? The assumption implicit in these statements is that reliability is a characteristic that is carried by the test itself. Such language implies a subtle but important misunderstanding of the concept of reliability. It is not the instrument itself that is or is not reliable. Rather, the term *reliability* properly refers to the scores generated by the instrument (Thompson, 1994). In other words, a given set of scores on a particular instrument—say the Beck Depression Inventory (BDI)—may have differing reliability depending on the population taking the test, the conditions under which the test is adminstered, and who is administering the test. Reliability coefficients are always specific to a particular setting and population and apply to scores generated by the test under specific conditions. The BDI itself does not have a reliability of 0.85 (or any other number). Scores from the BDI obtained under specified circumstances may have a reliability of about 0.85; scores obtained under different circumstances may have different reliability.

The implication is that the context in which the test is administered should be considered when estimating reliability. If the conditions of actually filling out the instrument are haphazard, reliability estimates should be lowered. This might be necessary, for example, if clients rush through filling in the instrument when late for an appointment, if measures are sent home with clients, or if different individuals hand out the instrument with inconsistent instructions. Similarly, the characteristics of the individuals taking the test should be considered. If it appears that clients are not taking the instrument seriously, are having trouble understanding the test questions, or are distracted by other things going on in the testing environment, then caution might be exercised when making assumptions about the reliability of the scores obtained.

Unfortunately, there is not a standard procedure that will provide an unambiguous answer to the question, "What is the reliability of this test?" Reliability coefficients are generally published in test manuals, or may be obtained in published summaries of a test instrument. As with individual test scores, however, the interpretation of the reliability estimates must be made in the context of the actual setting in which the instrument is being used. If in doubt as to which estimate to use, why not calculate both a liberal and a conservative estimate and fit both to the actual outcome data? It may then become clear whether the liberal, the conservative, or an intermediate value works best for a particular application. If all else fails and it seems impossible to make a decision as to which reliability estimate to use, consider reporting the data using both estimates. Fortunately the RCI is not especially sensitive to small variations in the reliability coefficient. Changing the reliability coefficient a few hundredths of a point in either direction usually has relatively little effect on the RCI.

DETERMINING THE RCI: SELECTING THE STANDARD DEVIATION

Two parameters must be specified in order to calculate a reliable change index. The first is a reliability coefficient for the scale, as discussed in the previous section. The second is an estimate of the variability of the scores on the scale, as indicated by a value for the standard deviation. Determining this value is easy if there is only a single distribution of scores with which to work. The standard deviation of the distribution is the one to use in the RCI equation. However, most often the normative data provide means and standard deviations for two or more populations, ranging from functional to dysfunctional. Again, if the standard deviations of these various distributions are approximately equal, there is little to decide. Simply calculate an average or a pooled value for the standard deviation and use it in the equation. (Use a pooled value weighted by the sample size if the sample sizes differ considerably between the groups. Use an average if the sizes of the various samples are about the same.)

In practice, selecting a value for the standard deviation to use in the equation for the RCI is often more complicated. This is because scores on many instruments are more variable in dysfunctional populations than in functional populations. The reason for this is fairly straightforward and stems from the nature of instruments used to assess distress and dysfunction. When given an instrument to fill out that measures psychological discomfort, most "normal" individuals will report relatively little difficulty. For example, if an individual is not particularly anxious, he or she can be expected to score low on a scale measuring anxiety. The consequence of this is that the scores of functional individuals tend to cluster at one end (the low end) of measures of distress, psychopathology, and the like. Very few functional individuals will generate high scores. Statistically, this means that for the functional population, there will be relatively little variability in the scores, and consequently the standard deviation will be relatively small. In contrast, there is much more room for variation in the scores of individuals from the dysfunctional population. This is because most instruments are designed to show a range of distress or psychopathology. Even in a clinical population, some individuals can be expected to report little or no distress (perhaps honestly, perhaps because of underreporting or minimizing). These individuals will yield low scores on an anxiety scale. Other individuals in a clinical population will report low levels of anxiety, with corresponding scores in the low-to-moderate range on an anxiety scale. Others will report a great deal of anxiety, reflected in high scores on the scale. An occasional individual with extremely high levels of anxiety might generate an extremely high anxiety score. The end result is that since the characteristic being measured varies over a considerable range, the standard deviation of scores in the dysfunctional population will often be larger than the standard deviation of scores in the functional population. This is not a problem. It simply reflects real variation of scores in the respective groups.

This pattern is clearly illustrated in the normative data reported previously for the Beck Depression Inventory (BDI). In Table 9.5 (see Chapter 9), standard deviations for groups in the general population, nondistressed groups, or nondepressed groups ranged from 4.5 to 5.8. In other words, the average standard deviation of scores on the BDI for the functional population seems to be around 5 points or a little higher. The standard deviation of scores from individuals who are depressed, however, ranged from 9.6 to 10.4 points. Although variability did not seem to increase as a function of level of depression, overall the BDI scores of depressed individuals seem to have an average standard deviation of around 10 points. This value is almost double the estimate for the functional population, illustrating the point that scores on a measure of psychological distress are more variable in dysfunctional than in functional populations.

There is not a clear-cut a rational basis for selecting one standard deviation over another, and there does not seem to be a generally accepted practice on the issue. To the extent that the population being assessed for outcome purposes is a clinical population, a case could be made for using the standard deviation of the dysfunctional population in the calculation of the RCI. In other words, the choice of an indicator of the amount of change necessary to be considered statistically reliable should be based on the typical variability of the measure in the population being assessed. On the other hand, the scores of a single individual are arguably unlikely to extend over the entire possible range of scores on the measure, and the true variability of the scores is arguably best reflected in the standard deviation of a relatively homogeneous group of individuals in the functional population. In some ways, the decision comes down to whether we wish to take a conservative or a liberal approach to the establishment of boundaries for reliable change. Use of the smaller standard deviation will result in a narrower range for the RCI, making it easier to conclude that there has been reliable improvement (or deterioration) in the individual client. Using the larger estimate for the standard deviation will result in a higher percentage of clients being classified as unchanged over the course of treatment.

Selecting a relatively large or small value for the standard deviation can have an effect on the RCI. For example, using the BDI and assuming a reliability coefficient of 0.85, the RCI is equal to 3.8 points if the standard deviation is assumed to be 5 points, but the RCI equals 7.6 points if the standard deviation is assumed to be 10 points. Similarly, using the Outcome Questionnaire (see Chapter 9), and again assuming a reliability coefficient equal to 0.85, the RCI is equal to 12.9 points if the standard deviation of the community sample is used, but equals 20.5 points if the standard deviation of a clinical sample is used. In practice, the difference between these estimates may not be as important as it might seem. Scores on the BDI range from 0 to more than 40, with depressed patients typically exhibiting scores of 20 points or higher. Over this range of scores, setting the RCI at 4 points or at 7 points will not necessarily make a great deal of difference in the overall outcome. A shift of 7 or 8 points on the BDI from before to after treatment is not uncommon; in fact, most therapists would consider such a shift minimal.

The practical implications of using the more liberal or the more conservative value for the standard deviation in calculating the RCI can be illustrated using the data from Table 9.3. Recall that this example from Chapter 9 reported an analysis of clinically significant change using the Outcome Questionnaire-45 (OQ-45). Reviewing the normative data for the OQ-45 presented in Chapter 9, the standard deviation of the functional population (a community sample) is approximately 17 points. Two dysfunctional populations are reported, an inpatient and an outpatient group. However, the standard deviations of both of these samples are very close and average about 27 points. To simplify calculations, we will assume that the reliability coefficient of the OQ-45 is equal to 0.90 (slightly smaller than the value of 0.93 used for the calculations in Chapter 9). Remembering that the formula for calculating the RCI is

$$\text{RCI} = 1.96\sqrt{2S^2(1 - r_{tt})}$$

liberal and conservative values can now be calculated. Using the standard deviation of 17 points from the community sample, the RCI is equal to 10.5 points. If the larger standard deviation of 27 points from the clinical populations is used, the RCI comes out to be 16.7 points. What difference do the two values make in classifying outcome? The impact can most clearly be seen by examining the data in Table 11.1. This table provides a frequency distribution of all of the change scores from the OQ-45 example in Chapter 9 (see Table 9.2). The first column lists all of the change scores in order from lowest to highest. (Note that a negative change score indicates that the client deteriorated over the course of treatment.) Overall, change scores for the sample ranged from −32 points (deterioration) to +66 points (improvement) from pre- to posttreatment assessment. Given this wide range of change scores, it should immediately be noted that the 6-point difference between the two RCIs just calculated is not particularly large. Using the narrower RCI of 10.5 points, based on the standard deviation of the community sample, a total of eight clients would be categorized as failing to show a reliable change over the course of treatment. This includes all clients with change scores between −3 and +9 in the table. If the RCI were set at the larger value of 16.7 points based on the standard deviation of the clinical populations, it would only affect the categorization of three clients. The two clients who had change scores of −13 would be reclassified as no change instead of deteriorated, and the single client who had a change score of 14 would be reclassified as no change instead of improved. Putting it another way, using the more liberal (i.e., narrower) RCI band, 8 out of 22 (36 percent) of the clients would be classified as showing no change. With the more conservative (i.e., broader) RCI band, 11 out of 22 (50 percent) of the sample would be categorized as failing to show a change over the course of treatment. Considering that of the three clients whose classification changed, two changed from deteriorated to no change, in this example there is some motivation for using the wider and more conservative estimate for the reliable change index!

DETERMINING THE CUTOFF FOR CLINICALLY SIGNIFICANT CHANGE

Once the RCI is established, the next major decision deals with setting the cutoff for clinically significant change. In theory, setting such a cutoff should be fairly straightforward: simply establish the most likely transition point on the scale to distinguish the scores of the functional and dysfunctional populations. In practice, of course, setting such a cutoff is not necessarily a clear-cut decision. Even in the original discussion by Jacobson and Truax (1991), three different approaches to setting the cutoff are described without a clear recommendation as to which is the best to use. Where to set the cut off for clinically significant change—or even whether to set such a cutoff—depends on the normative data available, the nature of the treatment population and setting, and the purposes of the clinician in conducting the analysis.

TABLE 11.1
Frequency Distribution of All Pre- to Posttreatment Change Scores on the OQ-45 for the Data Originally Presented in Table 9.2

Change Score	Frequency	Percent
32	1	4.5
−13	2	9.1
−3	1	4.5
1	1	4.5
2	1	4.5
3	1	4.5
5	2	9.1
8	1	4.5
9	1	4.5
14	1	4.5
17	1	4.5
19	1	4.5
22	1	4.5
25	1	4.5
28	1	4.5
31	2	9.1
38	1	4.5
41	1	4.5
66	1	4.5
Total	22	100.0

Negative numbers indicate deterioration.

The first decision is whether to establish a cutoff for return to normal functioning at all. This decision hinges mostly on the nature of the treatment population and the goals of the treatment. If the treatment population suffers from disorders or problems for which the treatment goal is a return to normal functioning, then setting a cutoff for clinically significant change makes sense. Such situations would likely include individuals seeking treatment for many of the common Axis I diagnostic categories like depression and anxiety. It could reasonably be argued that the goal of treatment for a client presenting with depression is to alleviate the depression to the point where the individual can function normally. A similar case could be made for the treatment of most anxiety-related disorders. It could also be argued that the goal of a return to normal functioning could be set in the context of couples therapy. The goal of such treatment is to help couples develop strategies for resolving issues such that the level of stress in the relationship is in the normative range. However, there are also many treatment populations for which the goal of return to normal functioning is either inappropriate or impossible.

In some situations, it seems appropriate not to set a cutoff for return to normal functioning. At the other extreme, it is also possible to consider setting more than one cutoff. This approach was suggested by Tingey, Lambert, Burlingame, and Hansen (1996), who argued that a client may pass through several stages on the way to a return to normal functioning. For example, one transition might be marked by a shift from severely disturbed to a moderate/mild level of disturbance. A severely disturbed client who made a reliable change from severely disturbed to moderately disturbed would be regarded as at least a partial success. At a later point, the same client may improve even further, and shift from a score typical of a moderately dysfunctional population to a score typical of the functional population. Tracking clinically significant change across these boundaries requires two cutoff scores. The first marks the transition from a severely dysfunctional population to a more moderately dysfunctional population; the second marks the transition from moderate dysfunction to normal functioning. Assuming normative data are available from these three populations, setting cutoff scores for clinically significant change can be accomplished using the procedures outlined previously. For additional details on using this approach, see Tingey et al. (1996) and Lambert and Lambert (1999).

Assuming that one or more cutoffs for clinically significant change are to be established, we will next consider the more detailed process of actually using normative data to set such a cutoff, focusing on the nature of the normative data available. In principle, the cutoff score should be placed at the boundary that most clearly separates the functional population's distribution of scores from the dysfunctional population's distribution of scores. The optimal placement of a cutoff score depends on both the shape of the two distributions and the degree of overlap of the two distributions.

The optimal pattern for establishing a clear cutoff is when there is relatively little overlap between the distribution of scores for the functional and the dysfunctional populations. In this situation, the means of the functional and dysfunctional distributions may be separated by three or even four standard deviations. This kind of optimal pattern is illustrated in Figure 11.1. As is evident in the graph, individuals in the functional population (for example, a community sample) tend to have low scores on the instrument. Very few individuals in the functional population have high scores on the instrument, yielding a curve with relatively little variability. Scores for individuals in the dysfunctional population are shifted to the right on the graph, consistent with the psychological distress this population is experiencing. Since the amount of distress varies considerably in this group, the variability of the scores for the dysfunctional population is larger than that for the functional population. In a typical instrument, scores for the dysfunctional population would also show a positive skew, reflecting the scores of a few individuals who report extremely high levels of distress.

If the distribution of scores for the functional and dysfunctional populations follows a pattern similar to that illustrated in Figure 11.1, a good case can be made for defining the cutoff score relative to the functional population. Recall from Chapter 8 that this is Cutoff b in the system suggested by Jacobson and Truax (1991). Although the criterion for Cutoff b is often a very liberal criterion that is easy to meet, in this case, given the separation of the two populations, relatively few members of either population will be misclassified. This example is similar to the analysis conducted on the Beck Depression Inventory in Chapter 9, in which the recommended cutoff of 13 points fell almost exactly two standard deviations above the mean of the functional population, but was well below the typical score of the depressed population.

Unfortunately, many instruments show a greater degree of overlap than illustrated in Figure 11.1. Although the functional distribution is clearly differentiated from the dysfunctional distribution, the distributions are separated only by about two standard deviations. This pattern is illustrated in Figure 11.2. Note that using a crite-

Figure 11.1

Distribution of scores for functional and dysfunctional populations when there is clear separation between the two. The cutoff is set at two standard deviations above the mean of the functional population.

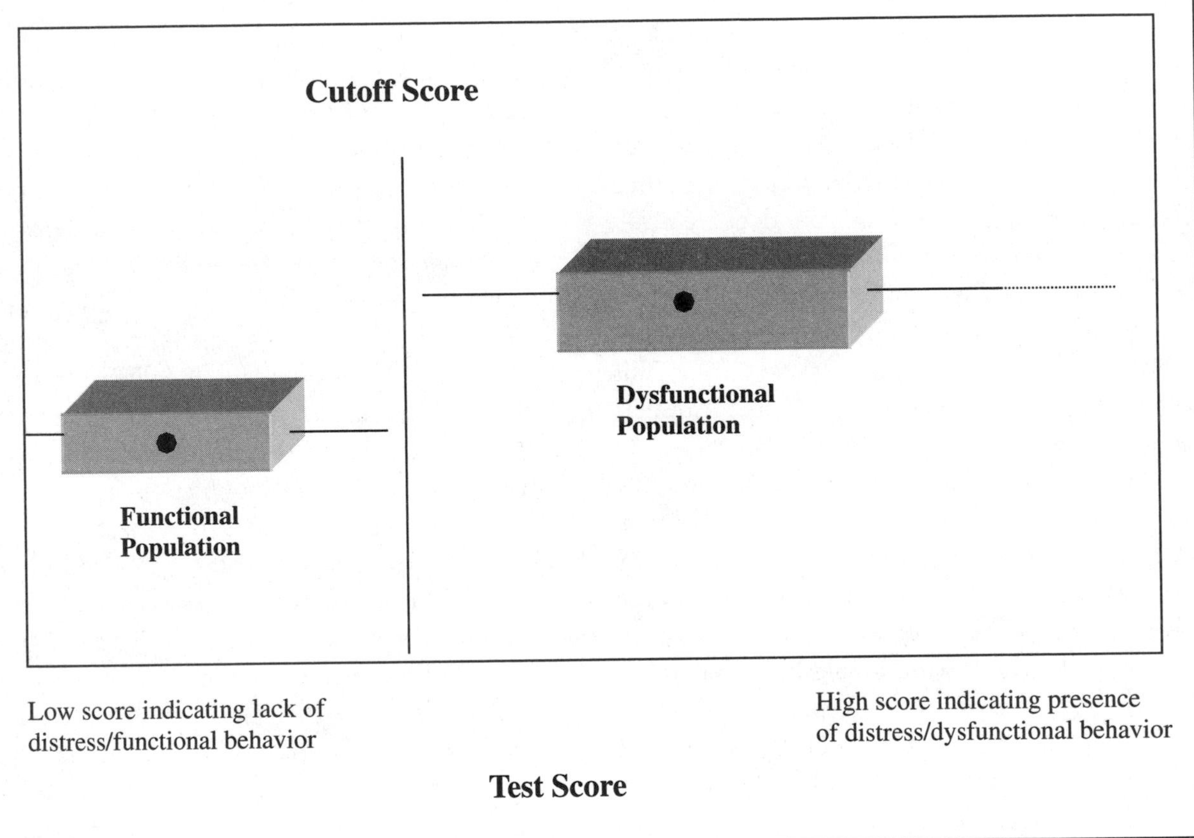

rion of two standard deviations above the mean of the functional population would place the cutoff far to the right, close to the mean of the dysfunctional population. This would not be an acceptable cutoff, since half or more of the dysfunctional group would be classified as recovered before treatment started. Similarly, setting a cutoff at two standard deviations below the mean of the dysfunctional population would mean that the cutoff would be near the mean of the functional population. This cutoff would require clients to improve to the point of scoring below more than 50 percent of the functional population before they could be classified as recovered. Given the degree of overlap of the two distributions, both of the two-standard-deviation criteria suggested by Jacobson and Truax (1991) are clearly unworkable. An intermediate cutoff must be established. In this example, a cutoff approximately one standard deviation from either mean seems to be most satisfactory. This cutoff also corresponds fairly closely to Cutoff c suggested by Jacobson and Truax (1991) (see Chapter 8), where the cutoff is placed halfway between the means of the functional and dysfunctional populations. The general pattern illustrated in Figure 11.2 is very similar to that described for both the OQ-45 and the SCL-90-R in Chapter 9.

Instruments that show more overlap than illustrated in Figure 11.2 are questionable for use as outcome measures, at least if a clinically significant change analysis is anticipated. As the distributions of the functional and dysfunctional populations overlap more and more, it is more and more difficult to determine whether a particular score comes from an individual suffering from psychological

Figure 11.2

Illustration of setting a cutoff score when there is considerable overlap between the functional and dysfunctional distributions. In this case, the cutoff is set one standard deviation from the means of both the functional and dysfunctional populations.

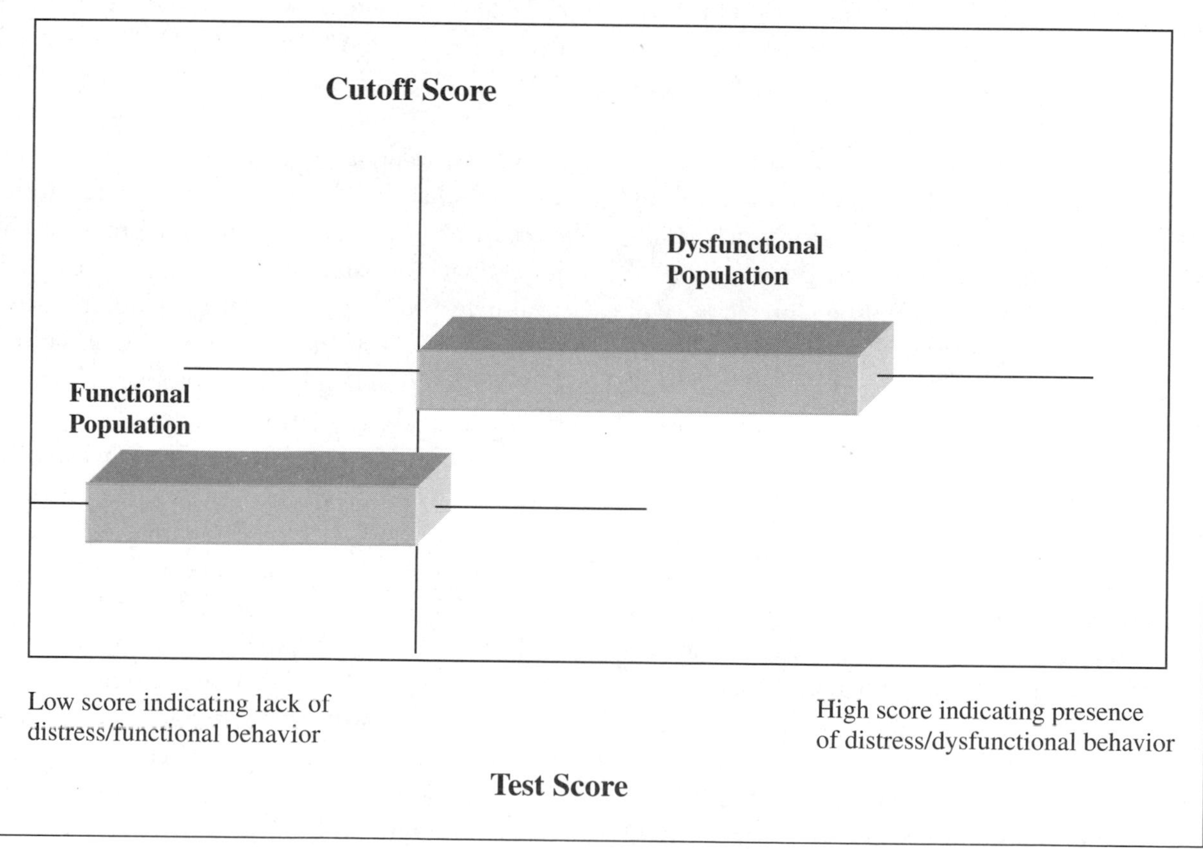

distress or whether the score might well be obtained by an individual in the general population who is not reporting symptoms of abnormal psychological distress or problematic behavior. In these situations, the instrument is not useful for discriminating between a functional and dysfunctional population, and should not be used for conducting normative outcome assessments.

Thus far we have considered examples where normative data are available for both the functional and dysfunctional populations. What if, however, normative data have only been collected from clinical populations? This is not uncommon, since most outcome measures are designed for use with a dysfunctional population of some kind. If an instrument is administered routinely, over a period of time a large number of scores may be obtained. These scores provide the basis for norms for various clinical populations. However, it is not as easy to obtain a set of scores from individuals who do not present for psychological or psychiatric treatment. Obtaining a sample from the general community can be time-consuming and expensive. Although samples may more easily be obtained from certain populations such as college students or prison inmates, these are special groups whose scores may not be representative of the more typical "functional population."

This situation is illustrated in Figure 11.3. When the distribution of scores of the functional population is unknown, the only reference point for setting a cutoff is the distribution of scores from the dysfunctional population. Certainly it would be possible to set a cutoff at one or two standard deviations below the mean of the dysfunctional population (Cutoff a according to Jacobson & Truax, 1991). This is risky, however. One possible scenario is that both the functional population and the dysfunctional population frequently register high scores, so that there is considerable overlap between the two distributions. In this case the use of the instrument as an outcome measure is questionable. It is true that this situation is probably unlikely with most clinical instruments. If the instrument really is assessing problematic behavior or distressing symptoms, individuals in the general population who are not seeking treatment may be considered to be unlikely to endorsc items on it. However, this cannot be determined for certain unless the appropriate normative data are collected.

A different situation is more commonly encountered when normative data for the functional population are not available and an attempt is made to set the cutoff relative to the dysfunctional population mean. With some instruments, scores in the functional population may be assumed to be close to zero, with average scores in the dysfunctional population ranging considerably higher. An example of such an instrument is the Addiction Severity Index (ASI) (McClellan, Kushner, et al., 1992; McClellan, Luborsky, Woody, & O'Brien, 1980). This instrument is designed to assess drug and alcohol use, and has been used extensively for initial assessment, to monitor treatment progress, and to evaluate outcome in chemical dependency treatment programs. Subscales include measures of alcohol use, drug use, employment difficulties, legal difficulties, family/social problems, medical problems, and psychiatric problems.

Administering the ASI requires an extensive interview by a trained rater, making its use problematic in some settings. However, the instrument has demonstrated good reliability and validity (e.g., Cacciola, Koppenhaver, McKay, & Alterman, 1999; Parker, Daleiden, & Simpson, 1999), and is useful with a population in which home self-administered self-report scales of alcohol and drug use may be expected to be unreliable. Scores on the various scales of the ASI can range from zero, indicating no problems or diffi-

Figure 11.3

Problems with setting a cutoff score when normative data from the functional population are not available. If the functional population is concentrated to the extreme right, leaving the dysfunctional population does not necessarily imply returning to normal functioning.

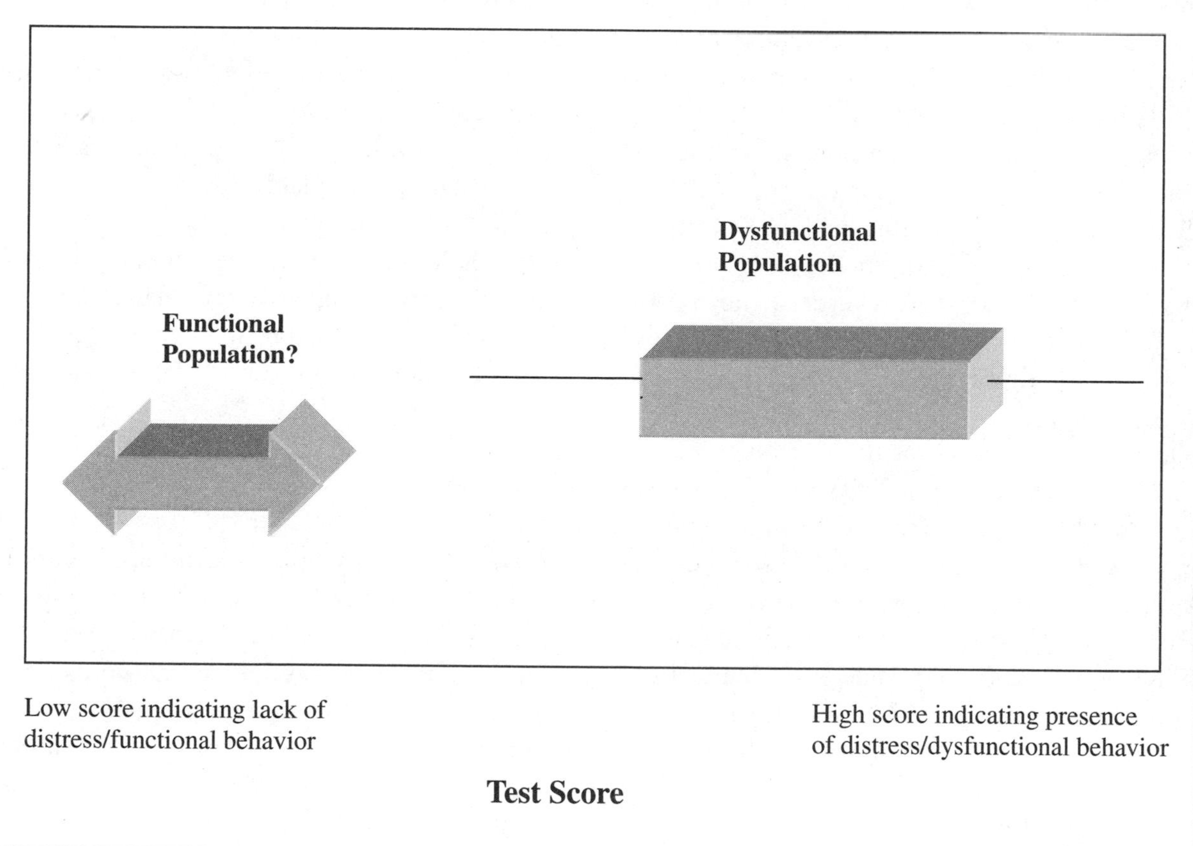

culties in that area, to much higher numbers indicating considerable problems in that area. It could reasonably be assumed that individuals who are not chemically dependent would report very few if any chemically related problems in these areas. In other words, scores in the functional population presumably should be close to zero, although normative data for the functional population have not been reported. This situation can be illustrated in Figure 11.3 if it is assumed that scores for the functional population have little variability and cluster close to a score of zero, to the extreme left of the graph. In this case, there is a considerable gap between typical scores from the dysfunctional population and scores from the functional population.

It may be tempting to set a criterion for return to normal functioning relative to the mean and standard deviations reported for the dysfunctional (currently chemically dependent) population. The difficulty with this approach is that such a cutoff may still be some distance from a score of zero, presumed to be necessary for a return to normal functioning. In other words, just because an individual moves one or even two standard deviations below the mean of the dysfunctional population does not guarantee that that person's score is now within the boundaries of the functional population. The higher the typical scores among the dysfunctional population, the more of an issue this will be. Jacobson, Roberts, Berns, and McGlinchey (1999) argued that in cases where there is little or no overlap between scores of the functional population and scores of the dysfunctional population, extreme caution must be exercised before setting a cutoff relative to the mean of the dysfunctional population. In doing so, the clinician runs the risk of mistakenly assuming that just because a client's score is no longer typical of the dysfunctional population, the client has necessarily obtained a score that is typical of the functional population. It is very possible that such an individual has improved, perhaps considerably, but still is experiencing significant difficulty, and cannot be judged to have recovered.

A final minor complication regarding the selection of cutoff scores has to do with possible differences in normative distributions for different demographic groups. This is most likely to be the case with gender. On some instruments (for example, the SCL-90-R), there are small but consistent differences between average scores for men and for women. Usually women from both functional and dysfunctional populations report greater distress than men do. In these circumstances, it is appropriate to use different norms for each gender. This means that the cutoff score for return to normal functioning would be set slightly lower for males than for females. However, it is likely that the gender differences are fairly small relative to the reliable change index. Hence, a good case can also be made for setting the cutoff based on the mean score for the entire sample and not being concerned about gender differences. For instruments on which there are not consistent gender differences, this is not an issue.

Other demographic differences may also need to be considered, particularly those relating to racially or ethnically diverse populations. If normative data are available for different populations, cutoff scores can be set accordingly. If, as is often the case, normative data broken down by racial or ethnic group are not available, appropriate caution must be taken in interpreting test scores for individuals from diverse populations.

DATA ANALYSIS

As long as the analysis of clinically significant change is considered on a case-by-case basis, the question of more complex statistical analysis of the data is not relevant. In other words, if the analysis is limited to considering whether John Doe or Jane Doe has shown no change, improvement, or recovery over the course of treatment, conclusions and analysis are made on an individual basis. These kinds of analyses and conclusions are often called *ideographic,* as they focus on and are limited to the individual case under consideration. To ask about the possible change in the status of a *particular* client from before to after treatment is to make an ideographic inquiry. If pre- and posttest scores are collected from a number of clients, it becomes possible to subject the group data to more complex statistical procedures. These kinds of analyses are called *nomo-*

thetic, and they focus on reaching conclusions about the data set as a whole. To ask whether on the *average* clients improved from pre- to posttreatment is to make a nomothetic inquiry.

Thus far the analysis of clinically significant change articulated in this book has focused on a few descriptive nomothetic analyses. Specifically, statistics were calculated that represented the percentage of clients falling into the categories of deteriorated, no change, improved, or recovered. The number of clients falling into these categories was illustrated graphically in the kinds of illustrations used repeatedly in previous chapters. Once sufficient data have been collected, however, the question of whether there is a significant difference between the pre- and the posttest scores may arise. This is an inferential statistical question, the answer to which requires conducting further statistical analysis. Specifically, one of the kinds of statistical tests covered in most introductory statistics courses needs to be applied to the data.

It is not mandatory to use tests of statistical significance to analyze outcome data. As discussed in Chapter 8, there is an important distinction between statistical significance and clinical significance. The focus of this book is on clinically significant change, not statistically significant change. It is appropriate, however, to conduct significance tests on data comparing pre- and posttreatment outcome assessment. The statistical question asked in such an analysis is the likelihood that the observed difference between the pretest mean score and the posttest mean score would have occurred under the assumption of the null hypothesis, which describes the distribution of differences that might have occurred by chance. The more common way the question is stated is whether there is a statistically significant difference between the mean of the pretest scores and the mean of the posttest scores.

The examples of an analysis of clinically significant change illustrated in this text are suitable for tests of statistical significance. In selecting an appropriate test, first consider the scale of measurement of the data themselves. Scores on standardized tests constitute what is termed *interval data;* hence parametric statistical tests are appropriate. Second, consider that in an analysis of clinically significant change, data are collected repeatedly from the same individual. Comparisons are thus being made within subjects (as opposed to between subjects). Consequently, statistical tests for repeated measures on the same individual are appropriate. In the simplest case where the means of pre- and posttest scores are being compared, the easiest statistical test to calculate is the paired *t*-test. If comparisons are made across three or more assessment periods (e.g., pretest, posttest, and follow-up), the traditional statistical test is the one-way repeated-measures analysis of variance. Details of how to conduct these analyses can be found in most statistics textbooks. These tests can also be calculated using most spreadsheets or other data handling and statistical analysis software.

To illustrate how to use a statistical test to analyze outcome data, we will analyze the data set from Table 9.6, illustrating the use of the BDI for the analysis of clinically significant change. Since only two means are being compared (pretest versus posttest), the paired *t*-test is an appropriate statistical procedure to use. The paired *t*-test is based on the change scores, or the difference between the pre- and the posttests. The necessary statistical information to conduct the paired *t*-test includes

N (total number of individuals) = 160
S_{diff} (standard deviation of the difference scores) = 12.29
$Mean_{Pre}$ (mean score at pretest) = 16.43
$Mean_{Post}$ (mean score at posttest) = 11.36

The value of the t statistic is given by

$$t = (\text{Mean}_{\text{Pre}} - \text{Mean}_{\text{Post}}) / (S_{\text{diff}} / \sqrt{N}) = (16.43 - 11.36) / (12.29 / \sqrt{160}) = 5.07 / 0.97 = 5.224$$

This value of t is statistically significant, $t(158) = 5.224$, $P < 0.001$. In other words, the assumption of chance differences is an unlikely explanation for the observed 5-point decrease in BDI scores from before to after treatment. Again, the reader is referred to any standard statistics text for additional details about these calculations.

A test of significance provides information about the likelihood that random chance factors can account for the observed differences between the pre- and posttest means. However, a statistically significant difference does not necessarily imply a large or important difference. The size or magnitude of the difference is better shown using an effect size statistic. Effect size statistics are typically reported in metanalytic studies of outcome research, as described in Chapter 1. The indicator of effect size typically reported in treatment outcome studies is the d statistic. The value of d gives the relative separation of the pre- and posttreatment means in standard deviation units. It is easily calculated by the formula

$$d = (\text{Mean}_{\text{Pre}} - \text{Mean}_{\text{Post}}) / S$$

or the difference between the pre- and posttest means divided by the standard deviation of the scores. In this example, d is given by

$$d = (16.43 - 11.36) / 9.0 = 0.55$$

In other words, approximately one-half of a standard deviation separates the pre- and posttest mean scores. This value is somewhat lower than usual for those found in treatment outcome studies, especially for comparisons within subjects (Lipsey & Wilson, 1993), although it represents a real and positive overall improvement in scores over the course of treatment.

The calculation of statistical significance tests and effect size statistics may be a useful adjunct to an analysis of clinically significant change. Such calculation may be especially convincing to individuals who are not familiar with the clinically significant change methodology but are conversant with more traditional statistical methods. At the same time, the clinician must remember that demonstrating a statistically significant improvement for the average client over the course of treatment does not necessarily imply that the average individual showed a clinically significant improvement, and in fact provides no information about the amount of the improvement. The calculation of an effect size statistic provides more information about the magnitude of the change than does a significance test. However, effect size statistics still provide information only about the aggregate amount of change for all clients in a sample. To obtain information about individual clients, the kinds of clinically significant change procedures described in this text must be employed.

SOURCES OF BIAS IN INTERPRETING CHANGE SCORES

The procedures for analyzing clinically significant change described in this book rely on the interpretation of changes in test scores over time. Assuming that clinically significant change is observed, at least for some clients, the next issue that often arises is the attribution of a reason for the change. In other words, why did the client demonstrate a positive change in test scores from before to after treatment? The primary goal of conducting an analysis of clinically significant change is to show that reliable improvement in functioning has been demonstrated for a client or a group of clients. This is a descriptive conclusion, merely stating that client John Doe has improved (or recovered), or that 65 percent of the clients have shown improvement (or recovery) over the course of treatment. What the methodology developed in this book does not allow the clinician to do is make a clearly definitive statement about what caused the change. To answer the causal question in an unequivocal manner requires experimental methodologies, including the use of a no-treatment control group. In other words, research aimed at determining whether clients who receive treatment fare better than they would if they did not receive treatment involves the kinds of efficacy research or large-scale effectiveness research strategies described in Chapter 1 of this text. In the absence of more methodologically demanding research designs, it is never clear that a client improved solely because of treatment. The possibility always remains that the client might have improved anyway, or that factors other than the treatment itself were responsible for all or part of the improvement.

The inability to make causal conclusions about treatment efficacy is not a failure of or a flaw in the analyses recommended in this book. Reaching cause and effect conclusions about treatment outcome is not the goal of either the individual or the normative approaches to outcome assessment described in this text. The individual clinician is not expected to prove that every client in his or her care improved strictly because of the clinician's interventions. Therapists know better than that! However, clinicians can legitimately be asked to evaluate whether clients in their care are showing change over the course of treatment. It is reasonable to assume that for most clients at least some of the improvement seen over the course of treatment can be attributed to the effects of the therapeutic intervention. This does assume that the clinician is competent and is using interventions recognized as effective and efficacious by the profession. A therapist who is using new and unproven methods of treatment cannot be as certain that his or her methods are efficacious.

It is important to recognize that factors other than the treatment itself can account for client changes over time, and it is worthwhile to briefly consider some of these kinds of factors. In experimental research methodology, the tendency for scores to improve on their own from before to after treatment is termed *regression to the mean.* This is a statistical phenomenon related to the tendency for individuals who score extremely high or low on a test to score closer to the mean if the test is repeated at a later time. This phenomenon is often cited as a threat to the internal validity of quasi-experimental research designs comparing scores from before and after treatment (Cook & Campbell, 1979). The concern is that the artifact of regression-to-the-mean effects will be misinterpreted as changes due to the treatment. Although most standard research methodologies warn against mistaking regression-to-the-mean effects for treatment effects (Kazdin, 1997; Pedhazur & Schmelkin, 1991), others (see Speer, 1998) have argued that regression-to-the-mean effects are not as pernicious as has been warned.

Our concern here is not so much with possible statistical artifacts as with the real reasons why clients' scores are changing over time. Since the goal of the outcome assessment is not to attempt to isolate the treatment as the independent variable that is causing client change, many of the traditional threats to internal validity are not of particular concern. However, clinically we are concerned about why people are changing. It is likely that some improvement in test scores would occur over time even in the absence of treatment. This is because clients tend to seek treatment when they are feeling worst. Some clients may also exaggerate symptoms at the beginning of treatment. At the end of treatment, there may be a similar but opposite tendency to report feeling better. Speer (1998) described these kinds of factors as "hello" and "goodbye" effects. He observed these phenomena at a psychiatric inpatient unit where patients were administered the SCL-90 at intake and discharge. At intake, many clients were desperate and reported extreme symptoms, perhaps partly to make sure they received care. At the end of treatment, most patients were anxious to be discharged, and hence underreported their symptoms. The result was an extremely dramatic reduction in SCL-90 scores from before to after treatment. Some of this change was undoubtedly due to the treatment received. However, Speer (1998) also argued that some of the change must be attributed to the hello and goodbye effects described. While it may not be possible to completely eliminate hello and goodbye effects, they can be minimized by carefully instructing clients to be honest and careful when they fill out the forms.

SUMMARY

There are many reasons why clients might improve (or fail to improve) over the course of treatment. Outcome assessment procedures can only provide information about the amount of change occurring, or whether reliable change is occurring at all. These procedures do not tell the clinician why the change is occurring. The analysis of reasons for change in client behavior remains in the province of the clinical skill and interpretive ability of the clinician.

This is arguably the most technical chapter in a book in which every effort has been made to remain nontechnical. In the course of conducting an analysis of clinically significant change in ax particular setting, numerous decisions must be made. The thrust of this chapter is that these decisions are usually best undertaken based on clinical considerations. In most cases, a statistics textbook or a research methods text will not provide the solution to the problem. A careful reading of the material in this chapter should provide hints, guideposts, and reassurance for the clinician conducting an analysis of clinically significant change. The chapter is designed more to help clinicians find their own answers to their questions than to provide ready-made answers for every contingency.

IV

INTEGRATION

12

INTEGRATING INDIVIDUAL AND NORMATIVE OUTCOME MEASURES

Many of the current outcome systems emphasize either individual or normative measures, but not necessarily both. Each procedure requires different data-gathering techniques, and different types of information are collected. Individual approaches make use of the treatment plan objectives as outcome measures, whereas normative measures incorporate standardized pretest and posttest (and sometimes intermediate) measures. Because different procedures are used and different types of information are gathered in normative and individual outcome measures, results can appear confusing. Thus, results may not be valid or reliable due to the procedures chosen, rather than to the actual state of clinical progress. Although results may appear discrepant at times, a clearer clinical picture is presented when both methods are incorporated.

The procedures in Parts III and IV may appear unrelated. Depending on the purposes of the outcome assessment, the practitioner may choose to use either or both methods. If the aim of the outcome assessment is primarily to track the progress of individual clients, the individualized procedures may be sufficient. If the aim is to provide an overall program evaluation, the normative procedures are more useful, since each individual client can be assessed using the same instrument. However, the authors strongly recommend the use of both normative and individualized approaches. These complement each other to provide a more complete picture of client progress. In reality, the two approaches are interdependent and, used together, provide a comprehensive evaluation. In this chapter we describe ways to integrate normative and individualized outcome measures and discuss ways to resolve possible discrepancies between the two methods.

An Analogy

The integration of individual and normative measures is analogous to describing a student's progress from the perspective of day-to-day classroom activities as described by the teacher versus the child's progress on national standardized tests. The child's day-to-day behaviors provide insight into his or her specific strengths and weaknesses within his or her immediate environment. A wide range of behaviors within the child's social, academic, maturational, physical, and emotional functioning can be monitored by the teacher and others involved in the child's life. Ultimately the teacher assesses day-to-day performance in the form of grades and behavior ratings at the end of each term. These cumulative ratings are based on the exams, assignments, behavioral observations, and other classroom contributions accumulated over the course of the term. Periodically, the child is also administered standardized achievement tests that are based on academics of children nationally. These tests provide summative information to compare the child's progress to that of a reference group, such as grade equivalents and age equivalents. However, they do not portray personality variables, level of motivation, social skills, or specific indices of personality, nor do they reflect day-to-day observation of the child's behavior and assessment of his or her performance. It should also be noted that most typically the standardized tests are referenced when evaluating the educational effort of an entire school, since only the standardized tests allow for school-to-school comparisons. In other words, standardized instruments are of most concern for program evaluation purposes in which the individual is compared to a larger group.

When the child's school records are scrutinized by others, both the standardized test scores and the ongoing behaviors are considered. For example, parents of a child applying to transfer to another school would be asked to provide both standardized achievement test scores and ongoing progress indicators such as grades, school activities, and teachers' recommendations as part of the application. It is possible to score low in one of the two areas, but adequately in the other. For example, a child may go through 12 years of schooling with adequate classroom performance, but fare poorly on standardized tests, or vice versa. The integration and comparison of the two types of measures is helpful in understanding the child's strengths and weaknesses.

This analogy is comparable to normative and individual mental health outcome measures. Although results are typically correlated, there is no guarantee that scores in both types of measures will be compatible due to individual differences.

Integrating Conflicting Results

There are several possible categories of outcome for both normative and individual outcome measures. At various points in this text, client outcome as been categorized as recovered, improved, unchanged, or deteriorated. For purposes of this discussion, these categories will be simplified into two: (1) improved (including both improved and recovered according to clinically significant change criteria), and (2) not improved (including both the no change and deteriorated categories). In the first case, the outcome measures clearly indicate that the treatment to date has been successful. Although additional treatment may still be needed, the outcome so far has been positive. In the second category, treatment has not been successful. The client has either not improved or gotten worse. The outcome is negative, and a change in treatment strategy is likely warranted.

Table 12.1 simplifies outcome results into a more easily understood strategy. Normative results are listed horizontally, with the client categorized as either improved/recovered (improved) or as no change/deteriorated (not improved). The results of the individual outcome assessment are listed vertically, using the same categories of either improved or not improved. Results numbered 1 and 4 represent consistent outcomes, where both normative and individualized measures yielded

TABLE 12.1
Integrating Individual and Normative Outcome Measures

		Normative Measures	
		Recovered/ Improved	**No Change/ Deteriorated**
Individual Measures	**Recovered/ Improved**	1	2
	No Change/ Deteriorated	3	4

similar conclusions. Results numbered 2 and 3 represent inconsistent outcomes, where the normative measure suggested one conclusion and the individualized measure another. This situation requires further clarification and discussion.

Outcome 1: Improvement in Both Normative and Individual Measures

This outcome is the most desirable outcome of mental health therapy. It provides both objective and subjective evidence that positive outcomes have taken place. There exists evidence that the client has improved when compared to both standardized measures and changes in specific problem areas defined as the goals of treatment. Since both measures yield a consistent outcome, interpretation is straightforward.

Outcome 2: Lack of Improvement in Normative Measures / Improvement in Individual Measures

Deterioration in normative measures suggests that the client's overall functioning in a given area has not been successfully addressed in treatment. Although noted improvements have been demonstrated in the individualized measures, it is possible that the treatment plan did not adequately identify sufficient problem areas. Perhaps the areas of concern that were treated were helpful, but they were not the client's core issues. Thus, the major areas of concern were left untreated. This client may be a candidate for long-term therapy.

Outcome 3: Improvement in Normative Measures / Lack of Improvement in Individual Measures

Normative improvement suggests an increase in the client's overall condition when compared on standardized tests at the beginning of treatment and at a later date. The more valid and reliable the measure used, the greater the confidence that improvements have taken place. Lack of improvement on individual measures suggests that the outcome indicators selected in the beginning and throughout therapy may not accurately depict the client's areas of need to restore adequate functioning. When the normative tests suggest improvement, but the individual measures indicate decline, it is possible that improvements have taken place, but the treatment plan needs revisions. Other possibilities may include, but are not limited to, misdiagnosis, noncompliance with treatment, and decreases in environmental stressors, but not change in behaviors.

Some clients improve as a function of time. In this case, scores on standardized tests could improve due to decreases in outside factors that led to undesirable subjective feelings. Individual outcome measures do not change, because the client has made no changes in measurable behaviors.

Outcome 4: Lack of Improvement in Both Normative and Individual Measures

Several concerns are noted when tests and measurements indicate lack of improvement on both normative and individual measures. Accordingly, neither standardized tests nor specific evidence from treatment documentation indicate that the client is progressing. There may be problems in the diagnosis, misunderstanding of the problem areas, inappropriate treatment, noncompliance, or unsatisfactory treatment. In any of these scenarios, major changes must be made in the treatment process, ranging from increasing the scope of services to termination, depending on the reason for the outcomes indicated. Even though the test results are consistent in this case, the outcome is clearly a cause for concern.

Troubleshooting Discrepancies between Normative and Individual Outcome Measures

There are no simple means of resolving discrepancies or contradictions in clinical outcomes. In clinical practice, few cases have clear-cut results in outcome assessment. Although some outcome indicators suggest clinical success, others may lead to the appearance of no clinical gains. Such findings are to be expected. However, when discrepancies exist between the normative and individual outcome indicators, interpretation is more clouded. The following suggestions are provided to help resolve such concerns.

Consider the Magnitude of the Discrepancy

No measure is perfectly reliable, and scores that barely meet or fail to meet an arbitrary criterion may be explained by measurement error. Assume that the individualized outcome measures clearly indicate improvement. Assume further that the normative outcome instrument fails to meet the improved category by a single point, and thus the client is classified as having experienced no reliable change. Given that the overall pattern of results suggests improvement, the fact that the normative measures missed classification as improved is not that critical. This client can be judged to have improved. Criteria for reliable and for clinically significant change cannot be applied by rote. Always consider the overall clinical picture of the client.

Review the Diagnosis

Once again, rule in and rule out other diagnostic possibilities based on information obtained during the course of treatment that may not have been available in the initial sessions. Consider a second opinion. An incorrect diagnosis with outcome measures that are concordant with the diagnosis but not with the client's true problem areas will lead to confusing results. It is crucial to spend sufficient time with the client to correctly rule in and rule out diagnostic possibilities. A questionable diagnosis can lead to ineffective treatment. All provisional and rule-out diagnoses should be resolved quickly.

For example, a client with a diagnosis of Major Depressive Disorder might have a treatment plan that describes goals and objectives in terms of alleviating vegetative symptoms of depression and increasing positive physical and social behaviors. If the correct diagnosis should have been Bipolar Affective Disorder, it is possible that behaviors associated with Bipolar Affective Disorder may interfere with specific treatment plan outcome indicators and standardized testing, thus yielding confusing results.

Discuss Other Potential Problem Areas with the Client

If normative measures suggest problem areas that have not been addressed in therapy, discuss them with the client. Perhaps there are areas of low insight or denial. Perhaps the therapist missed some important information.

Review the Client's Knowledge and Understanding of the Treatment Plan

The best treatment plan success rates in goal attainment are achieved when the client clearly understands the purpose and the process by which to attain the goals. Vague treatment plan goals and objectives lead to vague outcomes. Further evaluate for cognitive deficits that were not readily apparent in the initial interview. Rule out organic factors leading to cognitive deficits.

Examine the Incremental Steps in the Treatment Plan Objectives

Perhaps the focus of treatment has been too demanding for the client, leading to relapse or lack of progress. Consider placing fewer demands on the client. For some clients the reverse may be true; that is, they are not sufficiently challenged or motivated to change, and therefore progress does not take place.

Review Selection of Normative Outcome Measures

Examine the normative outcome measures to determine whether they are the most appropriate tests to provide evidence of outcomes for the client's problem areas.

Review Whether the Normative and Individual Outcome Measures Address Similar Constructs

It is not unusual for a clinician to assume that a normative test measures a construct that it is not, in fact, purported to measure. Perhaps the wrong test was used.

Double-Check the Standardized Test Procedures Employed

Common errors include incorrect scoring, incorrect use of norms, and improper interpretive strategies. It is unethical for clinicians to use tests if they have no training or supervised experience in the administration, scoring, and interpretation of those tests.

Consider Secondary Gain or Malingering as Possibilities

Some clients gain attention and sympathy and may be relieved of certain duties in the activities of daily living or gain in other areas when they present with mental health problems. To them, successful therapy denotes losing rewards they are receiving due to their mental health condition. Although they may believe they want to get better, there is no clear reward for doing so.

Malingerers purposely feign psychopathology to avoid a punishment (e.g., legal consequences) or gain a reward (e.g., disability benefits). In such cases, testing and individual measures are purposely sabotaged to avoid the appearance of progress. Such clients may be especially prone to "faking good" on standardized measures with high face validity.

Any of these concerns may affect outcome measures. The authors advise clinicians to refrain from arbitrarily assigning one of the aforementioned reasons when outcome measures do not demonstrate effective treatment. Sometimes treatment can be ineffective or even harmful to a client. Outcome measures are intended to benefit the client, not solely the therapist; therefore, negative outcomes can be viewed in a positive manner if they provide evidence leading to a change in the course of treatment.

Form 10 gives examples of both normative and individualized outcome results. Both standardized tests and specific individual treatment plan objectives are evaluated. Form 11 provides an example of a brief report for the client John Adams, whose paperwork has provided examples throughout this text. Although this client did not fully meet every treatment goal, he reached a level of mental health functioning in which services were no longer medically necessary. That is, by the end of treatment, he no longer suffered from the functional impairments he experienced in the beginning of treatment.

SUMMARY

The assessment of outcome is a part of the clinical process. It is important not to lose sight of that perspective. This book is about clinical practice. It is not about how to conduct research, at least not research in a traditional sense. The function of the methods described in this text is to determine whether individual clients are getting better on a case-by-case basis. They are not designed to prove whether or not treatment works, or to clarify which aspect of treatment is producing positive change. Assessment is a complex process. Valid and reliable measurement necessitates statistical reasoning and application.

When measuring outcomes, practitioners need to keep the clinical context and setting in mind. Decisions about such things as where to set criteria for clinically significant change, which behaviors to track over the course of treatment, and how to interpret ambiguous outcome statistics must all be considered in the context of the actual clinical setting. This book is not a cookbook with ready-made answers. It does not provide procedures that can be applied mechanically, that automatically fit every client without adjustment, or that are universally applicable in every clinical setting. The authors encourage clinicians to modify the forms, adjust the criteria, and select the measures that best meet their needs in their own settings.

One size of outcome assessment does not fit all, and outcome assessment procedures cannot easily be bought off the rack. Clinicians must be able to fit the procedure to the situation at hand, similarly to the way they employ therapeutic techniques or develop treatment plans. Clinicians select and interpret assessment and diagnostic instruments based on the population being tested and the purpose of the assessment. Similarly, outcome assessment procedures must fit the clinical settings in which they are applied. The authors have provided the tools, procedures, and examples to aid in that process.

FORM 10 TREATMENT OUTCOMES SUMMARY

Client *John Adams* Chart # ______

Date began *3-15-00* Date ended *6-27-00* Total # of sessions ______

___Therapy complete (as per estimated # of sessions) ___Therapy prematurely terminated

Comments ______

Normative Outcome Measures

(1) Test *SCL-90*

Subscale	Reliable change index	Cutoff score	Baseline score	End score	Change score	Outcome
GSI	*0.34*	*0.47*	*1.21*	*0.40*	*0.81*	*Recovered*
SOM	*0.34*	*0.62*	*1.01*	*0.65*	*0.36*	*Improved*
INT	*0.35*	*0.56*	*1.24*	*0.81*	*0.43*	*No change*
DBP	*0.36*	*0.59*	*2.11*	*0.55*	*1.56*	*Recovered*
ANX	*0.33*	*0.49*	*0.99*	*0.54*	*0.45*	*Improved*

Comments *Used subscales most relevant; pretest scores were functional on the other scales.*

(2) Test *BDI*

Subscale	Reliable change index	Cutoff score	Baseline score	End score	Change score	Outcome
BDI	*9*	*13*	*30*	*12*	*18*	*Recovered*

Comments ____

____

Use additional sheets for more tests.

Treatment Plan Goals/Objectives Progress (which are used as outcomes indicators)

Reasonable potential represents the expected level of goal attainment if therapy was completed in the amount of time intended for treatment.

Most recent objective represents the current objective level (in that therapy was terminated before treatment focused on the reasonable potential level).

Percentage attained represents the percentage of progress toward a specific behavioral objective. It is determined by the termination score minus the baseline score, divided by the reasonable amount of progress (the objective minus the baseline score). For example, a client enters therapy with a problem area of going to school only 1 day per week. A reasonable goal is set at 5 days per week. Therefore, there are 4 units of progress possible. Now the sessions are completed and the client is averaging 4 days per week at school. Therefore, 3 of the 4 units of reasonable progress have been attained.

Termination score (4) – Baseline score (1) = Change score (3). Change Score (3)/Reasonable progress (4) = 75% progress.
Note: For nominal data, simply use "Yes" and "No" to indicate completion goal at termination.

Objective # *1a: feel sad < 50% of time* Baseline *80* Termination *20*
Reasonable potential *20* Percent attained *100*
Most recent objective *20* Percent attained *100*
Comments *Goal met. Client satisfied.*

____

Objective # *1b: BDI score < 20* Baseline *30* Termination *12*
Reasonable potential *13* Percent attained *100+*
Most recent objective *12* Percent attained *100*
Comments *Normal range.*

____

Objective # *1c: (depression) SUD < 70* Baseline *90* Termination *50*
Reasonable potential *40* Percent attained *80*
Most recent objective *45* Percent attained *90*

Comments *Client claims minor distress, but able to cope and function adequately.*

Objective # *2b: attend work 32+ hours/week* Baseline *24* Termination *40*

Reasonable potential *40* Percent attained *100*

Most recent objective *40* Percent attained *100*

Comments *Returned to premorbid functioning*

Objective # *3a: 2+ hours/week with friends* Baseline *0* Termination *3.5*

Reasonable potential *4* Percent attained *87.5*

Most recent objective *4* Percent attained *87.5*

Comments *Now close to premorbid level.*

FORM 11 OUTCOME ASSESSMENT SUMMARY NARRATIVE REPORT

Client *John Adams* Chart # *JA032200* Intake date *3-22-00*

Total sessions *16* Individual ___ Group ___ Family *5* Other *Marital* Termination date *6-27-00*

Intake Diagnosis	**Discharge Diagnosis**
Axis I *296.32 Major Depression*	Axis I *Partner-Relationship Problem (mild)*
Partner-Relationship Problem (mod/severe)	*Major Depression in full remission*
Axis II *No diagnosis*	Axis II *No diagnosis*
	Avoidant and passive-aggressive features
Axis III *Defer to physician*	Axis III *Defer to Physician*
Axis IV *Occupational, social, marital*	Axis IV *Marital*
Axis V *50*	Axis V *75–80*

Outcome Summary

Client claims to be functioning at premorbid level prior to bout of depression. Met 6 of 9 treatment plan outcome indicator goals; other 3 nearly completed. Slight concerns in subjective depression, time spent with others, but steady improvement noted. Initially endorsed 8 DSM-IV symptoms of Major Depression as impairing; terminated endorsing only 1 symptom in which social withdrawal was described as mild. Has returned to work 40 hours per week, with quotas being met. No longer on probation at work. Spending significantly more time with family and friends, but not quite to premorbid levels. Client states that this will be attained, but does not want to rush things too quickly. Has progressed in resolving most marital issues. No longer threats of divorce. Denies feeling fatigued at any significant level. Describes current activities as pleasurable. Plans to return for additional services with spouse for monthly marital therapy to learn more effective means of meeting needs. Each normative measure of depression indicates clinically significant change with functioning in the normal range. Client agrees that termination at this time is appropriate, and will set up individual appointments if needed.

Therapist's signature/credentials *Jessie Brown, PhD* Date *6-28-00*

REFERENCES

Achenbach, T. M. (1999). The Child Behavior Checklist and related instruments. In M. E. Maruish (Ed.), *The use of psychological testing for treatment planning and outcomes assessment.* (2nd ed., pp. 429–466). Mahwah, NJ: Erlbaum.

Achenbach, T. M., & Edelbrock, C. S. (1983). *Manual for the Child Behavior Checklist and Revised Child Behavior Profile.* Burlington, VT: Department of Psychiatry, University of Vermont.

American Psychiatric Association (1994). *Diagnostic and statistical manual of mental disorders* (4th ed.). Washington, DC: Author.

Andrews, G. (1991). The changing nature of psychiatry. *Australian and New Zealand Journal of Psychiatry, 25,* 379–383.

Andrews, G., & Harvey, R. (1981). Does psychotherapy benefit neurotic patients? A re-analysis of the Smith, Glass and Miller data. *Archives of General Psychiatry, 38,* 1203–1208.

Attkisson, C., Cook, J., Karno, M., Lehman, A., McGlashan, T. H., Melzer, H. Y., O'Connor, M., Richardson, D., Rosenblat, A., Wells, K., Williams, J., & Hohman, A. A. (1992). Clinical services research. *Schizophrenia Bulletin, 18,* 389–406.

Attkisson, C. C., & Zwick, R. (1982). The Client Satisfaction Questionnaire: Psychometric properties and correlations with service utilization and psychotherapy outcome. *Evaluation and Program Planning, 5,* 223–237.

Barlow, D. H. (1993). *Clinical handbook of psychological disorders: A step-by-step treatment manual.* New York: Guilford.

Barlow, D. H. (1994). Psychological intervention in the area of managed competition. *Clinical Psychology: Science and Practice, 1,* 109–122.

Bass, B. M. (1968). How to succeed in business according to business students and managers. *Journal of Applied Psychology, 52,* 254–262.

Bass, B. M., Cascio, W. F., & O'Connor, E. J. (1974). Magnitude estimations of expressions of frequency and amount. *Journal of Applied Psychology, 59,* 313–320.

Beck, A. T. (1967). *Depression: Clinical, experimental and theoretical aspects.* New York: Harper & Row.

Beck, A. T., Rial, W. Y., & Rickels, K. (1974). Short form of depression inventory: Cross-validation. *Psychological Reports, 34,* 1184–1186.

Beck, A. T., Steer, R. A., & Garbin, M. A. (1988). Psychometric properties of the Beck Depression Inventory: Twenty-five years of evaluation. *Clinical Psychology Review, 8,* 77–100.

Bendig, A. W. (1954). Reliability of short rating scales and the heterogeneity of the rated stimuli. *Journal of Applied Psychology, 38,* 167–170.

Bergin, A. E. (1971). The evaluation of therapeutic outcomes. In A. E. Bergin & S. I. Garfield (Eds.), *Handbook of psychotherapy and behavior change* (pp. 217–270). New York: Wiley.

Bergin, A. E., & Garfield, S. L. (Eds.). (1994). *Handbook of psychotherapy and behavior change* (4th ed.). New York: Wiley.

Beutler, L. E., & Clarkin, J. (1991). Future research directions. In L. E. Beutler & M. Crago (Eds.), *Psychotherapy research: An international review of programmatic studies* (pp. 329–334). Washington, DC: American Psychological Association.

Beutler, L. E., Goodrich, G., Fisher, D., & Williams, O. B. (1999). Use of psychological tests/instruments for treatment planning. In M. E. Maruish (Ed.), *The use of psychological testing for treatment planning and outcomes assessment* (2nd ed., pp. 81–114). Mahwah, NJ: Erlbaum.

Beutler, L. E., Wakefield, P., & Williams, R. E. (1994). Use of psychological tests/instruments for treatment planning. In M. E. Maruish (Ed.), *The use of psychological testing for treatment planning and outcomes assessment* (2nd ed., pp. 55–74). Mahwah, NJ: Erlbaum.

Bieber, J., Wroblewski, J. M., & Barber, C. A. (1999). Design and implementation of an outcomes management system within inpatient and outpatient behavioral health settings. In M. E. Maruish (Ed.), *The use of psychological testing for treatment planning and outcomes assessment* (2nd ed., pp. 171–210). Mahwah, NJ: Erlbaum.

Black, M. M. (1991). Psychology internship training in a department of pediatrics: A 15-year follow-up. *Journal of Clinical Psychology, 20,* 184–190.

Boorse, C. (1976). What a theory of mental health should be. *Journal for the Theory of Social Behaviors, 6,* 61–84.

Bosco, M. R., Krebaum, S. R., & Rush, A. J. (1997). Outcome measures of depression. In H. Strupp, L. Horowitz, & M. Lambert (Eds.), *Measuring patient changes in mood, anxiety, and personality disorders.* Washington, DC: American Psychological Association.

Bowling, A. (1997). *Measuring health: A review of quality of life measurement scales* (2nd ed.). Philadelphia: Open University Press.

Brooks, R. H., & Lohr, K. N. (1985). Efficacy, effectiveness, variations, and quality: Boundary crossing research. *Medical Care, 23,* 710–722.

Broskowski, A. T. (1995). The evolution of health care: Implications for the training and careers of psychologists. *Professional Psychology: Research and Practice, 26,* 156–162.

Brown, J., Dreis, S., & Nace, D. K. (1999). What really makes a difference in psychotherapy outcome? In M. A. Hubble, B. L. Duncan, & S. D. Miller (Eds.), *The heart and soul of change: What works in therapy* (pp. 389–406). Washington, DC: American Psychological Association.

Browning, C. H., & Browning, B. J. (1996). *How to partner with managed care: A "do it yourself kit" for building working relationships and getting steady referrals.* (expanded ed.). New York: Wiley.

Cacciola, J. S., Koppenhaver, J. M., McKay, J. R., & Alterman, A. I. (1999). Test-retest reliability of the lifetime items on the Addiction Severity Index. *Psychological Assessment, 11,* 86–93.

Campbell, J., Ho, L., Evensen, R. C., & Bluebird, G. (1996). *Consumer satisfaction and treatment outcomes.* Paper presented at the Sixth Annual National Conference on State Mental Health Agency Services Research and Program Evaluation, Arlington, VA.

Carroll, L. (1981). *Alice's adventures in wonderland and through the looking glass.* New York: Bantam Books. (Originally published 1865 and 1871).

Carscddon, D. M., George, M., & Wells, G. (1990). Rural community mental health consumer satisfaction and psychiatric symptoms. *Community Mental Health Journal, 26,* 309–318.

Carter, R. K. (1983). *The accountable agency.* Beverly Hills, CA: Sage.

Chang, L. (1997). Dependability of anchoring labels of Likert-like scales. *Educational and Psychological Measurement, 57,* 800–807.

Ciarlo, J. A., Brown, T. R., Edwards, D. W., Kiresuk, T. J., & Newman, F. L. (1986). *Assessing mental health treatment outcome measurement techniques* (DHHS Publication No. ADM 86-1301). Washington, DC: Superintendent of Documents, U.S. Government Printing Office.

Clark, A., & Friedman, M. J. (1983). Nine standardized scales for evaluating treatment outcomes in a mental health clinic. *Journal of Clinical Psychology, 39,* 939–950.

Clement, P. W. (1988). Professional role modeling by faculty: The neglected child in doctoral training. *Professional Psychology: Research and Practice, 19,* 253–254.

Clement, P. W. (1996). Evaluation in private practice. *Clinical Psychology: Science and Practice, 3,* 145–159.

Clement, P. W. (1999). *Outcomes and incomes.* New York: Guilford.

Cliff, N. (1959). Adverbs as multipliers. *Psychological Review, 21,* 53–60.

Cohen, C. H. (1998). Fostering a culture of outcomes: How to get staff and patients on board. In K. Coughlin (Ed.), *The 1998 behavioral outcomes and guidelines sourcebook.* New York: Faulkner & Gray.

Cohen, J. (1990). Things I have learned (so far). *American Psychologist, 45,* 1304–1312.

Consumer Reports (1995, November). Mental health: Does therapy help? *11,* 734–739.

Conte, H. R., Plutchik, R., Buck, L., and Picard, S. (1991). Interrelations among ego functions and personality traits: Their relation to psychotherapy outcome. *American Journal of Psychotherapy, 45,* 69–77.

Cook, T. D., & Campbell, D. T. (1979). *Quasi-experimentation: Design and analysis issues for field settings.* Chicago: Rand McNally.

Coyle, J. T. (1996). Foreword. In L. I. Sederer & B. Dickey (Eds.), *Outcomes assessment in clinical practice* (pp. v–vii). Baltimore: Williams & Wilkins.

Cronbach, L. J. (1950). Further evidence on response sets and test design. *Educational and Psychological Measurement, 10,* 3–31.

Cummings, N. A. (1991). Ten ways to spot mismanaged mental health care. *Psychotherapy in Private Practice, 9,* 31–33.

Derogatis, L. R. (1994). *SCL-90-R administration, scoring, and procedures manual.* Minneapolis, MN: National Computer Systems.

Derogatis, L. R., & Savitz, K. (1999). The SCL-90-R, Brief Symptom Inventory, and matching clinical rating scales.

In M. E. Maruish (Ed.), *The use of psychological testing for treatment planning and outcomes assessment* (2nd ed., pp. 679–724). Mahwah, NJ: Erlbaum.

Dixon, P. N., Bobo, M., & Stevick, R. A. (1984). Response differences and preferences for all category-defined and end-defined Likert formats. *Educational and Psychological Measurement, 44,* 61–66.

Dornelas, E. A., Correll, R. E., Lothstein, L., and Wilber, C. (1996). Designing and implementing outcome evaluations: Some guidelines for practitioners. *Psychotherapy, 3,* 237–245.

Dworkin, R. J., Friedman, L. C., Telschow, R. L., Grant, K. D., Moffic, H. S., & Sloan, V. J. (1990). The longitudinal use of the Global Assessment Scale in multiple-rater situations. *Community Mental Health Journal, 26,* 335–344.

Edelman, R. E., & Chambless, D. L. (1993). Compliance during sessions and homework in exposure-based treatment of agoraphobia. *Behavior Research and Therapy, 31,* 767–773.

Edwards, D., Yarvis, R., Mueller, D., & Langsley, D. (1978). Does patient satisfaction correlate with success? *Hospital and Community Psychiatry, 29,* 188–190.

Edwards, D. W., Yarvis, R. M., Mueller, D. P., Zingale, H. C., & Wagman, W. J. (1978). Test-taking stability of adjustment scales: Can we assess patient deterioration? *Evaluation Quarterly, 2,* 276–291.

Eisen, S. V., & Culhane, M. A. (1999). Behavior Symptom Identification Scale (BASIS-32). In M. E. Maruish (Ed.), *The use of psychological testing for treatment planning and outcomes assessment* (2nd ed., pp. 759–790). Mahwah, NJ: Erlbaum.

Eisen, S. V., & Dickey, B. (1996). Mental health outcome assessment: The new agenda. *Psychotherapy, 33,* 181–189.

Eisen, S. V., Dill, D. L., & Grob, M. C. (1994). Reliability and validity of a brief patient-report instrument for psychiatric outcome evaluation. *Hospital and Community Psychiatry, 45,* 242–247.

Eisen, S. V., Wilcox, M., Schafer, E., Culhane, M. A., & Leff, H. S. (1997). *Use of the BASIS-32 for outcome assessment of recipients of outpatient mental health services.* Report to Human Services Research Institute, Cambridge, MA.

Ellason, J. W., & Ross, C. A. (1997). Childhood trauma and psychiatric symptoms. *Psychological Reports, 80,* 447–450.

Ellwood, P. M. (1988). Outcomes management: A technology of patient experience. *New England Journal of Medicine, 318,* 1549–1556.

Endicott, J., Spitzer, R. L., Fleiss, J. L., & Cohen, J. (1976). The Global Assessment Scale: a procedure for measuring overall severity of psychiatric disturbances. *Archives of General Psychology, 33,* 766–771.

Ericson, R. (1995). *Quality and clinical outcomes in managed mental health care.* St. Paul, MN: Decision Resources.

Eysenck, H. J. (1952). The effects of psychotherapy: An evaluation. *Journal of Consulting Psychology, 16,* 319–324.

Finn, R. H. (1972). Effects of some variations in rating scale characteristics on the means and reliabilities of ratings. *Educational and Psychological Measurement, 32,* 255–265.

Fischer, J., & Corcoran, K. (Eds.). (1994a). *Measures for clinical practice: A sourcebook: Vol. 1. Couples, families, and children* (2nd ed.). New York: Free Press.

Fischer, J., & Corcoran, K. (Eds.). (1994b). *Measures for clinical practice: A sourcebook: Vol. 2. Adults* (2nd ed.). New York: Free Press.

Flay, B. R. (1986). Efficacy and effectiveness trials (and other phases of research) in the development of health promotion programs. *Preventive Medicine, 15,* 451–474.

Fonagy, P. (1996). Evaluating the effectiveness of interventions in child psychiatry: The state of the art. Keynote address at the 16th Annual Meeting of the Canadian Academy of Child Psychiatry, Quebec City, Quebec, Canada.

Foxhall, K. (2000). Research for the real world. *Monitor on Psychology, 31,* 28–30.

Frisch, M. B. (1992). Use of the Quality of Life Inventory in problem assessment and treatment planning for cognitive therapy of depression. In A. Freeman & F. Dattilo (Eds.), *Comprehensive casebook of cognitive therapy* (pp. 27–52). New York: Plenum.

Frisch, M. B. (1994a). *Manual and treatment guide for the Quality of Life Inventory (QOLI).* Minneapolis, MN: National Computer Systems.

Frisch, M. B. (1994b). *Quality of Life Inventory (QOLI).* Minneapolis, MN: National Computer Systems.

Frisch, M. B. (1999). Quality of life intervention and the Quality of Life Inventory (QOLI). In M. E. Maruish (Ed.), *The use of psychological testing for treatment planning and outcomes assessment* (2nd ed., pp. 1277–1331). Mahwah, NJ: Erlbaum.

Frisch, M. B., Cornell, J., Villanueva, M., & Retzlaff, P. J. (1992). Clinical validation of the Quality of Life Inventory: A measure of life satisfaction for use in treatment planning and outcome assessment. *Psychological Assessment: A Journal of Consulting and Clinical Psychology, 4,* 92–101.

Froyd, J. E., Lambert, M. J., & Froyd, J. D. (1996). A review of practices of psychotherapy outcome measurement. *Journal of Mental Health, 5,* 11–15.

Fuerst, R. A. (1938). Problems of short term psychotherapy. *American Journal of Orthopsychiatry, 8,* 260–264.

Garfield, S. L., & Bergin, A. E. (Eds.). (1986). *Handbook of psychotherapy and behavior change* (3rd ed.). New York: Wiley.

Goldberg, L. R. (1981). Unconfounding situational attributions from uncertain, neutral, and ambiguous ones: A psychometric analysis of descriptions of oneself and various types of others. *Journal of Personality and Social Psychology, 41,* 517–552.

Goldfried, M. R. (1980). Toward the delineation of therapeutic change principles. *American Psychologist, 35,* 991–999.

Goldfried, M. R., & Wolf, B. E. (1996). Psychotherapy practice and research: Repairing a strained alliance. *American Psychologist, 51,* 1007–1016.

Goldman, B., & Mitchell, D. (Eds.). (1996). *Directory of unpublished experimental mental measures* (Vols. 1–7). Washington, DC: American Psychological Association.

Greenfield, T. K., & Attkisson, D. D. (1989). Steps toward a multifactorial satisfaction scale for primary care and mental health services. *Evaluation and Program Planning, 12,* 271–278.

Grissom, R. J. (1994a). Statistical analysis of ordinal categorical status after therapies. *Journal of Consulting and Clinical Psychology, 62,* 281–284.

Grissom, R. J. (1994b). Parametric analysis of ordinal categorical clinical outcome. *Psychotherapy Research, 4,* 136–140.

Hartman-Stein, P. E. (1999). Expect harsh, intensive scrutiny if your Medicare claims are audited. *The National Psychologist, 8,* 6–7.

Hawkins, R. P., Mathews, J. R., & Hamden, L. (1999). *Measuring behavioral health outcomes: A practical guide.* New York: Kluwer Academic/Plenum.

Holloway, R. G., and Ringel, S. P. (1988). Narrowing the evidence-practice gap: Strengthening the link between research and practice. *Neurology, 50,* 319–321.

Horowitz, L. M., Rosenberg, S. E., Baer, B. A., Ureño, G., and Villaseñor, V. S. (1988). Inventory of Interpersonal Problems: Psychometric properties and clinical applications. *Journal of Consulting and Clinical Psychiatry, 56,* 885–892.

Howard, K., Kopta, S., Krause, M., & Orlinsky, D. (1986). The dose-effect relationship in psychotherapy. *American Psychologist, 41,* 159–164.

Howard, K. I., Krause, M. S., & Lyons, J. (1993). When clinical trials fail: A guide for disaggregation. In L. S. Onken & J. D. Blaine (Eds.), *Psychotherapy and counseling in treatment of drug abuse.* Washington, DC: National Institute of Drug Abuse.

Howard, K. I., Lueger, R. J., Maling, M. S., & Martinovich, Z. (1993). A phase model of psychotherapy outcome: Causal mediation of change. *Journal of Consulting and Clinical Psychology, 61,* 678–685.

Howard, K. I., Orlinsky, D. E., & Lueger, R. L. (1994). Clinically relevant outcome research in individual psychotherapy: New models guide the researcher and clinician. *British Journal of Psychiatry, 165,* 4–8.

Hubble, M. A., Duncan, B. L., & Miller, S. D. (1999). *The heart and soul of change: What works in therapy.* Washington, DC: American Psychological Association.

Huck, S. W., & Jacko, E. J. (1974). Effect of varying the response format of the Alpert-Haber Achievement Anxiety Test. *Journal of Counseling Psychology, 21,* 159–163.

Hyink-Huttemier, K. (2000). *Effectiveness of psychotherapy in a local clinical setting.* Unpublished doctoral dissertation, Minnesota School of Professional Psychology, Minneapolis, MN.

Hyman, R., & Berger, L. (1965). Discussion of H. J. Eysenck's "The effects of psychotherapy." *International Journal of Psychiatry, 1,* 317–322.

Jacobson, N. S., Follette, W. C., & Ravenstorf, D. (1984). Psychotherapy outcome research: Methods for reporting variability and evaluating clinical significance. *Behavior Therapy, 52,* 336–352.

Jacobson, N. S., Roberts, L. J., Berns, S. B., & McGlinchey, J. B. (1999). Methods for defining and determining the clinical significance of treatment effects: Description, application, and alternatives. *Journal of Consulting and Clinical Psychology, 67,* 300–307.

Jacobson, N. S., & Truax, P. (1991). Clinical Significance: A statistical approach to defining meaningful change in psychotherapy research. *Journal of Consulting and Clinical Psychology, 59,* 12–19.

Johnson, L. D. (1995). *Psychotherapy in the age of accountability.* New York: Norton.

Joint Commission on Accreditation of Healthcare Facilities (1994). *A guide to establishing programs for assessing outcomes in clinical settings.* Oakbrook Terrace, IL: Author.

Kadera, S. W., Lambert, M. J., & Andrews, A. A. (1996). How much therapy is really enough? *The Journal of Psychotherapy Practice and Research, 5,* 132–151.

Katz, R., Katz, J., & Shaw, B. F. (1999). Beck depression inventory and hopelessness scale. In M. E. Maruish (Ed.), *The use of psychological testing for treatment planning and outcomes assessment* (2nd ed., pp. 921–934). Mahwah, NJ: Erlbaum.

Kazdin, A. E. (1997). *Research design in clinical psychology* (3rd ed.). Boston: Allyn & Bacon.

Kiesler, C. A., & Morton, T. L. (1988). Prospective payment system for inpatient psychiatry: The advantages of controversy. *American Psychologist, 43,* 141–150.

Kiresuk, J. J., & Sherman, R. E. (1968). Goal attainment scaling: A general method for evaluating comprehensive community mental health programs. *Community Mental Health Journal, 4,* 443–452.

Knesper, D. J., Pagnucco, D. J., & Kalter, N. M. (1986). Agreement on patient diagnosis, treatment, and referral across provider groups. *Professional Psychology: Research and Practice, 17,* 331–337.

Knight, B. (1996). Managed care and the future of mental health and aging. Keynote address. Representatives of State Mental Health Programs for Older Persons Annual Conference. Austin, TX.

Kopta, S. M., Lueger, R. J., Sanders, S. M., & Howard, K. I. (1999). Individual psychotherapy and process research: Challenges leading to greater turmoil or a positive transition? *Annual Review of Psychology, 50,* 441–469.

Kovacs, M. (1992). *The Children's Depression Inventory (CDI) manual.* Toronto, Ontario, Canada: Multi Health Systems.

Krawitz, R. (1997). A prospective psychotherapy outcome study. *Australian and New Zealand Journal of Psychiatry, 31,* 465–473.

Lambert, M. J. (1991). Introduction to psychotherapy research. In L. E. Beutler & M. Crago (Eds.), *Psychotherapy research: An international review of programmatic studies* (pp. 1–23). Washington, DC: American Psychological Association.

Lambert, M. J., Burlingame, G. M., Umphress, V., Hansen, N. B., Vermeersch, D., Clouse, G., & Yancher, S. (1996). The reliability and validity of a new psychotherapy outcome measure. *Clinical Psychology and Psychotherapy, 3,* 249–258.

Lambert, M. J., & Finch, A. E. (1999). The outcome questionnaire. In M. E. Maruish (Ed.), *The use of psychological testing for treatment planning and outcomes assessment* (2nd ed., pp. 831–870). Mahwah, NJ: Erlbaum.

Lambert, M. J., Hansen, N. B., Umphress, V., Lunnen, K., Okiishi, J., Burlingame, G. M., & Reisinger, C. W. (1996). *Administration and Scoring Manual for the OQ-45.* Stevenson, MD: American Professional Credentialing Services LLC.

Lambert, M. J., & Lambert, J. M. (1999). Use of psychological tests for assessing treatment outcome. In M. E. Maruish (Ed.), *The use of psychological testing for treatment planning and outcomes assessment* (2nd ed., pp. 115–152). Mahwah, NJ: Erlbaum.

Lambert, M. J., & McRoberts, C. H. (1993, April). Outcome measurement in JCCP: 1986–1991. Paper presented at the meetings of the Western Psychological Association, Phoenix, AZ.

Lambert, M. J., Okiishi, J. C., Finch, A. E., & Johnson, L. (1998). Outcome assessment: From conceptualization to implementation. *Professional Psychology: Research and Practice, 29,* 63–70.

Lambert, M. J., Shapiro, D. A., & Bergin, A. E. (1986). The effectiveness of psychotherapy. In S. L. Garfield & A. E. Bergin (Eds.), *Handbook of psychotherapy and behavior change* (pp. 157–211). New York: Wiley.

Lambert, W., Salzer, M. S., & Bickman, L. (1998). Clinical outcome, consumer satisfaction, and ad hoc ratings of improvement in children's mental health. *Journal of Consulting and Clinical Psychology, 2,* 270–279.

Likert, R. (1932). A technique for the measurement of attitudes. *Archives of Psychology, 140,* 1–55.

Lipsey, M. W., & Wilson, D. B. (1994). The efficacy of psychological, educational, and behavioral treatment: Confirmation from meta-analysis. *American Psychologist, 48,* 1181–1209.

Little, K. B. (1972). Bazelon challenge requires soul searching. *APA Monitor, 3,* 2.

Luborsky L., Singer, B., and Luborsky, L. (1975). Comparative studies of psychotherapies: Is it true that "Everybody has won and all must have prizes"? *Archives of General Psychiatry, 32,* 995–1008.

Lyons, J., Howard, K., O'Mahoney, M., & Lish, J. (1997). *The measurement and management of clinical outcomes in mental health.* New York: Wiley.

Maruish, M. E. (1999a). Symptom Assessment-45 Questionnaire (SA-45). In M. E. Maruish (Ed.), *The use of psychological testing for treatment planning and outcomes assessment* (2nd ed., pp. 725–758). Mahwah, NJ: Erlbaum.

Maruish, M. E. (Ed.). (1999b). *The use of psychological testing for treatment planning and outcomes assessment* (2nd ed.). Mahwah, NJ: Erlbaum.

Massey, O. T., & Wu, L. (1994). Three critical views of functioning: Comparisons of assessments made by individuals with mental illness, their case managers, and family members. *Evaluation and Program Planning, 17,* 1–7.

Masters, G. N. (1985). A comparison of latent trait and latent class analyses of Likert-type data. *Psychometrika, 50,* 69–80.

Masters, J. R. (1974). The relationship between number of response categories and reliability of Likert-type questionnaires. *Journal of Educational Measurement, 11,* 49–53.

McClellan, A. T., Kushner, H., Metzger, D., Peters, R., Smith, I., Grissom, G., Pettinati, H., & Argeriou, M. (1992). The fifth edition of the Addiction Severity Index. *Journal of Substance Abuse Treatment, 9,* 199–213.

McClellan, A. T., Luborsky, L., Woody, G. E., & O'Brien, C. P. (1980). An improved diagnostic evaluation instrument for substance abuse patients. *Journal of Nervous and Mental Disease, 168,* 26–33.

McNeilly, C. L., & Howard, K. I. (1991). The effects of psychotherapy: A reevaluation based on dosage. *Psychotherapy Research, 1,* 74–78.

Moldawsky, S. (1992). A proper education for private practice. *Psychotherapy in Private Practice, 11,* 37–42.

Moras, K., & Strupp, H. H. (1982). Pretherapy interpersonal relations, patients' alliance, and outcome in brief therapy. *Archives of General Psychiatry, 39,* 405–409.

Morrow-Bradley, C., & Elliott, R. (1986). The utilization of psychotherapy research by practicing psychotherapists. *American Psychologist, 41,* 188–197.

Moses, L. E., Emerson, J. D., & Hosseini, H. (1984). Analyzing data from ordered categories. *New England Journal of Medicine, 311,* 442–448.

Mueller, R. M., Lambert, M. J., & Burlingame, G. M. (1998). Construct validity of the outcome questionnaire: A confirmatory factor analysis. *Journal of Personality Assessment, 70,* 248–262.

Murphy, M., DeBernardo, C., & Shoemaker, W. (1998). Impact of managed care on independent practice and professional ethics: A survey of independent practitioners. *Professional Psychology: Research and Practice, 29,* 43–51.

Nathan, P. E., & Gorman, J. M. (1998). *A guide to treatments that work.* New York: Oxford University Press.

Newman, F. L., Ciarlo, J. A., & Carpenter, D. (1999). Guidelines for selecting psychological instruments for treatment planning and outcome assessment. In M. E. Maruish (Ed.), *The use of psychological testing for treatment planning and outcomes assessment* (2nd ed., pp. 153–170). Mahwah, NJ: Erlbaum.

Newman, R., & Bricklin, P. (1991). Parameters of managed mental health care: Legal, ethical and professional guidelines. *Professional Psychology: Research and Practice, 22,* 26–35.

Newstead, S. E., & Arnold, J. (1989). The effect of response format on ratings of teaching. *Educational and Psychological Measurement, 49,* 33–43.

Nietzel, M. T., Russell, R. L., Kelly, A., Hemmings, K. H., & Gretter, M. L. (1987). Clinical significance of psychotherapy for unipolar depression: A meta-analytic approach to social comparison. *Journal of Consulting and Clinical Psychology, 55,* 156–161.

Norquist, G., Lebowitz, B., & Hyman, S. (1999). Expanding the frontier of treatment research. *Prevention and Treatment,* Article 0001a. Available: http://journals.apa.org/prevention/volume2/pre002001a.html.

Nunnally, J. C. (1967). *Psychometric theory.* New York: McGraw-Hill.

Ogles, B., Lambert, M., & Masters, K. (1996). *Assessing outcome in clinical practice.* Boston: Allyn & Bacon.

Olson, R. P. (1999). A critique of Minnesota's managed mental health care with special reference to medical necessity determinations for outpatient psychotherapy. Unpublished manuscript. Available e-mail: olson@pclink.com.

Orlinsky, D. E., Grace, K., & Parks, B. K. (1994). Process and outcome in psychotherapy. In A. E. Bergin & S. L. Garfield (Eds.), *Handbook of psychotherapy and behavior change* (pp. 270–378). New York: Wiley.

Pallak, M. S., & Cummings, N. A. (1994). Outcomes research in managed behavioral health care: Issues, strategies, and trends. In S. A. Shueman, W. G. Trogy, & S. L Mayhugh (Eds.), *Managed behavioral health care* (pp. 205–221). Springfield, IL: Thomas.

Parker, J. D., Daleiden, E. L., & Simpson, C. A. (1999). Personality inventory substance abuse scales: Convergent and discriminant relations with the Addiction Severity Index in a residential chemical dependence treatment setting. *Psychological Assessment, 11,* 507–513.

Patterson, C. H. (1974). *Relationship counseling and psychotherapy.* New York: Harper & Row.

Paul, G. (1967). Strategy of outcome research in psychotherapy. *Journal of Consulting Psychology, 31,* 109–118.

Pearsall, D. F. (1997). Psychotherapy outcome research in child psychiatric disorders. *Canadian Journal of Psychiatry, 42,* 595–601.

Pedhazur, E. J., & Schmelkin, L. P. (1991). *Measurement, design, and analysis: An integrated approach.* Hillsdale, NJ: Erlbaum.

Pekarik, G. (1992). Relationship of clients' reasons for dropping out of treatment to outcome and satisfaction: Development of treatment to outcome and satisfaction. *Journal of Clinical Psychology: Research and Practice, 21,* 482–288.

Pekarik, G., & Wolff, C. B. (1996). Relationship of satisfaction to symptom change, follow-up adjustment, and clinical significance. *Professional Psychology Research and Practice, 27,* 202–208.

Persons, J. B. (1991). Psychotherapy outcome studies do not accurately represent current models of psychotherapy: A proposed remedy. *American Psychologist, 46,* 99–106.

Persons, J. B., Burns, D. D., & Perloff, J. M. (1988). Predictors of dropout and outcome in cognitive therapy for depression in a private practice setting. *Cognitive Therapy and Research, 12,* 557–575.

Phelps, R., Eisman, E., & Kohout, J. (1998). Psychological practice and managed care: Results of the CAPP practitioner survey. *Professional Psychology: Research and Practice, 29,* 31–36.

Phillips, E. L. (1991). George Washington University's international data on psychotherapy delivery systems: Modeling new approaches to the study of therapy. In L. E. Beutler & M. Crago (Eds.), *Psychotherapy research: An international review of programmatic studies* (pp. 263–273). Washington, DC: American Psychological Association.

Plankun, E. M., Muller, J. P., & Burkhardt, P. E. (1987). The significance of borderline and schizotypal overlap. *Hillside Journal of Clinical Psychology, 9,* 47–54.

Prioleau, L., Murdock, M., & Brody, N. (1983). An analysis of psychotherapy vs. placebo studies. *The Behavioral and Brain Sciences, 6,* 275–310.

Roth, A., & Fonagy, P. (1996). *What works for whom?: A critical review of psychotherapy research.* New York: Guilford.

Rothbaum, P., Bernstein, D., Haller, O., Phelps, R., & Kohout, J. (1998). New Jersey Psychologists' report on managed mental health care. *Professional Psychology: Research and Practice, 29,* 37–42.

Russo, J., Roy-Byrne, P., Jaffe, C., Ries, R., Dagadakis, C., Dwyer-O'Connor, E., & Reeder, D. (1997). The relationship of patient-administered outcome assessments to quality of life and physician ratings: Validity of the BASIS-32. *Journal of Mental Health Administration, 24,* 200–215.

Sanford, N. (1962). Discussion of papers on measuring personality changes. In H. H. Strupp & L. Luborsky (Eds.), *Research in psychotherapy* (Vol. 2, pp. 155–163). Washington, DC: American Psychological Association.

Sauber, S. R. (Ed.). (1996). *Mental health practice under managed care: Vol. 6. Treatment outcomes in psychotherapy and psychiatric interventions.* New York: Brunner/Mazel.

Schmidt, F. (1996). Statistical significance testing and cumulative knowledge in psychology: Implications for researchers. *Psychological Methods, 2,* 115–129.

Sederer, L. I, & Bennet, M. J. (1996). Managed mental health care in the United States: A status report. *Administration and Policy in Mental Health, 23,* 289–306.

Sederer, L. I., Dickey, B., & Hermann, R. (1996). The imperative of outcomes assessment in psychiatry. In L. I. Sederer & B. Dickey (Eds.), *Outcomes assessment in clinical practice* (Vols. 1–7). Baltimore: Williams & Wilkins.

Seligman, M. E. P. (1995). The effectiveness of psychotherapy: The *Consumer Reports* study. *American Psychologist, 50,* 965–974.

Seligman, M. E. P. (1996). Science as an ally of practice. *American Psychologist, 51,* 1072–1079.

Seligman, M. E. P., & Levant, R. F. (1998). Managed care policies rely on inadequate science. *Professional Psychology: Research and Practice, 29,* 211–212.

Shlien, J. M. (1966). Cross-theoretical criteria for the evaluation of psychotherapy. *American Journal of Psychotherapy, 1,* 125–134.

Shueman, S. A., Troy, W. G., & Mayhugh, S. L. (1999). *Managed behavioral health care: An industry perspective.* Springfield, IL: Thomas.

Shulman, J. M. (1994). *Does quality of behavioral health really matter?* Columbus, OH: INTERACT Behavior Healthcare Services.

Sitarenios, G., & Kovacs, M. (1999). Use of the Children's Depression Inventory. In M. E. Maruish (Ed.), *The use of psychological testing for treatment planning and outcomes assessment.* (2nd ed., pp. 267–298). Mahwah, NJ: Erlbaum.

Slaven, T. M. (1997). *Outcomes management in behavioral health.* Tucson, AZ: The Rehabilitation Accreditation Commission (CARF).

Sleek, S. (1998). Despite managed care, psychologists are committed to independent practice. *APA Monitor, 28,* 23.

Smith, M., & Glass, G. (1977). A meta analysis of psychotherapy outcome studies. *American Psychologist, 32,* 752–760.

Smith, M., Glass, G., & Miller, T. (1980). *The benefits of psychotherapy.* Baltimore: Johns Hopkins University Press.

Snyder, D. K. (1997). *Manual for the Marital Satisfaction Inventory—Revised.* Los Angeles: Western Psychological Services.

Snyder, D. K. & Aikman, G. G. (1999). Marital Satisfaction Inventory—Revised. In M. E. Maruish (Ed.), *The use of psychological testing for treatment planning and outcomes assessment* (2nd ed., pp. 1173–1210). Mahwah, NJ: Erlbaum.

Spanier, G. B. (1976). Measuring dyadic adjustment: New scales for assessing the quality of marriage and similar dyads. *Journal of Marriage and the Family, 38,* 337–347.

Spector, P. E. (1976). Choosing response categories for summated rating scales. *Journal of Applied Psychology, 3,* 374–375.

Speer, D. C. (1998). *Mental health outcome evaluation.* San Diego, CA: Academic.

Sperry, L., Brill, P. L., Howard, K. I., & Grissom, G. R. (1996). *Treatment outcomes in psychotherapy and psychiatric interventions.* New York: Brunner/Mazel.

Spielberger, C. D. (1983). *Manual for the State-Trait Anxiety Inventory (STAI) (Form Y).* Palo Alto, CA: Consulting Psychologists Press.

Spielberger, C. D., Gorusch, R. L., & Lushene, R. E. (1970). *The State-Trait Anxiety Inventory self evaluation questionnaire.* Palo Alto, CA: Consulting Psychologists Press.

Spielberger, C. D., Sydeman, S. J., Owen, A. E., & Marsh, B. J. (1999). Measuring anxiety and anger with the State-Trait Anxiety Inventory (STAI) and the State-Trait Anger Expression Inventory (STAXI). In M. E. Maruish (Ed.), *The use of psychological testing for treatment planning and outcomes assessment* (2nd ed., pp. 993–1021). Mahwah, NJ: Erlbaum.

Steuer, J. L., Mintz, J., Hammen, C. L., Hill, M. A., Jarvik, L. F., McCarley, T., Motoike, P., & Rosen, R. (1984). Cognitive-behavioral and psychodynamic group psychotherapy in treatment of geriatric depression. *Journal of Consulting and Clinical Psychology, 15,* 180–189.

Strategic Advantage Inc. (1997). *Manual for the Symptom Assessment-45 questionnaire (SA-45).* Minneapolis, MN: Author.

Stricker, G. (2000). The scientist-practitioner model: Ghandi was right again. *American Psychologist, 55,* 253–254.

Stricker, G., & Trierweiler, S. J. (1995). The local clinical scientist: A bridge between science and practice. *American Psychologist, 50,* 995–1002.

Strupp, H. H. (1989). Psychotherapy: Can the practitioner learn from the researcher? *American Psychologist, 44,* 717–724.

Strupp, H. H., Horowitz, L. M., & Lambert, M. J. (1997). *Measuring patient changes in mood, anxiety, and personality disorders: Toward a core battery.* Washington, DC: American Psychological Association.

Talley, F., Butler, S., & Strupp, H. (Eds.). (1994). *Research findings and clinical practice: Bridging the chasm.* New York: Basis.

Thompson, B. (1994). Guidelines for authors. *Educational and Psychological Measurement, 54,* 837–847.

Tingey, R. C., Lambert, M. J., Burlingame, G. M., & Hansen, N. B. (1996). Assessing clinical significance: Proposed extensions to method. *Psychotherapy Research, 6,* 109–123.

Trierweiler, S. J., & Stricker, G. (1998). *The scientific practice of professional psychology.* New York: Plenum.

Truax, C. B. (1966). Counseling and psychotherapy: Process and outcome. (Final Report: VRA Research and Demonstration Grant 906-P.) Little Rock, AR: University of Arkansas, Arkansas Rehabilitation Research and Training Center.

Tucker, L., & Lubin W. (1994). *National survey of psychologists. Report from Division 39, American Psychological Association.* Washington, DC: American Psychological Association.

Tyler, J. D., & Clark, J. A. (1987). Clinical psychologists reflect on the usefulness of various components of graduate training. *Professional Psychology: Research and Practice, 18,* 381–384.

Umphress, V. J., Lambert, M. J., Smart, D. W., Barlow, S. H., & Clouse, G. (1997). Concurrent and construct validity of the outcome questionnaire. *Journal of Psychoeducational Assessment, 15,* 40–55.

VandenBos, G. R. (Ed.). (1996). Outcome assessment of psychotherapy (Special issue). *American Psychologist, S1,* 10.

Vuori, H., (1999). Patient satisfaction—an attribute or indicator of the quality of care. *Quality Review Bulletin, 13,* 106–108.

Walborn, F. S. (1996). *Process variables: Four common elements of counseling and psychotherapy.* Pacific Grove, CA: Brooks/Cole.

Ware, J. E. (1999). SF-36 Health Survey. In M. E. Maruish (Ed.), *The use of psychological testing for treatment planning and outcomes assessment.* (2nd ed., pp. 1227–1246). Mahwah, NJ: Erlbaum.

Ware, J. E., Kosinski, M., & Keller, S. K. (1994). *SF-36 Physical and Mental Health Summary scales: A user's manual.* Boston, MA: New England Medical Center, The Health Institute.

Ware, J. E., Snow, K. K., Kosinski, M., & Gandek, B. (1993). *SF-36 Health Survey manual and interpretation guide.* Boston, MA: New England Medical Center, The Health Institute.

Wedding, D., Topolski, J., & McGaha, A. (1995). Maintaining the confidentiality of computerized mental health outcome data. *Journal of Mental Health Administration, 3,* 237–244.

Weisz, J. R., & Weiss, B. (1989). Assessing the effects of clinic-based psychotherapy with children and adolescents. *Journal of Consulting and Clinical Psychology, 57,* 741–746.

Weisz, J. R., Weiss, B., & Donenberg, G. R. (1992). The lab versus the clinic: Effects of child and adolescent psychotherapy. *American Psychologist, 47,* 1578–1585.

Wells, K. (1999). Treatment research at the crossroads: The scientific interface of clinical trials and effectiveness research. *American Journal of Psychiatry, 156,* 5–10.

Wells, M. G., Burlingame, G. M., & Lambert, M. J. (1999). Youth Outcome Questionnaire (Y-OQ). In M. E. Maruish (Ed.), *The use of psychological testing for treatment planning and outcomes assessment* (2nd ed., pp. 497–534). Mahwah, NJ: Erlbaum.

Whiston, S. C., & Sexton, T. L. (1993). An overview of psychotherapy outcome research: Implications for practice. *Professional Psychology: Research and Practice, 24,* 43–51.

Wiger, D. E. (1999a). *The psychotherapy documentation primer.* New York: Wiley.

Wiger, D. E. (1999b). *The clinical documentation sourcebook* (2nd ed.). New York: Wiley.

Wilkinson, L. (1999). Statistical methods in psychology journals: Guidelines and explanations. *American Psychologist, 54,* 594–604.

Williams, B. (1994). Patient satisfaction: A valid concept? *Social Science and Medicine, 38,* 509–516.

Wilson, S. A., Becker, L. A., and Tinker, R. H. (1995). Eye movement desensitization and reprocessing (EMDR) treatment for psychologically traumatized individuals. *Journal of Consulting and Clinical Psychology, 63,* 928–937.

Wilson, S. A., Becker, L. A., & Tinker, R. H. (1997). Fifteen-month follow-up of eye movement desensitization and reprocessing (EMDR) treatment for posttraumatic stress disorder and psychological trauma. *Journal of Consulting and Clinical Psychology, 65,* 1047–1056.

APPENDIX: FORMS

USE OF FORMS

The following information provides directions for using the forms included in this text. A 3½-inch IBM-compatible disk with all forms is included with this text.

1. Limits of Confidentiality—Use of Client Information
2. Initial Assessment—Adult
3. Personal History—Adult
4. Individual Treatment Plan
5. Progress Notes
6. Behavioral Observations: Weekly Tally Sheet
7. Hourly Behavioral Observation Tally Sheet
8. Treatment Plan Objectives Progress Chart
9. Treatment Plan Objectives Progress Chart—Individual Objectives
10. Treatment Outcomes Summary
11. Outcome Assessment Summary Narrative Report

FORM 1: LIMITS OF CONFIDENTIALITY—USE OF CLIENT INFORMATION

Form 1 is self-explanatory and needs no filling out other than signatures and some brief information on how to contact the client. It is a necessary document for ethical and legal reasons. The limits of confidentiality and specific agency procedures are explained to help avoid potential problem areas. Several areas in which it is possible to breach a client's confidence are explained on the form. The client's signature is requested in two places to assure confirmation of understanding the limits of confidentiality and permission to use client data in outcome assessment. Although Form 1, in itself, is not an outcome procedure, it gains the client's permission to use clinical information to study outcomes. Without such permission, the clinician may be subject to ethical violations.

FORM 2: INITIAL ASSESSMENT—ADULT

Form 2 provides a sample assessment form designed to fit information requested by the Joint Commission on Accreditation of Healthcare Organizations (JCAHO) and most third parties. The material is designed to be collected in one session and to coordinate with *Diagnostic and Statistical Manual of Mental Disorders*—Fourth Edition (*DSM-IV*) criteria. Several of the most popular *DSM-IV* diagnoses are listed with their respective diagnostic symptoms to aid the clinician in validating the diagnosis during the interview. Important *DSM-IV* aspects depicting the level of functional impairments such as baseline measures of frequency, duration, and severity of symptoms are emphasized. The same data are incorporated into the treatment plan problem areas and objectives. Both client strengths and weaknesses are sought to best aid in treatment. The information collected includes a biopsychosocial assessment, diagnostic interview, mental status exam, and validation of the diagnosis. It parallels the format of Form 3, in which similar information is filled out by the client. The two forms complement each other. Form 2 is important in outcome assessment because it defines specific problem areas that will be assessed throughout treatment. The information attained is directly incorporated into the treatment plan and other forms evaluating outcomes.

FORM 3: PERSONAL HISTORY—ADULT

Form 3 is used in conjunction with Form 2. It is filled out by the client (not the therapist, as in Form 2). If the client fills out the form prior to the interview with the clinician, it is especially helpful in ruling in and ruling out client problem areas from several aspects in the client's life. It follows a JCAHO format.

FORM 4: INDIVIDUAL TREATMENT PLAN

Form 4 is an example of a treatment plan that also includes some baseline outcome measures. An overview of writing the treatment plan is provided in Chapter 6. The problems portion of the treatment plan summarizes specific areas in the client's life that will be treated. These reflect functional impairments in areas such as occupational, social, educational, and other areas of significant distress. Outcomes are based on providing empirical evidence that the problem areas have been treated effectively. The goals and objectives section describes specific observable outcome measures by which the effects of therapy will be evaluated. Goals and objectives should be written in such a manner that objectives are set to incrementally return the client to a level of adequate functioning. Treatment plan goals and objectives are the same information used to assess outcomes of intraindividual change. The treatment strategies area of the treatment plan describes specific therapeutic interventions by which the objectives will be met.

FORM 5: PROGRESS NOTES

Form 5 provides a format for writing progress notes. An overview of writing progress notes is provided in Chapter 7. Progress notes provide session-by-session evidence of outcomes. They are designed to provide evidence of treatment plan objectives and indicate progress and setbacks in all areas of treatment.

FORM 6: BEHAVIORAL OBSERVATIONS: WEEKLY TALLY SHEET

Form 6 provides a tally sheet on which specific target behaviors can be tallied on a daily basis.

The information may be provided by the client or by a collateral. Besides simply counting the frequency of the behavior, each incident can also be rated for duration and intensity. A scale of 1 to 100 is suggested to rate the severity of each behavioral occurrence (or the rater might choose another scaling system). Instructions are provided on the form.

FORM 7: HOURLY BEHAVIORAL OBSERVATION TALLY SHEET

Form 7 is similar to Form 6 in providing a tally of behavior. It differs in that it provides an hourly tally of behaviors, rather than a summation of each day as in Form 6. Form 7 is especially helpful in behavioral programming or in identifying at what times of the day and/or on which days of the week the behavior takes place. The information can be helpful in identifying antecedents and reinforcers of the behavior. Directions are provided on the form.

FORM 8: TREATMENT PLAN OBJECTIVES PROGRESS CHART

Form 8 provides a session-by-session summary of each treatment plan objective. Although this one-page form does not provide any descriptions or explanations of progress, it helps the clinician to quickly view the baseline and current progress of each objective on one sheet. When objectives are written in terms of ordinal or interval data, the numbers filled in on the form are the specific numbers. For example, if the client's objectives include applying for jobs, and the client applies for four jobs in a particular week, the number 4 is written for the session. Nominal or nonnumerical data can be plotted by stating "Yes" or "No" as to whether an objective has been fulfilled. For example, an objective of making an appointment for a medical evaluation is not quantifiable, but it can be written as "Yes" once the behavior has taken place.

FORM 9: TREATMENT PLAN OBJECTIVES PROGRESS CHART—INDIVIDUAL OBJECTIVES

Form 9 is used to graph, summarize, and evaluate very specific information for each treatment plan objective. The form provides directions as to how to fill it out. Generally, this form is only used for treatment plan objectives that have been chosen to be specific outcome indicators.

FORM 10: TREATMENT OUTCOMES SUMMARY

Form 10 is divided into two parts, summarizing standardized and individual outcome results. First, pre- and posttest scores are compared to evaluate the client's scores on standardized tests in an effort to determine clinical significance when comparing the client to a normal population. The second part of the form evaluates progress in treatment plan objectives.

FORM 11: OUTCOME ASSESSMENT SUMMARY NARRATIVE REPORT

Form 11 provides a brief description of the client's individual and normative outcomes. It defines areas of progress and continued concerns and provides empirical evidence of the effects of treatment.

BLANK FORMS

FORM 1 LIMITS OF CONFIDENTIALITY—USE OF CLIENT INFORMATION

Confidentiality

The contents of a counseling, intake, or assessment session are considered confidential. Verbal information and/or written records about a client cannot be shared with another party without the written consent of the client or the client's legal guardian. It is the policy of this clinic not to release any information about a client without a signed release of information. Noted exceptions are as follows in points 1–8 below.

(1) Duty to Warn and Protect

When a client discloses intentions or a plan to harm another person, the health care professional is required to warn the intended victim and report this information to legal authorities. In cases when the client discloses or implies a plan for suicide, the health care professional is required to notify legal authorities and make reasonable attempts to notify the family of the client.

(2) Abuse of Children and Vulnerable Adults

If a client states or suggests that he or she is abusing a child (or vulnerable adult) or has recently abused a child (or vulnerable adult), or a child (or vulnerable adult) is in danger of abuse, the health care professional is required to report this information to the appropriate social service and/or legal authorities.

(3) Prenatal Exposure to Controlled Substances

Health care professionals are required to report admitted prenatal exposure to controlled substances that are potentially harmful.

(4) In the Event of a Client's Death

In the event of a client's death, the spouse or parents of a deceased client have a right to access their child's or spouse's records.

(5) Professional Misconduct

Professional misconduct by a health care professional must be reported by other health care professionals. In cases in which a professional or legal disciplinary meeting is being held regarding the health care professional's actions, related records may be released in order to substantiate disciplinary concerns.

(6) Court Orders

Health care professionals are required to release client records due to a court order.

(7) Minors/Guardianship

Parents or legal guardians of nonemancipated minor clients have the right to access the client's records.

(8) Other Provisions and Procedures

When fees for services are not paid in a timely manner, collection agencies may be utilized in collecting unpaid debts. The specific content of the services (e.g., diagnosis, treatment plan, case notes, testing) is not disclosed. If a debt remains unpaid it may be reported to credit agencies, and the client's credit report may state the amount owed, the time frame, and the name of the clinic.

Insurance companies and other third-party payers are given information that they request regarding services to clients. Information that may be requested includes type of services, dates/times of services, diagnosis, treatment plan, description of impairment, progress of therapy, case notes, and summaries.

Form 1 Limits of Confidentiality

Information about clients may be disclosed in consultations with other professionals in order to provide the best possible treatment. In such cases the name of the client, or any identifying information, is not disclosed. Clinical information about the client is discussed. In some cases notes and reports are dictated/typed within the clinic or by outside sources specializing in (and held accountable for) such procedures.

When couples, groups, or families are receiving services, separate files are kept for individuals for information disclosed that is of a confidential nature. The information includes (a) testing results, (b) information given to the mental health professional not in the presence of other person(s) utilizing services, (c) information received from other sources about the client, (d) diagnosis, (e) treatment plan, (f) individual reports/summaries, and (h) information that has been requested to be kept separate. The material disclosed in conjoint family or couples sessions, in which each party discloses such information in the other's presence, is kept in each file in the form of case notes.

In the event the clinic or mental health professional must telephone the client for purposes such as appointment cancellations or reminders, or to give/receive other information, efforts are made to preserve confidentiality. Please list where we may reach you by phone and how you would like us to identify ourselves. For example, you might request that when we phone you at home or work, we do not say the name of the clinic or the nature of the call, but rather the mental health professional's first name only.

If this information is not provided to us (below), we will adhere to the following procedure when making phone calls: First we will ask to speak to the client (or guardian) without identifying the name of the clinic. If the person answering the phone asks for more identifying information we will say that it is a "personal call." We will not identify the clinic (to protect confidentiality). If we reach an answering machine or voice mail we will follow the same guidelines. It is possible that the clinic could be identified through Caller ID or similar means over which we may have no control.

Please check where you may be reached by phone. Include phone numbers and how you would like us to identify ourselves when phoning you.

______HOME Phone number______________________________

How should we identify ourselves?______________________

May we say the clinic name?____Yes ____No

______WORK Phone number______________________________

How should we identify ourselves?______________________

May we say the clinic name?____Yes ____No

______OTHER Phone number______________________________

How should we identify ourselves?______________________

May we say the clinic name?____Yes ____No

I agree to the above limits of confidentiality and understand their meanings and ramifications.

Client's name (please print) ________________________________

Client's (or guardian's) signature X ________________________________ Date _____/____/______

Use of Client Information in Outcome Research

Client information is often used to evaluate the effectiveness of types of therapy, treatment procedures, the therapist, and/or other factors in which a more careful study may help in the delivery of mental health services. Client names are not used when client information is evaluated for outcome evaluation purposes.

I agree to allow data from my record (not my name) to be used for outcome purposes.

Client's name (please print) ________________________________

Client's (or guardian's) signature X ________________________________ Date _____/____/______

FORM 2 INITIAL ASSESSMENT—ADULT

Client's name ______________________________ Date ______________

Starting time ______________ Ending time ______________ Duration ______________

PART A. BIOPSYCHOSOCIAL ASSESSMENT

1. Presenting Problem

____

____

____

____

2. Signs and Symptoms (*DSM* based) Resulting in Impairment(s)
(Include current examples for treatment planning, e.g., social, occupational, affective, cognitive, physical)

____

____

____

____

3. History of Presenting Problem

Events, precipitating factors, or incidents leading to need for services ______________

____

____

____

Frequency/duration/severity/cycling of symptoms ______________________

____

____

____

Was there a clear time when symptoms worsened? ______________________

Family mental health history ______________________________

____

____

____

4. Current Family and Significant Relationships (See Personal History Form)

Strengths/support ______________________________

Stressors/problems ______________________________

Recent changes ______________________________

Changes desired ______________________________

Comment on family circumstances ______________________________

5. Childhood/Adolescent History (See Personal History Form)

(Developmental milestones, past behavioral concerns, environment abuse, school, social, mental health)

____

____

____

____

6. Social Relationships (See Personal History Form)

Strengths/support ______________________________

Stressors/problems ______________________________

Recent changes ______________________________

Changes desired ______________________________

7. Cultural/Ethnic (See Personal History Form)

Strengths/support ______________________________

Stressors/problems ______________________________

Beliefs/practices to incorporate into therapy ______________________________

8. Spiritual/Religious (See Personal History Form)

Strengths/support ______________________________

Stressors/problems ______________________________

Beliefs/practices to incorporate into therapy ______________________________

Recent changes ______________________________

Changes desired ______________________________

9. Legal (See Personal History Form)

____

____

Status/impact/stressors ______________________________

10. Education (See Personal History Form)

Strengths ______________________________

Weaknesses ______________________________

11. Employment/Vocational (See Personal History Form)

Strengths/support ______________________________

Stressors/problems ______________________________

12. Military (See Personal History Form)

____

Current impact ______________________________

13. Leisure/Recreational (See Personal History Form)

Strengths/support ______________________________

Recent changes ______________________________

Changes desired ______________________________

14. Physical Health (See Personal History Form)

____

____

Physical factors affecting mental condition ______________________________

15. Chemical Use History (See Personal History Form)

____

____

Patient's perception of problem ______________________________

16. Counseling/Prior Treatment History (See Personal History Form)

____

____

Benefits of previous treatment ______________________________

Setbacks of previous treatment ______________________________

PART B. DIAGNOSTIC INTERVIEW

Mood

Common mood disorders listed below (rule in and rule out signs and symptoms: validate with *DSM*)
Predominant mood during interview ______________________________

Current Concerns (give examples of impairments, severity [s], frequency [f], duration [d])

Adjustment Disorder

(within 3 mo of identified stressor, symptoms persist <6 mo after stressor, marked distress)

___Depressed ___Anxiety ___Mixed anxiety and depression ___Conduct

___Emotions and conduct ___Unspecified

Specify disturbance ___Acute (<6 mo) ___Chronic (>6 mo) ______________________________

____

Impairment(s) ___Social ___Occupational/educational ___Affective ___Cognitive ___Other

Examples of impairment(s) ____

____

Major Depression (2 or more wks) ___Usually depressed or ___Anhedonia (4+ of following)

___Weight +/(−) 5%/mo ___Appetite +/(−) ___Sleep +/(−) ___Psychomotor +/(−)

___Fatigue ___Worthlessness/guilt ___Concentration ___Death/suicidal ideation

Other ___Crying spells ___Withdrawal ___Additional symptoms ____________________

____

Impairment(s) ___Social ___Occupational/educational ___Affective ___Cognitive ___Other

Examples of impairment(s) ____

____

Dysthymia (2 or more years) ___Depressed most of time (2+ of following)

___Low/high appetite or eating ___In-/hypersomnia ___Low energy/fatigue ___Low self-esteem

___Low concentration/decisions ___Hopelessness ___Other ____________________

____

Impairment(s) ___Social ___Occupational/educational ___Affective ___Cognitive ___Other

Examples of impairment(s) ____

____

Mania (3+)

___Grandiosity ___Low sleep ___Talkativeness ___Flight of ideas ___Distractibility

___Goals/agitation ___Excessive pleasure

____

Impairment(s) ___Social ___Occupational/educational ___Affective ___Cognitive ___Other

Examples of impairment(s) ____

____

Panic Attacks (4+, abrupt development of)

___Palpitations ___Sweating ___Trembling ___Shortness of breath ___Feeling of choking

___Chest pain ___Nausea ___Dizziness ___Light-headedness ___Derealization
___Fear of losing control ___Fear of dying ___Numbness ___Chills/hot flashes

____

Impairment(s) ___Social ___Occupational/educational ___Affective ___Cognitive ___Other
Examples of impairment(s) ____

____

Anxiety (GAD 3+, most of time, 6 mo)
___Restlessness ___Easily fatigued ___Concentration ___Irritability
___Muscle tension ___Sleep disturbance

____

Impairment(s) ___Social ___Occupational/educational ___Affective ___Cognitive ___Other
Examples of impairment(s) ____

____

Other Diagnostic Concerns or Behavioral Issues
(e.g., ___Dissociation ___Eating ___Sleep ___Impulse control ___Thought disorders ___Anger
___Relationships ___Cognitive ___Phobias ___Substance abuse ___Medical conditions
___Somatization ___Sexual PTSD, etc.)

____

Impairment(s) ___Social ___Occupational/educational ___Affective ___Cognitive ___Other
Examples of impairment(s) ____

____

USE ADDITIONAL PAPER AS NECESSARY

Mental Status

(Check appropriate level of impairment: N/A or OK signifies no known impairment. Comment on significant areas of impairment.)

Appearance	N/A or OK	Slight	Moderate	Severe
Unkempt, disheveled	(___)	(___)	(___)	(___)
Clothing dirty, atypical	(___)	(___)	(___)	(___)
Odd physical characteristics	(___)	(___)	(___)	(___)
Body odor	(___)	(___)	(___)	(___)
Appears unhealthy	(___)	(___)	(___)	(___)

Posture	N/A or OK	Slight	Moderate	Severe
Slumped	(___)	(___)	(___)	(___)
Rigid, tense	(___)	(___)	(___)	(___)

Body Movements	N/A or OK	Slight	Moderate	Severe
Accelerated, quick	(___)	(___)	(___)	(___)
Decreased, slowed	(___)	(___)	(___)	(___)
Restlessness, fidgety	(___)	(___)	(___)	(___)
Atypical, unusual	(___)	(___)	(___)	(___)

Speech	N/A or OK	Slight	Moderate	Severe
Rapid	(___)	(___)	(___)	(___)
Slow	(___)	(___)	(___)	(___)
Loud	(___)	(___)	(___)	(___)
Soft	(___)	(___)	(___)	(___)
Mute	(___)	(___)	(___)	(___)
Atypical (e.g., slurring)	(___)	(___)	(___)	(___)

Attitude	N/A or OK	Slight	Moderate	Severe
Domineering, controlling	(___)	(___)	(___)	(___)
Submissive, dependent	(___)	(___)	(___)	(___)
Hostile, challenging	(___)	(___)	(___)	(___)
Guarded, suspicious	(___)	(___)	(___)	(___)
Uncooperative	(___)	(___)	(___)	(___)

Affect	N/A or OK	Slight	Moderate	Severe
Inappropriate to thought	(___)	(___)	(___)	(___)
Increased lability	(___)	(___)	(___)	(___)
Blunted, dull, flat	(___)	(___)	(___)	(___)
Euphoria, elation	(___)	(___)	(___)	(___)
Anger, hostility	(___)	(___)	(___)	(___)
Depression, sadness	(___)	(___)	(___)	(___)
Anxiety	(___)	(___)	(___)	(___)
Irritability	(___)	(___)	(___)	(___)

Perception	N/A or OK	Slight	Moderate	Severe
Illusions	(___)	(___)	(___)	(___)
Auditory hallucinations	(___)	(___)	(___)	(___)
Visual hallucinations	(___)	(___)	(___)	(___)
Other hallucinations	(___)	(___)	(___)	(___)

Cognitive	N/A or OK	Slight	Moderate	Severe
Alertness	(___)	(___)	(___)	(___)
Attention span, distractibility	(___)	(___)	(___)	(___)
Short-term memory	(___)	(___)	(___)	(___)
Long-term memory	(___)	(___)	(___)	(___)

Judgment	N/A or OK	Slight	Moderate	Severe
Decision making	(___)	(___)	(___)	(___)
Impulsivity	(___)	(___)	(___)	(___)

Thought Content	N/A or OK	Slight	Moderate	Severe
Obsessions/compulsions	(___)	(___)	(___)	(___)
Phobic	(___)	(___)	(___)	(___)
Depersonalization	(___)	(___)	(___)	(___)
Suicidal ideation	(___)	(___)	(___)	(___)
Homicidal ideation	(___)	(___)	(___)	(___)
Delusions	(___)	(___)	(___)	(___)

Estimated level of intelligence ______________________________

Orientation ___Time ___Place ___Person

Able to hold normal conversation? ___Yes ___No

Eye contact ______________________________

Level of insight

___Complete denial ___Slight awareness

___Blames others ___Blames self

___Intellectual insight, but few changes likely

___Emotional insight, understanding, change can occur

Client's view of actions needed to change ______________________________

Comments

____
____
____
____
____
____
____

PART C. DIAGNOSIS VALIDATION

Diagnosis 1 _______________________________ Code _______

DSM criteria

____
____
____

Examples of impairment/dysfunction ____
____
____
____

Additional validation (e.g., testing, previous records, self-report)_______________
____
____
____

Diagnosis 2 _______________________________ Code _______

DSM criteria

____
____
____

Examples of impairment/dysfunction ____
____
____
____

Additional validation (e.g., testing, previous records, self-report)______________________________

Diagnosis 3 ____ Code ______

DSM criteria

Examples of impairment/dysfunction ________________________________

Additional validation (e.g., testing, previous records, self-report)______________________________

		Diagnosis	Code
Axis I	1		
	2		
	3		
Axis II	1		
	2		
Axis III			
Axis IV			

Axis V Current GAF = ______ Highest GAF past year = ______

Prognosis ___Poor ___Marginal ___Guarded ___Moderate ___Good ___Excellent

Qualifiers to prognosis ___Med compliance ___Treatment compliance ___Home environment ___Activity changes ___Behavioral changes ___Attitudinal changes ___Education/training

Other ____

Treatment Considerations

Is the patient appropriate for treatment? ___Yes ___No

If no, explain and indicate referral made ______________________________

Treatment modality ___Individual ___Conjoint ___Family ___Collateral ___Group

Frequency ________ ________ ________ ________ ________

If conjoint, family, or collateral, specify with whom ______________________________

Adjunctive Services Needed

___Physical exam ___School records (specify)______________________________

___Laboratory tests (specify)______________________________

___Patient records (specify) ______________________________

Therapist's Questions/Concerns/Comments ___Psychiatric evaluation ___Psychological testing

____

____

____

Therapist's signature/credentials ______________________________ Date ____/____/____

Supervisor's Remarks

____

____

____

Supervisor's signature/credentials ______________________________ Date ____/____/____

Therapist's Response to Supervisor's Remarks

____

____

Therapist's signature/credentials ______________________________ Date ____/____/____

FORM 3 PERSONAL HISTORY—ADULT

Client's name ______________________________ Date ______________

Gender ___F ___M Date of birth ______________ Age ________

Form completed by (if someone other than client) ______________________________

Address ______________________________ City ______________ State_____ Zip________

Phone (home) ______________________ (work)______________ ext ________

If you need any more space for any of the questions, please use the back of the sheet.

Primary reason(s) for seeking services

___Anger management ___Anxiety ___Coping ___Depression
___Eating disorder ___Fear/phobias ___Mental confusion ___Sexual concerns
___Sleeping problems ___Addictive behaviors ___Alcohol/drugs
___Other mental health concerns (specify)______________________________

Family Information

Relationship	Name	Age	Living Yes	Living No	Living with you Yes	Living with you No
Mother	______	___	___	___	___	___
Father	______	___	___	___	___	___
Spouse	______	___	___	___	___	___
Children	______	___	___	___	___	___
	______	___	___	___	___	___
	______	___	___	___	___	___

Significant others (brothers, sisters, grandparents, step-relatives, half-relatives—please specify relationship)

Relationship	Name	Age	Living Yes	Living No	Living with you Yes	Living with you No
______	______	___	___	___	___	___
______	______	___	___	___	___	___
______	______	___	___	___	___	___
______	______	___	___	___	___	___
______	______	___	___	___	___	___
______	______	___	___	___	___	___

Marital Status (more than 1 answer may apply)

___Single

___Divorce in process
Length of time ______

___Unmarried, living together
Length of time ______

___Legally married
Length of time ______

___Separated
Length of time ______

___Divorced
Length of time ______

___Widowed
Length of time ______

___Annulment
Length of time ______

Total number of marriages ______

Assessment of current relationship (if applicable) ___Good ___Fair ___Poor

Parental Information

___Parents legally married

___Mother remarried (number of times)______________

___Parents have ever been separated

___Father remarried (number of times) ______________

___Parents ever divorced

Special circumstances (e.g., raised by person other than parents, information about spouse/children not living with you, etc.) ____

Development

Are there special, unusual, or traumatic circumstances that affected your development? ___Yes ___No

If yes, please describe ____

Has there been a history of child abuse? ___Yes ___No

If yes, which type(s)? ___Sexual ___Physical ___Verbal

If yes, the abuse was as a ___Victim ___Perpetrator

Other childhood issues ___Neglect ___Inadequate nutrition ___Other (please specify)_______

Comments regarding childhood development____

____

Social Relationships

Check how you have related to or gotten along with other people most of your life (check all that apply)

___Affectionate ___Aggressive ___Avoidant ___Fight/argue often ___Follower

___Friendly ___Leader ___Outgoing ___Shy/withdrawn ___Submissive

___Other (specify) ____

Have your social relationships changed recently? ___Yes ___No

If yes, describe ____

Sexual orientation ______________ Comments ______________

Sexual dysfunctions? ___Yes ___No

If yes, describe____

Any current or history of being a sexual perpetrator? ___Yes ___No

If yes, describe____

Cultural/Ethnic

To which cultural or ethnic group do you belong? ________________________

Are you experiencing any problems due to cultural or ethnic issues? ___Yes ___No

If yes, describe____

Other cultural/ethnic information ______________________________

Spiritual/Religious

How important to you are spiritual matters? ___Not ___Little ___Moderate ___Much

Are you affiliated with a spiritual or religious group? ___Yes ___No

If yes, describe____

Were you raised within a spiritual or religious group? ___Yes ___No

If yes, describe____

Would you like your spiritual/religious beliefs incorporated into the counseling? ___Yes ___No

If yes, describe____

Legal

Current Status

Are you involved in any active cases (traffic, civil, criminal)? ___Yes ___No

If yes, please describe and indicate the court and hearing/trial dates and charges________________

Are you presently on probation or parole? ___Yes ___No

If yes, please describe ____

Past History

Traffic violations	___Yes	___No	DWI, DUI, etc.	___Yes	___No
Criminal involvement	___Yes	___No	Civil involvement	___Yes	___No

If you responded yes to any of the above, please fill in the following information.

Charges	Date	Where (city)	Results

Education

Fill in all that apply. Years of education ______Currently enrolled in school? ___Yes ___No

___High school grad/GED

___Vocational Number of years ___ Graduated ___Yes ___No Major________________

___College Number of years ___ Graduated ___Yes ___No Major________________

___Graduate Number of years ___ Graduated ___Yes ___No Major________________

Other training ____

Special circumstances (e.g., learning disabilities, gifted)________________________

Employment

Beginning with most recent job, list job history.

Employer	Dates	Title	Reason for leaving	How often do you miss work?

Currently __FT __PT __Temp __Laid off __Disabled __Retired __Soc. Sec. __Student

Other (describe) ____

Military

Military experience? ___Yes ___No Combat experience? ___Yes ___No

Where ____

Branch ______________________ Discharge date ______________________

Date drafted ______________________ Type of discharge ______________________

Date enlisted ______________________ Rank at discharge ______________________

Leisure/Recreational

Describe special areas of interest or hobbies (e.g., art, books, crafts, physical fitness, sports, outdoor activities, church activities, walking, exercising, diet/health, hunting, fishing, bowling, traveling, etc.)

Activity	How often now?	How often in the past?

Medical/Physical Health

___AIDS	___Dizziness	___Nosebleeds
___Alcoholism	___Drug abuse	___Pneumonia
___Abdominal pain	___Epilepsy	___Rheumatic fever
___Abortion	___Ear infections	___Sexually transmitted diseases
___Allergies	___Eating problems	___Sleeping disorders
___Anemia	___Fainting	___Sore throat
___Appendicitis	___Fatigue	___Scarlet fever
___Arthritis	___Frequent urination	___Sinusitis
___Asthma	___Headaches	___Small pox
___Bronchitis	___Hearing problems	___Stroke
___Bed-wetting	___Hepatitis	___Sexual problems
___Cancer	___High blood pressure	___Tonsillitis
___Chest pain	___Kidney problems	___Tuberculosis
___Chronic pain	___Measles	___Toothache
___Colds/coughs	___Mononucleosis	___Thyroid problems
___Constipation	___Mumps	___Vision problems
___Chicken pox	___Menstrual pain	___Vomiting
___Dental problems	___Miscarriages	___Whooping cough
___Diabetes	___Neurological disorders	___Other (describe) ______________
___Diarrhea	___Nausea	______________________

List any current health concerns ____

List any recent health or physical changes ________________________________

Nutrition

Meal	How often (times per week)	Typical foods eaten	Typical amount of food eaten			
Breakfast	____/week	____________________	___No	___Low	___Med	___High
Lunch	____/week	____________________	___No	___Low	___Med	___High
Dinner	____/week	____________________	___No	___Low	___Med	___High
Snacks	____/week	____________________	___No	___Low	___Med	___High

Comments ____

Current prescribed medications	Dose	Dates	Purpose	Side effects
____________	____	____	______	______
____________	____	____	______	______
____________	____	____	______	______
____________	____	____	______	______

Current over-the-counter meds	Dose	Dates	Purpose	Side effects
____________	____	____	______	______
____________	____	____	______	______
____________	____	____	______	______
____________	____	____	______	______

Are you allergic to any medications or drugs? ___Yes ___No

If yes, describe____

____

	Date	Reason	Results
Last physical exam	____	__________	__________
Last doctor's visit	____	__________	__________
Last dental exam	____	__________	__________
Most recent surgery	____	__________	__________
Other surgery	____	__________	__________
Upcoming surgery	____	__________	__________

____

Family history of medical problems________________________________

____

Please check if there have been any recent changes in the following

___Sleep patterns ___Eating patterns ___Behavior ___Energy level

___Physical activity level ___General disposition ___Weight ___Nervousness/tension

Describe changes in areas you checked above ______________________

____

Chemical Use History

	Amount	Frequency of use	Age of first use	Age of last use	Used in last 48 hours? Yes	No	Used in last 30 days? Yes	No
Alcohol	______	______	____	____	__	__	__	__
Barbiturates	______	______	____	____	__	__	__	__
Valium/Librium	______	______	____	____	__	__	__	__
Cocaine/crack	______	______	____	____	__	__	__	__
Heroin/opiates	______	______	____	____	__	__	__	__
Marijuana	______	______	____	____	__	__	__	__
PCP/LSD/mescaline	______	______	____	____	__	__	__	__
Inhalants	______	______	____	____	__	__	__	__
Caffeine	______	______	____	____	__	__	__	__
Nicotine	______	______	____	____	__	__	__	__
Over-the-counter drugs	______	______	____	____	__	__	__	__
Prescription drugs	______	______	____	____	__	__	__	__
Other drugs	______	______	____	____	__	__	__	__

Substance(s) of preference

1 ______________________ 3 ______________________

2 ______________________ 4 ______________________

Substance Abuse Questions

Describe when and where you typically use substances ______________________

____

Describe any changes in your use patterns______________________

____

Describe how your use has affected your family or friends (include their perceptions of your use)_____

____

Reason(s) for use

___Addicted ___Build confidence ___Escape ___Self-medication

___Socialization ___Taste ___Other (specify)

How do you believe your substance use affects your life?______________________

Who or what has helped you in stopping or limiting your use?______________________

Does/has someone in your family present/past have/had a problem with drugs or alcohol?

___Yes ___No If yes, describe ______________________

Have you had withdrawal symptoms when trying to stop using drugs or alcohol? ___Yes ___No

If yes, describe____

Have you had adverse reactions or overdose to drugs or alcohol? (describe)____

____

Does your body temperature change when you drink? ___Yes ___No

If yes, describe____

Have drugs or alcohol created a problem for your job? ___Yes ___No

If yes, describe____

Counseling/Prior Treatment History

Information about client (past and present)

	Yes	No	When	Where	Your reaction to overall experience
Counseling/psychiatric treatment	___	___	___	___	___
Suicidal thoughts/attempts	___	___	___	___	___
Drug/alcohol treatment	___	___	___	___	___
Hospitalizations	___	___	___	___	___
Involvement with self-help groups (e.g., AA, Al-Anon, NA, Overeaters Anonymous)	___	___	___	___	___

Information about family/significant others (past and present)

	Yes	No	When	Where	Your reaction to overall experience
Counseling/psychiatric treatment	___	___	___	___	___
Suicidal thoughts/attempts	___	___	___	___	___
Drug/alcohol treatment	___	___	___	___	___
Hospitalizations	___	___	___	___	___
Involvement with self-help groups (e.g., AA, Al-Anon, NA, Overeaters Anonymous)	___	___	___	___	___

Please check behaviors and symptoms that occur more often than you would like.

___Aggression ___Elevated mood ___Phobias/fears

___Alcohol dependence ___Fatigue ___Recurring thoughts

___Anger
___Antisocial behavior
___Anxiety
___Avoiding people
___Chest pain
___Cyber addiction
___Depression
___Disorientation
___Distractibility
___Dizziness
___Drug dependence
___Eating disorder
___Gambling
___Hallucinations
___Heart palpitations
___High blood pressure
___Hopelessness
___Impulsivity
___Irritability
___Judgment errors
___Loneliness
___Memory impairment
___Mood shifts
___Panic attacks
___Sexual addiction
___Sexual difficulties
___Sick often
___Sleeping problems
___Speech problems
___Suicidal thoughts
___Thoughts disorganized
___Trembling
___Withdrawing
___Worrying
___Other (specify) ____________________

Comments ____

Briefly discuss how the above symptoms impair your ability to function effectively____________

Any additional information that would assist us in understanding your concerns or problems ______

What are your goals for therapy? ____

____

____

____

____

____

____

Do you feel suicidal at this time? ___Yes ___No

If yes, explain ____

____

____

____

For Staff Use

Therapist's signature/credentials ______________________________ Date _____/____/______

Supervisor's comments ____

____

____

________________________________Physical exam ___Required ___Not required

Supervisor's signature/credentials______________________________ Date _____/____/______

(Certifies case assignment, level of care and need for exam)

FORM 4 INDIVIDUAL TREATMENT PLAN

Client ______________________________Chart # __________Date______________
Diagnosis(es)____Therapist___________
Estimated # of sessions Individual ___Group ___Family ___Other _______________________
Impairments ___ Social ___ Occupational ___Academic __Physical __Affective distress
___Other ____
Initial GAF _________Target GAF ___________

Normative Outcome Measures

Test #1 _____________________________________

Subscale	Baseline score	Target score	Subscale	Baseline score	Target score

Test #2 _____________________________________

Subscale	Baseline score	Target score	Subscale	Baseline score	Target score

TP Problem #1 ____
____
Frequency________________ Duration ________________ Severity ________________
Goal 1____
Objective 1a ______________________________________Target date ____________
Objective 1b ______________________________________Target date ____________
Objective 1c ______________________________________Target date ____________
Treatment strategies ____
____

TP Problem #2 ____

____

Frequency________________ Duration ________________ Severity ________________

Goal 2____

Objective 2a ______________________________Target date ____________

Objective 2b ______________________________Target date ____________

Objective 2c ______________________________Target date ____________

Treatment strategies ____

____

TP Problem #3 ____

____

Frequency________________ Duration ________________ Severity ________________

Goal 3____

Objective 3a ______________________________Target date ____________

Objective 3b ______________________________Target date ____________

Objective 3c ______________________________Target date ____________

Treatment strategies ____

____

TP Problem #4 ____

____

Frequency________________ Duration ________________ Severity ________________

Goal 4____

Objective 4a ______________________________Target date ____________

Objective 4b ______________________________Target date ____________

Objective 4c ______________________________Target date ____________

Treatment strategies ____

____

TP Problem #5 ____

____

Frequency________________ Duration ________________ Severity ________________

Goal 5____

Objective 5a ______________________________ Target date __________
Objective 5b ______________________________ Target date __________
Objective 5c ______________________________ Target date __________
Treatment strategies ____

____

TP Problem #6 ____

____

Frequency____________ Duration ____________ Severity ____________
Goal 6____
Objective 6a ______________________________ Target date __________
Objective 6b ______________________________ Target date __________
Objective 6c ______________________________ Target date __________
Treatment strategies ____

____

(Use additional sheets as needed for more problem areas.)

I have discussed the above information, various treatment strategies, and their possible outcomes. I have received and/or read my copy of my rights as a client and procedures for reporting grievances. I concur with the above diagnosis and treatment plan.

Client's signature ______________________________ Date ______________

Guardian's signature ______________________________ Date ______________

Therapist's signature ______________________________ Date ______________

Supervisor's signature ______________________________ Date ______________

FORM 5 PROGRESS NOTES

Client ______________________ Chart # __________ Session # ______ Date __________

Diagnosis ____

Outcome indicators measured prior to session __________________________________

____

____

Treatment plan objectives for this session ____________________________________

____

____

____

____

____

____

____

____

____

____

____

____

____

____

____

____

____

____

____

____

____

____

Time started ________ Time finished ________ Duration _____ Next appt. ______ @ ________

Procedure ____________________ Therapist's signature/credentials ______________________

FORM 6 BEHAVIORAL OBSERVATIONS: WEEKLY TALLY SHEET

Name of person observed ______________________ Observation date(s) __________

Observed by ______________________________ Relationship________________

Behavior observed/tallied ____

How will the observations take place? ______________________________

Check which aspects of the behavior will be observed and tallied.

(A)___Frequency (how often does the behavior take place in each time period?)

(For example: January 13; 3 anger outbursts took place)

(B)___Duration (how long it takes place) ___Sec ___Min ___Hr ___Other (specify)______

(For example: January 13; anger outbursts lasted 15, 18, and 12 minutes)

(C)___Severity (describe severity scale used, such as SUD, Mild/Moderate/Severe, or other descriptors)

(For example: January 13; the severity [IRS] of anger outbursts was 80, 85, and 70)

Example (from the above data)

5-Mon	(A) Frequency	(B) Duration	(C) Severity	Comments
July 7	Total 3	Average 15	Average 83.3	Decreased duration when ignored

Average = Sum or durations or severities/Frequency—for example: Average duration = (15 + 18 + 12)/3 = 15

Day Date	**(A) Frequency** ______	**(B) Duration** __Sec__Min__Hr	**(C) Severity** ______	**Comments**
1 _____	______	______	______	______
_____	Total ______	Average ______	Average ______	______
2 _____	______	______	______	______
_____	Total ______	Average ______	Average ______	______
3 _____	______	______	______	______
_____	Total ______	Average ______	Average ______	______
4 _____	______	______	______	______
_____	Total ______	Average ______	Average ______	______
5 _____	______	______	______	______
_____	Total ______	Average ______	Average ______	______
6 _____	______	______	______	______
_____	Total ______	Average ______	Average ______	______

7 ____ __________ __________ __________ ____________________

_____ Total ________ Average _____ Average_____ ____________________

Average frequency per day = Total of averages/Number of days listed ______/ ______=________

Weekly average of daily averages = Total of average scores/Number of days measured

Duration weekly average = ______/ ______=_______

Severity weekly average = ______/ ______=_______

FORM 7 HOURLY BEHAVIORAL OBSERVATION TALLY SHEET

Name of person observed ______________________________ Observation dates ______________

Observed by ____ Relationship __________________

Behavior(s) observed/tallied ____

Time period	Sun	Mon	Tue	Wed	Thu	Fri	Sat	Total	# Days	Daily hourly average
6:00–7:00 A.M.	____	____	____	____	____	____	____	____	____	________
7:00–8:00 A.M.	____	____	____	____	____	____	____	____	____	________
8:00–9:00 A.M.	____	____	____	____	____	____	____	____	____	________
9:00–10:00 A.M.	____	____	____	____	____	____	____	____	____	________
10:00–11:00 A.M.	____	____	____	____	____	____	____	____	____	________
11:00–12:00 A.M.	____	____	____	____	____	____	____	____	____	________
12:00–1:00 P.M.	____	____	____	____	____	____	____	____	____	________
1:00–2:00 P.M.	____	____	____	____	____	____	____	____	____	________
2:00–3:00 P.M.	____	____	____	____	____	____	____	____	____	________
3:00–4:00 P.M.	____	____	____	____	____	____	____	____	____	________
4:00–5:00 P.M.	____	____	____	____	____	____	____	____	____	________
5:00–6:00 P.M.	____	____	____	____	____	____	____	____	____	________
6:00–7:00 P.M.	____	____	____	____	____	____	____	____	____	________
7:00–8:00 P.M.	____	____	____	____	____	____	____	____	____	________
8:00–9:00 P.M.	____	____	____	____	____	____	____	____	____	________
9:00–10:00 P.M.	____	____	____	____	____	____	____	____	____	________
10:00–11:00 P.M.	____	____	____	____	____	____	____	____	____	________
11:00–12:00 P.M.	____	____	____	____	____	____	____	____	____	________
12:00–1:00 A.M.	____	____	____	____	____	____	____	____	____	________
1:00–2:00 A.M.	____	____	____	____	____	____	____	____	____	________
2:00–3:00 A.M.	____	____	____	____	____	____	____	____	____	________
3:00–4:00 A.M.	____	____	____	____	____	____	____	____	____	________
4:00–5:00 A.M.	____	____	____	____	____	____	____	____	____	________
5:00–6:00 A.M.	____	____	____	____	____	____	____	____	____	________
										Weekly

Daily totals	___	___	___	___	___	___	___		________
# of Observations	___	___	___	___	___	___	___		________
***Daily averages**	___	___	___	___	___	___	___	*****Total hourly average**	________

*Daily average = Daily total/# of observations

Note: Daily averages should be based on the number of hours the behavior was observed, not 24 hours, unless it is observed 24 hours per day.

**Daily hourly average = Hourly total/# of observations for time period

***Total hourly average = Weekly total/Total # of observations for week

Remarks ____

____

____

FORM 8 TREATMENT PLAN OBJECTIVES PROGRESS CHART

Client ______________________ **Chart #**__________ **Intake date** __________

Objective # ______ Describe ____

Initial objective level ____________ Revisions in level of objective ______________

Date __ __ __ __ __ __ __ __ __ __ __ __ __ __ __ __ Date completed

Data __ __ __ __ __ __ __ __ __ __ __ __ __ __ __ __ __________

Objective # ______ Describe ____

Initial objective level ____________ Revisions in level of objective ______________

Date __ __ __ __ __ __ __ __ __ __ __ __ __ __ __ __ Date completed

Data __ __ __ __ __ __ __ __ __ __ __ __ __ __ __ __ __________

Objective # ______ Describe ____

Initial objective level ____________ Revisions in level of objective ______________

Date __ __ __ __ __ __ __ __ __ __ __ __ __ __ __ __ Date completed

Data __ __ __ __ __ __ __ __ __ __ __ __ __ __ __ __ __________

Objective # ______ Describe ____

Initial objective level ____________ Revisions in level of objective ______________

Date __ __ __ __ __ __ __ __ __ __ __ __ __ __ __ __ Date completed

Data __ __ __ __ __ __ __ __ __ __ __ __ __ __ __ __ __________

Objective # ______ Describe ____

Initial objective level ____________ Revisions in level of objective ______________

Date __ __ __ __ __ __ __ __ __ __ __ __ __ __ __ __ Date completed

Data __ __ __ __ __ __ __ __ __ __ __ __ __ __ __ __ __________

Objective # ______ Describe ____

Initial objective level ____________ Revisions in level of objective ______________

Date __ __ __ __ __ __ __ __ __ __ __ __ __ __ __ __ Date completed

Data __ __ __ __ __ __ __ __ __ __ __ __ __ __ __ __ __________

Objective # ______ Describe ____

Initial objective level ____________ Revisions in level of objective ______________

Date __ __ __ __ __ __ __ __ __ __ __ __ __ __ __ __ Date completed

Data __ __ __ __ __ __ __ __ __ __ __ __ __ __ __ __ __________

Objective # _______ Describe ____

Initial objective level _______________ Revisions in level of objective ___________________________

Date __ __ __ __ __ __ __ __ __ __ __ __ __ __ __ __ __ Date completed

Data __ __ __ __ __ __ __ __ __ __ __ __ __ __ __ __ __ ____________

Use additional sheets as necessary.

FORM 9 TREATMENT PLAN OBJECTIVES PROGRESS CHART—INDIVIDUAL OBJECTIVES

Client____ Chart #__________ Intake date _______

Presenting problem ____ Therapist ________

Objective (A) __Increase __Decrease (*B) __Duration __Frequency __Rating __Test score

___Other ____

Outcome description of objective (*C) ____

(*D) Baseline measurement (number or descriptor) __________, is based on ___Average or ___Total per (time period)

(E) Charted below as __Session number __Weekly __2 Weeks __Dates as listed __Other ______

Use one form for each treatment plan objective used as an outcome indicator.

Treatment plan objective # ____________Remarks (i.e., factors affecting objectives; include dates)

____

____

____

____

____

High

(*C) Outcome
behavior or
name of test
or outcome
measure

____
____
____
____

(Fill in increments
of measurement
from low to high,
e.g., 5, 10, or
never to always.
Fill in or skip
spaces as needed.)

Low
Measurement
(*D) Baseline
Session number
Date

Comments ____
____
____
____

FORM 10 TREATMENT OUTCOMES SUMMARY

Client ______________________________ Chart # ______________

Date began ____________ Date ended ____________ Total # of sessions ____________

___Therapy complete (as per estimated # of sessions) ___Therapy prematurely terminated

Comments ____

____

Normative Outcome Measures

(1) Test ______________________________

Subscale	Reliable change index	Cutoff score	Baseline score	End score	Change score	Outcome
______	______	______	______	______	______	______
______	______	______	______	______	______	______
______	______	______	______	______	______	______
______	______	______	______	______	______	______
______	______	______	______	______	______	______
______	______	______	______	______	______	______
______	______	______	______	______	______	______

Comments ____

____

(2) Test ______________________________

Subscale	Reliable change index	Cutoff score	Baseline score	End score	Change score	Outcome
______	______	______	______	______	______	______
______	______	______	______	______	______	______
______	______	______	______	______	______	______
______	______	______	______	______	______	______
______	______	______	______	______	______	______
______	______	______	______	______	______	______
______	______	______	______	______	______	______

Comments ____

____

Use additional sheets for more tests.

Treatment Plan Goals/Objectives Progress (which are used as outcomes indicators)

Reasonable potential represents the expected level of goal attainment if therapy was completed in the amount of time intended for treatment.

Most recent objective represents the current objective level (in that therapy was terminated before treatment focused on the reasonable potential level).

Percentage attained represents the percentage of progress toward a specific behavioral objective. It is determined by the termination score minus the baseline score, divided by the reasonable amount of progress (the objective minus the baseline score). For example, a client enters therapy with a problem area of going to school only 1 day per week. A reasonable goal is set at 5 days per week. Therefore, there are 4 units of progress possible. Now the sessions are completed and the client is averaging 4 days per week at school. Therefore, 3 of the 4 units of reasonable progress have been attained.

Termination score (4) – Baseline score (1) = Change score (3). Change Score (3)/Reasonable progress (4) = 75% progress.
Note: For nominal data, simply use "Yes" and "No" to indicate completion goal at termination.

Objective # ______________________ Baseline ________ Termination ________

Reasonable potential ____________ Percent attained ________

Most recent objective ____________ Percent attained ________

Comments ____

____

Objective # ______________________ Baseline ________ Termination ________

Reasonable potential ____________ Percent attained ________

Most recent objective ____________ Percent attained ________

Comments ____

____

Objective # ______________________ Baseline ________ Termination ________

Reasonable potential ____________ Percent attained ________

Most recent objective ____________ Percent attained ________

Comments ____

____

FORM 10 TREATMENT OUTCOMES SUMMARY

Objective # ______________________________ Baseline ________ Termination __________

Reasonable potential __________ Percent attained _______

Most recent objective __________ Percent attained _______

Comments ____

____

Objective # ______________________________ Baseline ________ Termination __________

Reasonable potential __________ Percent attained _______

Most recent objective __________ Percent attained _______

Comments ____

____

Objective # ______________________________ Baseline ________ Termination __________

Reasonable potential __________ Percent attained _______

Most recent objective __________ Percent attained _______

Comments ____

____

Use additional sheets for more.

FORM 11 OUTCOME ASSESSMENT SUMMARY NARRATIVE REPORT

Client______________________________________ Chart #__________ Intake date _______

Total sessions ___Individual ___Group___Family___Other____________Termination date _______

Intake Diagnosis

Axis I ________________________________

____

Axis II ________________________________

____

Axis III _______________________________

Axis IV _______________________________

Axis V ________________________________

Discharge Diagnosis

Axis I ___________________________________

____

Axis II __________________________________

____

Axis III _________________________________

Axis IV _________________________________

Axis V __________________________________

Outcome Summary

____

____

____

____

____

____

____

____

____

____

____

____

____

____

____

____

Therapist's signature/credentials ______________________________ Date________

ABOUT THE AUTHORS

Donald Wiger received his PhD from Fordham University and is a licensed psychologist in Minnesota and in Michigan, where he operates mental health clinics. He conducts seminars nationally in clinical documentation procedures for diverse groups of mental health professionals and is the host of a daily radio program in Detroit, Michigan, "Family Life Perspectives." Dr. Wiger is the author of *The Clinical Documentation Primer* and *The Psychotherapy Documentation Sourcebook,* which are in the Wiley Practice Planner Series.

Kenneth Solberg received his PhD from the University of Wisconsin—Madison, and is a licensed psychologist in the state of Minnesota. He is a full-time faculty member at the Minnesota School of Professional Psychology, where he teaches the statistics and research sequence and supervises student research. Dr. Solberg also teaches specialized courses in outcome research methods, has presented numerous seminars on this topic, and serves as a consultant to individual practitioners and agencies on the design and analysis of outcome research.

ABOUT THE DISK

Introduction

The forms on the enclosed disk are saved in Microsoft Word for Windows version 7.0. In order to use the forms, you will need to have word processing software capable of reading Microsoft Word for Windows version 7.0 files.

System Requirements

- IBM PC or compatible computer
- 3.5-inch floppy disk drive
- Windows 95 or later
- Microsoft Word for Windows version 7.0 (including the Microsoft converter*) or later or other word processing software capable of reading Microsoft Word for Windows 7.0 files

*Word 7.0 needs the Microsoft converter file installed in order to view and edit all enclosed files. If you have trouble viewing the files, download the free converter from the Microsoft Web site. The URL for the converter is http://officeupdate.microsoft.com/downloadDetails/wd97cnv.htm.

Microsoft also has a viewer that can be downloaded, which allows you to view but not edit documents. This viewer can be downloaded at http://officeupdate.microsoft.com/downloadDetails/wd97vwr32.htm.

NOTE: Many popular word processing programs are capable of reading Microsoft Word for Windows 7.0 files. However, users should be aware that a slight amount of formatting might be lost when using a program other than Microsoft Word. If your word processor cannot read Microsoft Word for Windows 7.0 files, unformatted text files have been provided in the TXT directory on the floppy disk.

How to Install the Files onto Your Computer

To install the files, follow these instructions:

1. Insert the enclosed disk into the floppy disk drive of your computer.
2. From the Start Menu, choose Run.
3. Type A:\SETUP and press OK.

4. The opening screen of the installation program will appear. Press OK to continue.
5. The default destination directory is C:\OUTCOMES. If you wish to change the default destination, you may do so now.
6. Press OK to continue. The installation program will copy all files to your hard drive in the C:\OUTCOMES or user-designated directory.

Using the Files

Loading Files

To use the word processing files, launch your word processing program. Select File, Open from the pulldown menu. Select the appropriate drive and directory. If you installed the files to the default directory, the files will be located in the C:\OUTCOMES directory. A list of files should appear. If you do not see a list of files in the directory, you need to select WORD DOCUMENT (*.DOC) under Files of Type. Double-click on the file you want to open. Edit the file according to your needs.

Printing Files

If you want to print the files, select File, Print from the pulldown menu.

Saving Files

When you have finished editing a file, you should save it under a new file name by selecting File, Save As from the pulldown menu.

User Assistance

If you need assistance with installation or if you have a damaged disk, please contact Wiley Technical Support at:

Phone:	212-850-6753
Fax:	212-850-6800 (Attention: Wiley Technical Support)
E-mail:	techhelp@wiley.com

To place additional orders or to request information about other Wiley products, please call 800-225-5945.

For information about the disk see the About the Disk section on page 283.